How to Read the
Old Testament

Etienne Charpentier

How to Read the
Old Testament

SCM PRESS LTD

Translated by John Bowden from the French
Pour lire l'Ancien Testament
published 1981 by Les Éditions du Cerf,
29 bd Latour-Maubourg, Paris

334 02057 3

First published in English 1982
by SCM Press Ltd, 26–30 Tottenham Road, London, N1 4BZ
Fifth impression 1987

Photoset by Input Typesetting Ltd, London
and printed in Great Britain by
Richard Clay Ltd, Bungay, Suffolk

A Guide to the Bible

This book is for those who want to read the Bible but don't know how to go about it. It has been planned as a modest, yet ambitious guide to the Old Testament. There is a companion volume on the New Testament.

A travel guide

When we go on a trip, we may like to buy one of those guides that we can take with us, suggesting places to visit, telling us the sights to see and giving us a brief history of the country to which we shall be going. This guide is meant to help you to discover the Bible in just the same way.

It is a modest guide. It is very simple. Those who have never opened a Bible or who have tried, but given up, should find no difficulty with it (though they will have to do some work!). Before I wrote it, I tried out its contents for a long time with a great many groups. It is short. Each chapter is divided into sections of two or three pages which can be read on their own.

At the same time, however, it is an ambitious guide, because it sets out to offer you all the equipment you will need for reading the Bible on your own. The plan is as follows.

After a general introduction, there are eight chapters, each constructed on the same lines, and containing:

● A summary of the history of Israel. These two pages (always with a grey border) begin the chapter, but they are also a self-contained whole. You can read them one after another right through the book to have an overall view of the history of Israel.

● An introduction to the biblical writings produced during this period. We shall see the gradual growth of the different traditions which one day will become the Law (sometimes called the Pentateuch); we shall hear the prophets who were active in preaching during the periods concerned; we shall discover the way in which the wise men reflected on the human condition, life, love, death, and how their reflections one day culminate in the great works of wisdom literature.

- Parts of the Bible to read (indicated by 📖). These draw attention to the more important texts that you should read, by yourself or in a group.

- Documentation (contained in the boxes). This varies a great deal and includes explanations of important or difficult words, helps towards reading the texts, ancient texts which can be compared with the Bible, theological and spiritual reflections, and so on.

How to use this guide

You can use this guide by yourself. It can also be used for group study, in schools or churches. That's why it has been divided into eight chapters: a group, meeting only once a month, could use it to go through the Old Testament in a year.

Reading a travel guide before a trip gives us a general idea of what we shall be seeing and whets our appetite; but we know that some of the things it says will not mean anything to us until we actually arrive. We also know that we shall not be able to visit all the monuments listed in the guide. The same thing is true of this book.

You will be well advised to begin by reading each chapter straight through. That will give you a general idea, and you will know the texts that you will be 'visiting', while being well aware that you won't have time to see them all: at least you will be able to note the ones you would like to study. Then go back through the chapter again, Bible in hand. If you are part of a group, the work can be shared between you; thus at each meeting one person will have studied one particular part of the chapter more attentively than others, and will be able to help them to understand this part better.

You have your guide . . . but what specific country are you going to visit? In other words, which edition of the Bible are you going to use?

Which Bible?

There are plenty of good versions of the Bible. Translations vary, and some are more faithful than others. In particular, those which concentrate above all on putting the Bible into a truly modern idiom, like the *Good News Bible* (*Today's English Version*), can be rather free with the original text. However, in the end it does not really matter which edition of the Bible you use. If you have a Bible, you can use this guide.

We had to choose one particular translation of the Bible to quote in the pages which follow, and after a great deal of deliberation, finally decided on the *Revised Standard Version*. This was one of the earliest of the new translations, and is still one of the best – and one of the most widely used. Mention should also be made of the *Jerusalem Bible*, which is a very close contender. If you plan to buy a new Bible, you might well consider the Standard Edition of the Jerusalem Bible, which also has introductions and notes to each book. It will be a good source of extra information, but unfortunately it is not cheap!

Why read the Old Testament. . .

. . . especially now that we have the New Testament? If you've bought this guide, you will already have decided that the Old Testament is important. If you still need to be convinced, turn to pages 109–111.

Who is the author of this guide?

Who is the author? Certainly not me! Granted, I produced it, but that would not have been possible without the countless biblical scholars who are my friends, among whom I have worked, and from whom I have 'stolen' ideas or pictures in the course of meetings, lectures, conferences or my own reading. Nor can I forget the friendship of all those peoples in groups both in Chartres and throughout France where I have learned what I would like to share with you. This guide is as much their work as mine. Thank you, everybody!

Étienne Charpentier

This picture from the tomb of a certain Beni-Hassan, in Egypt (about 1890 BC), gives us some idea of the world of the patriarchs. A caravan of thirty-seven Arab nomads is paying its respects to the local governor. Men, women and children all seem to be in glowing health. They are wearing woollen garments in various colours. The men are well armed. Their chief (who does not appear in this part of the picture, but see p. 17) is offering as a present an ibex caught in the desert (see Genesis 12.10).

Getting Ready for our Journey

Suppose you decide to have a holiday in Spain. You have a number of choices. You can spend a couple of weeks in a town or a resort, in which case you will know that place well, but not the rest of the country. You can manage on your own and make no fixed plans. Or you can go to a travel agency which will suggest a choice of package tours: you can cover the whole of Spain by coach in a month.

However, even the last kind of holiday could be organized in two different ways. One way, the itinerary might be completely fixed. The coach stops at such and such a sight, the guide takes you round it, you get back in the coach which puts you down at a particular museum, and so on. Alternatively, the arrangements could be much simpler. The coach stops for two days in one town, three in another; at each stop the agency gives you a leaflet with the things to see and you make your own plans: if you want to, you can make use of the services of the guide suggested by the agency for this church or that museum. The itinerary is marked out: you are offered various options and make your own choice.

This book suggests something like this second kind of holiday. Each chapter makes up one of the eight stops in a journey through the Old Testament. At each stop you will be told what there is to visit, and you will be offered a guided tour of one or other of the more important texts. However, it is up to you to choose. You certainly won't be able to see everything. So choose!

Of course, it's a bit frustrating: we find our mouths watering, we want to see everything, study everything, and there just isn't time. The coach, the next chapter, calls us to join it, and we have to go. . . Obviously, by the end of a trip of this kind we cannot claim to know Spain – or the Bible. But we have got to know it a bit; lots of things have fallen into place, and we can go on to read a particular book, return to a certain city or study a particular prophet. We shall no longer be disorientated, because we shall be able to see where they fit into a whole.

Before beginning a journey, we pack our bags and get ready. We learn a bit about the geography and the history of the place to which we are going, we read up the language of the country and learn one or two essential words and phrases. We gather together our things, and they will differ depending on whether we are leaving for the mountains or for the sea.

So in this first chapter, before we really begin, we are going to gather together some essential ideas so that we don't get too lost.

This is what you will find on the next few pages:

1. *The Bible: book or library?* Some practical advice about getting to know the Bible itself (pages 6–7).

2. *A people rereads its life.* A more theoretical reflection on the Bible: not 'eye-witness accounts' but the reflections of believers (pages 8–10).

3. *Reading and studying a text.* Two methods of analysing a text, and a 'tool box' (pages 11–15).

4. *A people stamped by its geography.* The geographical and historical environment of Israel (pages 16–17).

5. *A people stamped by the mentality of the Near East.* A survey of the thought-patterns of the people with whom Israel is in contact (pages 18–21).

6. *A thousand years of history.* The great moments of Israel (pages 22–23).

1. The Bible: book or library?

We shall begin by getting to know something about the Bible itself. If you are already familiar with it, you can go straight on to page 8.

Names

The word Bible comes from the Greek; it is a plural noun, *ta biblia*, and means 'the books'. When this word was taken over into Latin, it became singular, the Bible.

The Bible is more than a book; it's a library. In it you will find a number of very different works, collected together in two large groupings, the Old Testament and the New Testament (usually abbreviated as OT and NT). The word 'testament' here does not mean what we might take it to mean in modern English: it is the same word as the Latin *testamentum*, which translates the Hebrew word meaning covenant. So the Bible is the collection of books which tells us about the covenant, the agreement, which God made with Israel through Moses (the old covenant) and which he fulfilled in Jesus (the new covenant).

The Bible is often called scripture, the scriptures, or holy scripture. That is important, and means at least two things. First, this is the Word of God set down in writing – so there can be a Word of God which is not written. Furthermore, it is the writings which are the Word of God for us, and not the events or the words spoken before they were composed. We shall come back to this point.

Books

The first part of the Bible, the Old Testament, is common to both Jews and Christians, but with some differences.

The Jews, followed by Protestants, recognize only the books written in Hebrew, forty of them; Catholics also recognize six books written in Greek. Protestants call these latter books 'apocryphal'; Catholics call them 'deutero-canonical', that is, books which entered the canon, or rule of faith, at a secondary stage (see the box on p. 86).

The New Testament, which is identical for all Christians, consists of twenty-seven books.

So the Christian 'library' – the Bible – contains either sixty-seven or seventy-three books. They are usually referred to by means of abbreviations (you will find a list on p. 125). Thus Gen. refers to Genesis and Rev. to Revelation. The system of abbreviations is almost uniform, but you will find slight differences between one edition of the Bible and another, and between different books about the Bible.

Classification

If you are putting books on the shelves of a library, you have several possible ways of doing it.

If you want to be aesthetic, you will arrange them according to size. So in the Bible, the letters of Paul are arranged in order of decreasing length.

If you want to be practical, you will arrange the books according to subject. So in the Bible, we find all the prophets, or all the books of Paul, together.

If you want to follow the development of ideas, you can arrange the books in the order in which they appeared. You might have all the books published before the Second World War, then all the books published before the assassination of President Kennedy, and so on. That is the order we shall try to follow in this book.

The books of the New Testament are arranged in the same way in all Christian Bibles.

The books of the Old Testament are arranged in two different ways.

The Jewish Bible contains three parts: the Law or Torah (which we call the Pentateuch); the Prophets or Nebiim, divided into two groups, the former prophets (which we wrongly call the 'historical' books) and the latter prophets (Isaiah, Jeremiah, Ezekiel and the twelve others); and lastly the Writings or Kethubim. By taking the first letters of each of these Hebrew titles (Torah, Nebiim, Kethubim), the Jews formed the word TaNaK, which is their name for the Bible. This is the arrangement you will find in the Jerusalem Bible, which adds at the end those books which are not recognized by Catholics.

Most Bibles have adopted an order inspired by the Greek Bible, which arranges the books in four parts: the Pentateuch, the historical books, the prophetic books and the wisdom books.

Languages

The whole of the Old Testament is written in Hebrew (there are just a few passages in Aramaic). Like Arabic, these two languages are written with consonants only; the reader has to add the vowels according to the way in which he understands the text. Beginning in the seventh century of our era, Jewish scholars known as 'Massoretes' fixed the meaning of a text by adding vowels in the form of little points above and below the consonants. This is why the Hebrew text is sometimes called the 'Massoretic text'.

The Old Testament was translated into Greek in Alexandria, from about the third century BC onwards. According to legend, seventy scribes working independently all arrived at exactly the same translation. The significance of this legend is important. It indicates that a translation of this kind must have been inspired by God. As a result, the translation is known as the Septuagint (Greek for seventy: the usual abbreviation is LXX). There were other ancient Greek translations, by Aquila, Symmachus and Theodotion.

The New Testament was written entirely in Greek, in the common language spoken at the time. This Greek, which is not the same as classical Greek, is called *koine* (Greek for common, i.e. language).

Specialist scholars work with and translate from the original texts, i.e. Hebrew for the Old Testament and Greek for the New Testament.

Of the other ancient translations or versions I should mention the translations into Syriac, Coptic and Latin. The Latin version known as the Vulgate (*editio vulgata* or popular edition) is the work of St Jerome (end of the fourth and beginning of the fifth century of our era).

Chapters and verses

To make it easy to find one's way around the Bible, Stephen Langton, Archbishop of Canterbury, had the idea of dividing each book into numbered chapters: this was done in 1226. During a carriage journey from Lyons to Paris in 1551, the printer Robert Estienne numbered almost every phrase of these chapters: hence our modern division into verses.

The division into chapters and verses does not always match the meaning of the text; you don't have to take account of it to understand the meaning. However, it is very practical, because all Bibles have adopted it. So to indicate a passage in the Bible, it is enough to give the reference, i.e. to indicate the book, the chapter and the verse, e.g. 2.4. In the box you will find the system of abbreviations and references generally used today.

How a reference works

First comes an abbreviated form of the title of the book (for a list of abbreviations see p. 125).

The first figure indicates the chapter, and the second, separated from the first by a full stop (sometimes a colon), indicates the verse.

Thus Gen. 2.4 denotes Genesis, chapter 2, verse 4.

A hyphen is used in indicating several chapters or verses. Gen. 2–5 denotes Genesis, chapters 2 to 5 (inclusive); Gen. 2.4–8 denotes Genesis, chapter 2, verses 4 to 8 (inclusive).

A semi-colon separates two different references. Gen. 2; 5 denotes Genesis, chapters 2 and 5.

A comma separates different verses in the same chapter. Gen. 2.4, 8, 11 denotes verses 4, 8 and 11 of chapter 2.

An f. added to a figure indicates the following verse (ff. indicates an indeterminate number of subsequent verses). Thus Gen. 2.4f. denotes Genesis chapter 2, verses 4 and 5.

Some verses are particularly long. If you want to indicate just part of the verse, you add letters to the numbers. Thus Gen. 2.4a denotes the first part of Genesis chapter 2, verse 4.

Here is an example: Gen. 2.4–6, 8; 3.5f.; 4.1–6.8 denotes: Genesis, chapter 2, verses 4 to 6 (inclusive) and verse 8, then chapter 3, verses 5 and 6; chapter 4, verse 1 to chapter 6, verse 8.

This system may seem very complicated, but it is no more difficult than looking up a number in a telephone directory. You'll soon get used to it.

Qumran manuscript. Temple Scroll. Before 70 BC.

2. A people rereads its life

The Bible, and above all the Old Testament, is a disconcerting book. Even those who have never opened it know that it is the holy book of Jews and Christians and expect to find in it the 'word of God in a pure form', a kind of catechism or handbook of morality.

And when they do open it . . . they find stories about the past of a tiny people, which are often quite insignificant, stories of an unedifying and immoral kind which one cannot read aloud without blushing, wars, murders, poems with which it is difficult to pray even if one turns them into 'psalms', the counsels of an antiquated morality, out of date and deliberately misogynist. . .

A disconcerting book. . . But is it in fact a book?

In the first place, it is a library, consisting of seventy-three books, the writing of which extends over more than a thousand years. Put side by side on the shelves of your bookcase *Gawain and the Green Knight* and a collection of Snoopy cartoons, the Canterbury Tales and a mediaeval theological treatise, Winston Churchill's memoirs of the Second World War, some Elizabethan love lyrics and sermons by Newman, the songs of the American Civil War and Tolkien's *Lord of the Rings*, together with some modern books on theology and some on science. You will have representative works written in English over the past thousand years or so, but you will end up rather disorientated. . .

The Bible is in fact more than a fixed library; it is a world we have to enter for ourselves, an adventure to which we are summoned: that of a people seized with a passion for God.

Perhaps a little story will make things clearer.

It was the eve of their golden wedding. When I arrived, they were alone. Their children had already left. We spent the evening together, and it was marvellous.

I thought I knew these old friends well enough: simple people who had lived together for half a century, sharing joys and sorrows. That evening, however, I saw them with new eyes, because they showed me their 'treasure': a plain cardboard box held it all. Of course there were photographs, from the family wedding photograph, posed and very solemn, to snaps of a child's smile or a holiday view. There were postcards, trite and conventional, some in pieces because he had carried them round in his uniform pocket all through the war. As I looked through them, the couple gave me a commentary and explained why they had kept them, and these common objects became sad or happy mementoes of moments in their lives.

And it was their lives which took shape through their family papers. The family genealogy, a monotonous list of old-fashioned names, here became pride at belonging to a line, at having roots in a particular area. A lease was no longer a pretentious and minutely detailed document, but the final realization of a life-long dream of work and savings: they had their own house. Letters exchanged during their engagement ('Hey, you mustn't let him read that,' the old man protested, delighted that it would show me the tenderness of their love) had been put next to prayers composed for the great moments of their life. Their marriage sermon lay next to rather a bad poem sent by a grandchild.

The evening went like a dream. I thought I knew these old friends well, and all of a sudden, with them and alongside them, I discovered the meaning of their life. All these papers and photographs were trivial, valueless. Yet for us they became priceless: they were no longer just objects, but the whole of a life, summed up and interpreted. Each one of these commonplace things had a place in a story of which it formed part of the fabric.

Now we must go back to some of the important points of this illustration.

1. Life turned into a 'text'

This married couple showed me photographs and documents; these objects were interesting, not only in themselves, but above all because they were so to speak the life of the couple in concentrated form. Through them and by means of them, I was able to go a little way into the world of my friends and share in their adventure of love.

Similarly, the various books of the Bible can often seem trite and uninteresting to us. But through them we shall discover the adventure of a people of believers, and will be able to enter into their world.

2. You understand afterwards

'That's our first love letter,' my old friend said to me with a wicked smile. I read it in amazement: it was an algebra problem. At that time he and his future wife were still at school. Because she was away ill, he had been given the task of writing to her with the maths homework. An ordinary enough letter, but it had started something, and it had been followed by others. Taken by itself, the letter would have been completely uninteresting; kept by chance and reread after their marriage, it had really become their first love letter.

So there are events which make no sense by themselves: they make some sense by becoming part of our history. At the moment when they are taken, photographs are not very interesting; looked at afterwards, they become important.

Thus each event can carry within it a number of meanings which we may not see all at once; if, however, it is important, we shall be led to think about it again, and by thinking about it, we shall discover its riches. The more one goes on, the richer the original event becomes.

Describing an event is not the same as giving an exact account, like a photograph of what happened; it is rather like recreating this event and showing the meaning that it now has for us. And as we talk about it later, we discover yet other things. For example, a friend may tell us something; we don't pay too much attention, and then later, often a good deal later, we exclaim, 'So that's what he wanted to tell me. . .' How are we going to describe the friend's original statement – in terms of what he told us or in terms of how we now understand it? In other words, are we going to reproduce his exact words or add the meaning that he truly wanted to convey?

3. Exact or true?

Sometimes we hear people asking, 'Is what is in the Bible true? Did miracles really happen?' Before we answer, we ought perhaps to ask ourselves what we mean by 'true'. It can have a number of meanings. For example, someone might say, 'This story is true, this novel is true, this poem is true. . .' We immediately realize that the meaning of true here isn't always the same. In a novel, everything has been made up, but it can be true if we identify easily with it, if it is a good reflection of the realities of human life. Nothing is exact or historical, but everything is true.

It is always dangerous to use labels, but at least that allows us to see clearly. So let us take these two words, exact and true.

We use the word exact to refer to what actually happened in history: what the camera or the tape recorder might have registered. In this perspective my old friends' first love letter is no more than sending on maths homework: what this friend actually said will be reproduced exactly as it was.

But it is true that these algebra sums are a 'love letter', and the way in which I reproduce the phrase used by my friends will be more true than if it were exact.

Is the Bible, then, true? Yes, but in this sense of the word. Of course we shall find inaccuracies, and the way in which events are narrated or speeches reported will not always be exact, but it will be true because it includes the meaning which has been discovered.

4. Believing in order to understand

The essential reality of the event cannot be seen with the eyes; we have to infer it through the historical features of the event, through what we can see. For example, we might see a man and a woman kissing. That is an exact, historical fact. But we cannot infer anything from it. Sometimes we are obliged to kiss people we do not like or love. If someone tells me that this couple is in love, then the kiss takes on meaning: it becomes a sign of their love. 'If someone tells me. . .': that means that I believe what I am told, and it is because I believe that I understand this kiss as a gesture of love. If we are to understand, we need to believe, and the fact of understanding reinforces our belief. In this way, then, we progress as though up a spiral staircase: we keep going round, but at each turn we progress further.

It is the same with the Bible. That applies to those who wrote it. They told of events, but these events took on meaning because they believed. And that applies to us who read it today: we can study it whether or not we are believers, and we can understand what the texts tell us. But we understand them differently if we share the same faith as the authors, and if we enter on the same quest as theirs.

All that might seem rather complicated, but we shall return to it, and things will become clearer as we go along. For the moment, let us draw one important consequence from what has been said so far. What is the meaning of a text? What is reading?

5. The meaning of a text

When we are confronted with a text, above all an ancient text, we instinctively think rather like this. The author had something to say, a meaning to communicate. He wrapped up this meaning in his own words and his own culture. So our task today consists of unwrapping this meaning and wrapping it up again in our own words. We imagine that there is an objective meaning in the text, a hard core that we have to extract.

By now, we should be beginning to understand that things are not quite as simple as this. As I listened to my old friends describing their life to me, of course I was trying to understand what they wanted to say; but as I listened, I transformed it. After that evening I had a picture of them which doubtless was not quite the picture they had of themselves, and which was not the picture that would have been presented to another friend who might have been there. As we read a text, we reshape it in the light of what we are ourselves. That is quite normal: in that way we continue the life of the event that is being narrated, adding the meaning that we discover in it.

Reading is a matter of getting hold of a text and making it tell us something for today, something that will make us live.

In that case, though, can we make a text say virtually anything? That is where the study of the text comes in, and the use of different methods of study.

A miraculous history?

'Why should the Bible interest me? It tells a miraculous story in which God is talking all the time (to Abraham, to Moses, to the prophets. . .), and in which he is always performing miracles to free the oppressed, heal the sick. . . What has that to do with my ordinary, common, everyday life, or with the life of the world? God chattered on for two thousand years, and now he is silent. But people are still oppressed and wretched. Why doesn't he act any more?'

That's a real objection. But what I have already said should enable you to guess that those who make this objection are comparing histories at two different levels.

The historian who studies the history of Israel will find it to be the ordinary history of a tiny people in the Near East, no different from the others.

The believers who produced the Bible read in these events the word and the intervention of their God, in the same way that the couple I mentioned discovered a love letter in some maths homework.

The history of Israel is as common, ordinary, wretched as our history today. It is the same. And the unbeliever will not discover any trace of God in it.

But to read the Bible should lead us to reread our existence with the eyes of the believer. If we do, we shall discover that God continues to speak to us as he spoke to the prophets, and he continues to act. And the whole of our life will appear to us to be a history full of miracles.

3. Reading and studying a text

What I have just said suggests that we should distinguish between reading a text and studying it.

Reading a text is making it produce a meaning for its present-day reader. That's what we do naturally; we say, 'That's what this text says to me. . . What strikes me about this text. . .', and that is the kind of reading that we must finally achieve. But there is an obvious danger: can you make a text say virtually anything? That is where study comes in.

Study, that is, working on the text with the help of different methods of analysis, is aimed at helping us to discover that there is a distance between us and this text, that we cannot just rush straight into it, and that it is dangerous to project our feelings and our psychology on to it too quickly. This study should also make us read the text very carefully. There are texts which we know so well (or think that we know so well), from the Gospels, for example, that we no longer actually read them: we skip over them and repeat what people have always told us about them.[1]

Two methods of analysis

In fact, when confronted with a text, we instinctively use two ways of studying it. Let me give you a trivial example.

Old aunt Bertha has written to you. As you read her letter, you imagine her there and interpret the text from what you know of her.

Suppose for a moment that your aunt is complaining; if you know that she moans all the time, you will not pay much attention, and will simply say, 'That's just like her!' On the other hand, if you know that she is a very tough person, you may wonder why she is complaining, and feel that perhaps she is really ill. Or again, when you read a sentence in which she is attacking the young or a particular social group, you may say, 'It's her age,' or, 'It's the way she was brought up.' Here, then, you go beyond the text to imagine your aunt, and you try to see what she is trying to convey in the light of what you know of her.

Now suppose that while reading you come across a phrase you can't understand. For a few moments you stop looking for the meaning and pay attention to the grammar, that is, you try to sort out the elements which allow a phrase to make sense: 'Where is the subject? What is the object?' Once you have these elements in place, you read the text to make sense of it. Or again, you note that the letter begins in a pessimistic tone and ends in a better frame of mind; the atmosphere has changed a bit. You read the text once more to see what has caused this transformation (for example, it could be quite simply the fact of telling her troubles to someone). Here, you do not leave the text behind, but try to understand it in itself.

Specialists have taken up these two major ways of studying a text and have perfected them. We are now going to see how they use them, and how we can make use of them too.

1. Historical analysis

If you were reading a letter from aunt Bertha, you would ask yourself, 'What does she want to say?', and to find an answer, you would set the letter against the background of her life, past or present.

That is also the question that we ask when confronted with a biblical text: 'What does Luke want to say? What does the author of Genesis want to say?'

However, things are rather more complicated than that. You know your aunt Bertha. I don't, and if I read her letter I shall get some idea of her from her writing, the references she makes to particular events, the mentality she displays. I shall be able to put an age to her, detect something of her background and ideas, and I shall interpret the letter in terms of this person I have begun to imagine. Of course that's rather dangerous, and we have to be aware of that: I am inventing a person from the text and then interpreting the text in the light of what I think I know of the person.

Similarly, we know Luke or the author of Genesis only from their texts. So we must tread carefully, and constantly check what we are saying.

1. For example, we always talk about the 'adoration of the shepherds' in connection with Luke 2.1–20. But read the text! You will see that the shepherds do not come to adore, but only to deliver a 'sermon' to Mary!

How to place an author

It is easy enough to place aunt Bertha, because she is a contemporary. But as soon as she refers to the 1914–1918 war, I am obliged to recall what I have read in books. The books of the Bible were put together two or three thousand years ago. To place them, we shall have to use, among other things, information coming from:

- **History** which we know from the Bible and also from the documents of other peoples.

- **The literature** of the time: the Jews, exiled in Babylon, heard the great Mesopotamian legends about the flood; Jewish sermons from the time of Jesus show us how people understood scripture in those days.

- **Archaeology:** the city of Jericho was in ruins when Joshua took it; the pool with five porticos, mentioned by John, has been discovered in Jerusalem.

This work is obviously restricted to specialists. Fortunately, however, they are concerned to pass on the most important results of their research. There are plenty of excellent popular accounts, some of which are mentioned on page 115. And you can use the introductions and notes in your Bible, which will provide essential information.

How to place a story

We imagine all too easily that the author of a story is no more than a tape recorder giving an exact rendering of words and actions. Now an author speaks to us as much about his life and about his age as about the event which he reports. Here are some examples.

Luther lived in the sixteenth century. Suppose we read two books about him by Catholics, one written about 1900 and the other today. The first will say something like this. By his pride Luther, a defrocked monk who seduced a nun, set Europe and the church on fire and caused a great deal of bloodshed. The second will say: Luther had his failings, like all of us, but above all he was a monk with a passionate concern for God, haunted by the question of man's salvation. He saw that the church needed to be reformed and to return to the Bible, and the church pushed him out. We can learn things about Luther from these two books, but above all we shall learn how ecumenism has made its mark on Catholics between 1900 and today!

The old couple I mentioned earlier were describing their marriage on the eve of their golden wedding. To understand that marriage, I have to put it in the context of 1930.

But I also have to put it in the context of 1980, because they were also describing it in terms of the half century which has since passed.

Similarly, a biblical author tells the story of Abraham differently, depending on whether he is writing in the happy days of David or, five hundred years later, in a camp of exiles in Babylon. The words of Jesus must be understood in the light of the history of the thirties, but also in the light of the communities who wrote them down towards 80 or 90.

That, very briefly, is the concern of historical analysis: to put a text back in its historical context, in the different moments of history when it came into being, in an attempt to see what the author wanted to say. (The method is sometimes called historical-critical, to show that we keep a critical point of view when putting ourselves in the context of this history.)

Materialist analysis

'That shows the way she was brought up', we might think in reading some remark in aunt Bertha's letter. That means that when we speak, although we imagine the words are ours, they are often our social background and our education talking through us.

In placing texts in their historical context, materialist analysis is attentive to this aspect. A text is also a product of the social, economic and political conditions of its day. This method is called 'materialist' because it deliberately uses the analytical framework developed by Marxism. (You can use this framework without being compelled to accept all Marxist theory.)

2. Structuralist analysis

Let's go back to aunt Bertha's letter. Faced with an incomprehensible sentence, we shall stop looking for its meaning for a moment to sort out the elements in it (subject, object and so on) which allow a sentence to have meaning.

Now from the beginning of the twentieth century a new science of the study of language has come into being: semiotics (from a Greek word *semeion*, meaning sign) studies these signs, which are the elements of language or the conditions of meaningful language.

Specialists in semiotics teach us that there is not only a grammar of phrases but also a grammar of the text. Just as when writing a sentence we respect a certain number of rules (fortunately, without thinking about them!), so when we write a text (a letter, a story. . .), we respect other rules. We cannot study them here. You will find some of them in the explanation given on page 15.

We must note just one of the chief characteristics of this method. With the historical method, we go beyond the text to interpret it in the light of what the author wanted to say. Here, we try not to go beyond the text, but to study it in itself, independently of the intentions of the author ('the author is dead!'); we move around the text, in every direction, forgetting what we already know (or think we know) of it, and leaving aside what we want to find there, looking at it only for itself. For us, that is the chief advantage of this method.

Imagine a couple of friends taking a walk in the woods. One loves mushrooms. That's all he sees; for him, woods mean mushrooms. His friend is unaware of them, and treads on them without noticing; for him woods mean birds, or stones, or trees. It is the same when we read a text. Unconsciously, we already have some idea: we are in search of a particular piece of information or we are looking for some form of comfort, and that is all we see. That explains why we so easily misunderstand one another. You might imagine these friends beginning by paying as comprehensive a visit as possible to the woods, each forgetting their own interests: they will try to see everything, birds, trees, mushrooms. . . After that, if they so wish, they can go out looking for mushrooms. They will no longer be tempted to say that woods mean mushrooms; they will know that they have chosen to look for mushrooms, but that woods offer other possibilities.

The advantage of structuralist analysis, even practised in a very rough and ready way, is to force us to look at the text from the greatest possible number of perspectives, forgetting our own viewpoint as we look at the text. After that, in our own personal reading, we may perhaps retain only one perspective, but we shall know that others exist. And our reading will be enriched.

3. A parable

I shall sum up what I've just said with the help of a parable. I am listening to a record with a friend – say it is a Mozart symphony. Each of us will hear it differently; I may find it joyful while my friend finds it sad. Each person listens as they are, as they are feeling at that moment, and they project their feelings on to the work.

Our interpretations are so different that we decide to study the symphony, so that we are better able to come to some agreement. With the help of a score, we study the work itself, analysing the movements, the entries of the various subjects, the instrumentation, and so on. Then we leave the work and read a book on the life of Mozart, to see what he wanted to do. By using these two methods we shall discover a great deal, and dispense with certain personal interpretations. That's interesting. But a symphony wasn't written to be studied, but to be listened to.

Now we put the record on again, to listen to it anew. Our study will have helped us to do that better, but now we forget this study and simply devote ourselves to the pleasure of hearing the symphony. We give it a meaning, we discover in it a new delight in life. And that is the essential thing.

Substitute read for listen and book for record and you have the essentials of what I have tried to say in this section.

Seal belonging 'to Shema', servant of Jeroboam'. Found at Megiddo (eighth century BC)

A 'tool box'

First contact

Read the text. Note your spontaneous reactions: what strikes you, what you like, what amazes you, what raises questions for you.

Studying the text

Go back to the text without any explanatory notes from your Bible or any other help. If it is not too long, you might copy it out. Go through it (if necessary, using coloured pencils) and mark:

The text itself

- words or expressions which keep recurring, correspond or contrast.
- those involved in the action (people or things): note what they do, what they say, what happens to them.
- places and movements. Are certain places connected with a particular person or idea?
- indications of time: the tenses of verbs, other pointers.

As a result of all this, see what is happening in the text. Who is doing or looking for what? Who (or what) is helping in this search? is getting in the way? What happens between the beginning and the end of the text? Can you see any change? In whom or in what? How does it happen? What stages are involved? Who or what brings about this change?

The text put back in its context

This text is part of a larger whole (book, chapter). How does it fit into this whole? What is its place? What does it contribute?

The text in the setting of its time

With the help of the notes in your Bible or other aids, you can ask yourself:
- When was this text written? What was the situation of the people or the author at that particular time?
- Do some words or expressions have a meaning peculiar to that particular time?
- What is the literary genre of this text (see page 25)?
- Are there similar texts to this period, in the Bible or outside it? Does this OT text take up themes from the Bible? What does it add? Does it take up themes known in Egyptian or Mesopotamian literature? What are the similarities? What are the differences? Does this NT text take up Jewish themes from the time of Christ? or OT texts? In that case, how do they illuminate it?
- If there are similar texts in the Bible, in particular in the Gospels (you may often find references in the margin of your Bible), compare them. Note the similarities and the differences. How does this help you to understand the text better?
- This text was produced by a community for a community. Who is talking to whom? What question are they answering?

A check

Go back to the questions you noted down at the beginning. Can you answer them?

Reading the text

Now put aside this book and your 'tool box', and read the text. What does it say to you? How does it help you to live?

When you get out your tool box, the aim is not to use the tools but, say, to strip down an engine. Here I have brought together a number of tools which may help you to strip down a text: the aim is not to use all of them.

First contact

This first reading is too often the only one that we do. It allows us to discover a little about the text, but above all to discover ourselves: what are our chief interests, our preoccupations.

If you are working as a group, put down the questions but do not try to answer them straight away: you will run the risk of getting bogged down in minor problems. Take them up again after your study.

Studying the text

Here we make use of the important methods I mentioned above. The first questions are inspired more by structuralist analysis, and the later ones by the historical method. The aim is not to make the method work perfectly, but to study a text.

The text itself

These questions may seem to be too scholarly or too childish. Their chief concern is to make you look at the text very closely, forgetting preconceived ideas. Do not hesitate to spend time on them: you will find that this pays off.

Above all, pay attention to all the contrasts. We can only think by means of contrasts. Saying that a house is large makes sense, only because we compare it – in our minds, at any rate – with an apartment and not a tower block.

A story begins when there is a need, and it ends when this need has been met. The whole aim of the story is to show us the stages which are gone through for this aim to be achieved, and the obstacles that have to be surmounted on the way. The various elements in the action (people or things) are organized around this search for what is lacking; they can be rearranged into six categories:

sender → object → recipient
↑
support → subject ← opposition.

Here is a trivial illustration. I see that my neighbour Paul is thirsty: the object that he lacks is a drink. I ask Peter to go and get him something to drink. As the sender, I set up Peter as the subject to go to look for what Paul, the recipient, needs. If Peter is truly to be the subject, he must be willing (he might refuse), knowledgeable (where to find the drink) and able (he must have some money). He will find support from those who tell him what he needs to know (where the refrigerator is), or what he needs to have (money), and opponents who may put obstacles in his way. A number of people may be in opposition, help one another, lack something, but they will form a single group.

You must remember that at this point we are not yet looking for meaning: we are trying to sort out the elements which allow a text to make sense. Be ready to spend time on this research: you will find that as a result the text says much more to you.

The text in its context

We have become far too accustomed to reading texts in tiny fragments, particularly as a result of lectionaries at the mass or in other services. Put them back in their proper contexts; they will often take on a new flavour.

The text in its time

This is the point at which we use the historical method. Now is the time to read the introductions and notes in your Bible, or other aids (commentaries, which go through a text verse by verse); usually you will find that they provide all the information you need. You may also find an atlas of the Bible useful.

The last question is important: do not forget to ask why people wanted to report this event or these words; they do not do so as a matter of course, but in answer to a question that was raised at the time.

Check

By now you should have found an answer to the questions you asked at the beginning. If not, write them down and ask someone with more knowledge when you have a chance.

Reading the text

This is the object of all the work that you have been doing so far. Spend time on it. You might like to try to rewrite the text in such a way that it speaks to you now.

4. A people stamped by its geography

Look at the map of the Near East on the opposite page. Note where there are seas and deserts. That explains how civilizations grew up and developed in three main regions, in the plains and the valleys.

The great civilizations

To the south, in the Nile valley, from about 3000 BC Egypt becomes an important people, governed by dynasties of kings (Pharaohs) living sometimes in the north (Memphis) and sometimes in the south (Thebes). The history of Egypt is usually divided up in terms of dynasties. Thus the Exodus probably took place under the Nineteenth Dynasty (about 1250).

To the north, on the plains of Asia Minor, the Hittites flourished. They were extremely powerful for about 1500 years, but had virtually disappeared by biblical times.

To the east we have the expanses of Mesopotamia (from the Greek, meaning the area between the rivers). This region is also called the fertile crescent. Magnificent civilizations grew up there side by side and gave way to one another, disappearing only to return to power some centuries later. Chief of these in the south are Sumer, Akkad and Babylonia, with Assyria in the north. This is the region which is now Iraq. Further east, in present-day Iran, the Medes emerged, to be followed by the Persians.

Other peoples later came from the west, from present-day Europe, to invade the Near East: the Greeks, three centuries before Christ, and the Romans, in the first century BC.

What happens when great peoples are neighbours? They fight! 'At the return of spring, when kings set out to war,' says the Bible, as naturally as we say, 'At the return of autumn, when people go out hunting again. . .' But in order to fight, they have to make contact with or to invade one another, and to do that it was necessary to move through the narrow corridor between the Mediterranean and the Arabian desert.

The one problem was that the tiny people in whom we are interested, Israel, lived in this corridor! So we can understand how much its life depended on the power of other nations. As a buffer state between the great powers, it served as a forward post for now one, now another. And it was tempted to make alliances with one or the other.

To have an idea of the way in which these powers succeeded one another, you should now read the contents of the boxes in the map on the right. The numbers indicate the order in which they intervened in the history of Israel. If you want more detail, look at an atlas or a chronological table of the history of Israel. There may be one in your Bible.

Canaan

In the Bible or in extra-biblical texts the word Canaan sometimes denotes a people and sometimes a country.

The country of Canaan is roughly equivalent to present-day Palestine. You will find a schematic map of it on page 44. Look at the map. The country is divided, vertically, into several regions.

A coastal plain extends along the Mediterranean, divided by Mount Carmel.

The central region is made up of a plain (Galilee) and hill country (Samaria Judah).

Finally, to the east we have the strange valley of the Jordan. Look at the indications of height: the source of the river, at the foot of Mount Hermon, is about 200 metres above sea level. At Lake Huleh, it is still 68 metres above sea level, but by Lake Tiberias, about 15 kilometres lower, it is already 212 metres below sea level and it flows into the Dead Sea at 392 metres below sea level.

This is the country in which, in the twelfth century BC, those tribes settled which, around 1000 BC, became the kingdom of David and Solomon. On Solomon's death the kingdom divided into two: in the south, the kingdom of Judah, with Jerusalem as its capital, and in the north, that of Israel, the capital of which was Samaria.

Also round about the twelfth century the Philistines settled to the south, on the Mediterranean coast. Some centuries before the birth of Christ the Greeks gave their name to the country: Palestine, or the land of the Philistines.

Another small kingdom was to play an important role in the history of Israel, that of Damascus.

We can already imagine to what extent the history of Israel would depend on that of other peoples. It remains for us to see how its thought and ideas would be stamped by other civilizations.

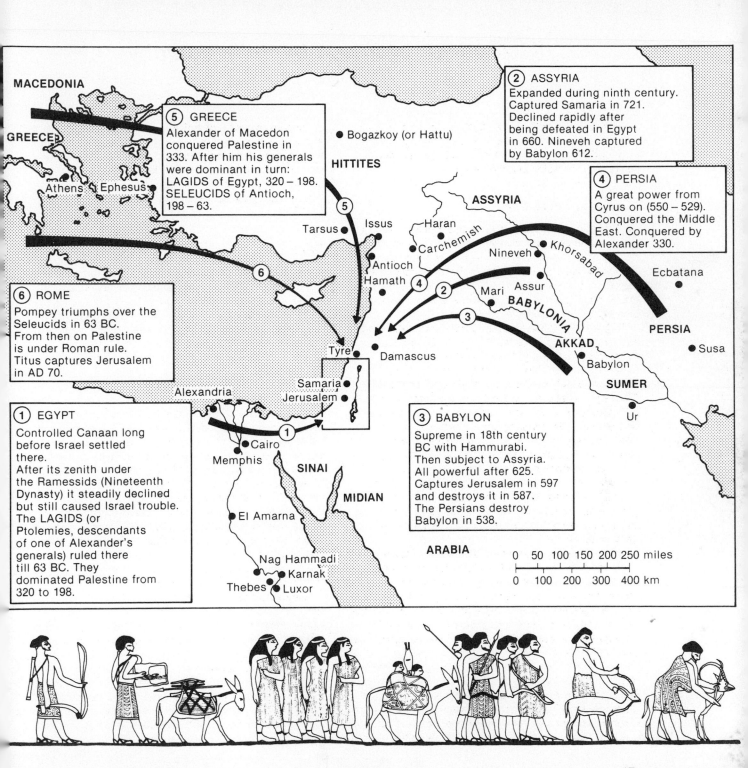

MACEDONIA

GREECE

⑤ **GREECE**
Alexander of Macedon conquered Palestine in 333. After him his generals were dominant in turn: LAGIDS of Egypt, 320 – 198. SELEUCIDS of Antioch, 198 – 63.

• Bogazkoy (or Hattu)

HITTITES

② **ASSYRIA**
Expanded during ninth century. Captured Samaria in 721. Declined rapidly after being defeated in Egypt in 660. Nineveh captured by Babylon 612.

④ **PERSIA**
A great power from Cyrus on (550 – 529). Conquered the Middle East. Conquered by Alexander 330.

• Athens Ephesus

⑤

Tarsus Issus

Haran •

ASSYRIA

• Carchemish

Nineveh • • Khorsabad

• Ecbatana

⑥

Antioch •
Hamath •

④ ② Mari • Assur •

BABYLONIA

PERSIA

⑥ **ROME**
Pompey triumphs over the Seleucids in 63 BC. From then on Palestine is under Roman rule. Titus captures Jerusalem in AD 70.

③

AKKAD

Tyre •

Damascus

• Susa

• Babylon

Alexandria

Samaria •
Jerusalem •

SUMER

① **EGYPT**
Controlled Canaan long before Israel settled there.
After its zenith under the Ramessids (Nineteenth Dynasty) it steadily declined but still caused Israel trouble. The LAGIDS (or Ptolemies, descendants of one of Alexander's generals) ruled there till 63 BC. They dominated Palestine from 320 to 198.

①

• Cairo

Memphis •

SINAI

MIDIAN

• Ur

③ **BABYLON**
Supreme in 18th century BC with Hammurabi. Then subject to Assyria. All powerful after 625. Captures Jerusalem in 597 and destroys it in 587. The Persians destroy Babylon in 538.

ARABIA

• El Amarna

Nag Hammadi
• Karnak

Thebes • • Luxor

```
0  50  100 150 200 250 miles
0    100   200   300   400 km
```

5. A people stamped by the mentality of the Near East

Throughout its history, Israel was in contact with neighbouring peoples and was familiar with their chief literary works. We shall have occasion to reread some extracts from them. Here I shall try to put these great civilizations in context.

Egyptian hymn to the sun god Aten

Here are some extracts from this hymn, composed by Pharaoh Akhenaten.

You shine out in beauty on the horizon of heaven,
O living disc, the beginning of life.
When you have appeared on the eastern horizon,
you have filled every land with your perfection.
When you set on the western horizon,
the earth lies in darkness as in death.
The earth lies in silence,
for the one who created it has gone to rest on his horizon.
Then the earth becomes bright: you have arisen on the horizon.
As solar disc, you shine by day.
Men awaken and stand on their feet.
Their arms are bent in worship, because you appear.
The whole land goes to work.
All beasts are satisfied with their pasture,
the trees and plants become green.
The birds flutter in their nests,
raising their wings in worship before your spirit.
The ships sail upstream and down.
The fish in the river dart before your face.
You make the seed grow in women,
make fluid into mankind.
How manifold are your works!
They are hidden from the face of man,
O sole God, apart from whom there is no other.
You have made people for yourself,
the Lord of all of them,
wearying himself with them,
the Lord of the whole land, rising for them.
You are in my heart. . .

(from *Near Eastern Religious Texts relating to the Old Testament*, SCM Press and Westminster Press 1978, pp. 16ff.)

Egyptian thinking was shaped by the country. The Egyptian lived in a radiant part of the world: he felt a degree of anxiety as he watched the sun setting in the evening, though experience had taught him that it would appear the next morning, having conquered the powers of the night. Divinized under various names, the sun was the first of the gods, who had engendered other gods and men. In the adjacent box you can read some passages of the great hymn to the sun god composed about 1350 BC by Pharaoh Akhenaten; the author of Psalm 104 may have been inspired by it.

The Nile tended to flood, but this happened at fixed times and the floods brought the fertile alluvium and the water needful for life.

The Egyptian temperament was naturally optimistic; the gods were good and watched over men. After death, a new and splendid life awaited the faithful, even if this life was somewhat impersonal.

In contrast, **Mesopotamian thinking** was by and large fundamentally pessimistic. Those who lived in this area inhabited a valley in which the floods were unpredictable, sometimes producing real 'deluges' of which many traces have been found in archaeological excavations. There were frequent invasions of nomads from the Arabian desert, or surging in from the plains of Iran.

So, too, the Mesopotamian gods were usually capricious, constantly struggling among themselves: man tends to appear as a terrified mortal seeking to avoid the repercussions of their anger. According to the Gilgamesh epic, the gods have given him death for his portion and they have filled him with deceit. The kingdom of the dead is a sorry one: the shades of the dead are reunited for a joyless destiny.

Here are some of the great myths from which we shall have occasion to quote extracts.

The epic of Atrahasis (which means the very intelligent) is known to us from a copy found in Babylon and dating from 1600 BC. In this long poem of 1645 lines, we are shown the gods wearied by all the chores they have to do. They decide to create man to do the work; they form him of clay mixed with the blood of a god whose throat has been cut. But mankind proliferates, makes trouble and wearies the gods, who inflict various scourges, culminating in the flood. However, the god Ea warns a man who builds a boat, and puts his family in it, along with a pair of every animal.

The poem Enuma Elish (named after its first two words, meaning 'when on high') is also very ancient; in its present form it must have been written about 1100 BC. At the very beginning there were two sexual principles, Apsu, the sweet water, and Tiamat (whose name can be found again in the *tehom* – abyss – of Gen. 1.2), the salt waters of the sea. All the gods take their origin from these. Because they annoy her, Tiamat wants to kill them, but Marduk overcomes her, divides her in half like an oyster, and makes her into the vault of heaven. Then he creates man from the blood of a rebel god.

The Gilgamesh epic is beyond question the most famous work from ancient Mesopotamia. Created in Sumer, it developed over more than a thousand years in Assyria and Babylon, and was known by the Hittites, having been copied again in Palestine. In its present form it is composed of twelve cantos.

Gilgamesh, a Sumerian hero, becomes unbearable to the gods because of his pride. They produce a rival, Enkidu, a monster living with the wild beasts. He is humanized by a woman and becomes a friend of Gilgamesh: together, they accomplish all kinds of exploits. However, one day Enkidu dies; Gilgamesh discovers the atrociousness of death and sets off in search of immortality. The hero of the flood gives him the secret of the herb of life. Gilgamesh succeeds in getting hold of it, but a serpent snatches it from him, and Gilgamesh has to resign himself to death.

Canaanite thought has been better known since the discovery, in 1929, of the library of the city of Ugarit, present-day Ras Shamra in Syria. The heyday of Ugaritic civilization was in 1500 BC, about the time of the patriarchs: Abraham, Isaac and Jacob.

The chief god is called El, often presented in the form of a bull. (One of the names for God in the Bible is Elohim, a solemn plural of the word El – the equivalent of our 'royal we'.) This religion pays homage to the deified forces of nature: Baal, god of storm and rain, sometimes called 'the rider on the clouds' (like God in Ps. 68.5), and Anath, his sister, later called Astarte: she is the goddess of war, love and fertility.

Israel, and above all the kingdom of Samaria, was to be attracted by Canaanite religion and the sexual cult offered to the naked goddess in the high places, with its rites aimed at obtaining fertility for land and flocks.

The organization of the universe in Babylon

The poem Enuma Elish tells of the birth of the gods through Apsu, the male principle, and Tiamat, the female principle. Tiamat wants to destroy the young gods, who are disturbing her. They delegate their power to Marduk (the god of Babylon). He kills Tiamat and the gods allied with her. Then he forms the world from her body.

Marduk strengthened his hold on the vanquished gods,
and turned back to Tiamat whom he had bound.
With his unsparing mace he crushed her skull,
then the lord rested and contemplated her corpse,
intent on dividing the form and doing skilful works.
He split it like a dried fish,
set up one half and made it the firmament,
drew a skin over it, posted guards
and instructed them not to let its water escape.

(*Near Eastern Religious Texts*, p. 83)

One might compare this myth with the story in Gen. 1 and also with a different myth often represented in Egyptian sculpture.

The organization of the universe in Egypt

Shu, the god of the air, separates Nut, his daughter, the heavenly vault, from Geb, his son, the earth (Egyptian papyrus from between 1100 and 950 BC).

A hymn, written about 1400 BC, celebrates the sun god Amon, who goes through the night to rise upon sleeping humanity. He is father of all the gods, and they sing his praises:

They say to you, 'Welcome, father of the fathers of all the gods,
who raised the heaven and laid out the earth,
who made what is and created what will be,
we offer hymns to you because you have wearied yourself with us.'   (*Near Eastern Religious Texts*, p. 15).

We shall discover the nature of **biblical thinking** as we go along. However, it is good to emphasize here a basic feature which distinguishes it from the other patterns of thinking to which I have referred.

Shema Israel, Adonai hedad! Hear, O Israel, the Lord is one! That is the essential faith of the people as Deuteronomy puts it (6.4). Israel is aware of being addressed by its God, and the people respond to him in love. By way of a caricature, we might represent mythical thought by an arrow which begins with man and returns to him: man projects a deity on to the beyond and then, by means of ritual, he tries to gain control over this deity, to enlist his service.

In the Bible, the arrow goes the other way. God addresses man and man responds. Here ritual becomes the expression of the response.

The ritual may be the same, but it has changed its meaning. Here is an example. A child may give its mother a bunch of flowers in order to be allowed to go to the cinema; the same child may give the same bunch of flowers to its mother on Mothering Sunday. In the latter case this is a disinterested gesture meant to express a response to its mother's love. It is a form of recognition. That is the basic attitude of eucharist, thanksgiving, to which we shall have occasion to return later.

However, now that we have put these various tools in our luggage, it is time to set off to discover the Bible.

The god Hadad (called Baal in the Ugaritic texts) standing on a bull which serves as a pedestal. He is holding bolts of lightning in his hand (eighth century BC). This calls to mind the cult of the Baals and the bulls which were installed by king Jeroboam at Dan and Bethel.

Nature myths in Canaan

A poem found at Ugarit celebrates Baal and Mot. Baal is the god of storms and rain, Mot is the god of death. So here we have an evocation of the agonizing problem of fertility. Baal aids men by making the soil fertile with his rain; in this way he has been absorbed by Mot, the god of the underworld. Will the water remain captive in the earth, bringing about a drought?

This extract from the poem shows El, the supreme God, guessing that Baal will be reborn, that the rain will return.

Someone announces the dream that El is going to have:

If the all-powerful Baal is alive,
if the prince, the lord of the earth, exists,
in a dream, kindly El benign,
the heavens rain down fat,
the torrents flow with honey.

El has this dream and rejoices:

In a dream, the kindly El benign,
in a vision the Creator of creatures sees
the heavens rain down fat,
the torrents flow with honey.
Joyfully the kindly El cries out,
'Now I can sit and rest,
for all-powerful Baal is alive,
the prince exists, the Lord of the earth.'

In the Bible we can find the formula 'a land flowing with milk (or fatness) and honey' (see, for example, Ex. 3.8). We shall come up against this problem of fertility – to whom is it to be attributed, to the Baals or to God? – when we study the northern kingdom (page 47).

Towards the end of this book (on p. 115), you will find a list of others which will help you to make a fuller study of the subjects covered in this guide, if you so wish. However, remember that the essential thing is to read the texts themselves. You can sort things out very well with a good Bible, its introduction and notes, and this book.

You will find Walter Beyerlin, *Near Eastern Religious Texts relating to the Old Testament*, a useful source book for exploring the thought world of the peoples of Mesopotamia, Ugarit and Canaan (SCM Press and Westminster Press 1978, 299pp.).

MYTH

On a number of occasions we have come across the word 'myth'. What does it mean?

The ancient myths appear as stories presenting gods, goddesses and ancient heroes. On a first reading we may be somewhat disconcerted, but we shall very soon be caught up in them, because we can see that they are concerned with the great questions that we ask ourselves and which are taken further here. Where does the world come from? Why does man exist at all? Why is there suffering and death? Why is there this mysterious attraction between the sexes? What relationship do human beings have with the divine?

However, instead of discussing these problems in profound and difficult books, as happens today, the myths discuss them in 'strip cartoons'.

Let's take a present-day example: the Miss World contest. In a time when royalty hardly exists any more, a queen is chosen and surrounded by her courtiers.

Our existence is often a grey one, with all the tedium of daily life; this queen is crowned and receives magnificent presents. All this helps to put this contest in another world, a dream world, an unreal world. But it expresses the desire of every woman to be beautiful, to be rich, to succeed, and the desire of every man to admire feminine beauty. However, there is another side to it. A woman might be alienated by this myth, might no longer be free to be herself. For example, we can see how girls copy the hair-style of Miss World or try to reproduce her measurements, though it may not suit their kind of beauty. The photo-romances in some magazines in which the secretary marries the boss's son play the same role: they allow the secretary to dream, perhaps enable her to live, but she does so in a dream world, and in the end she neglects her work and thinks of nothing but how to seduce her boss's son.

Putting it at its simplest, we might say: myth consists of taking a great question that we ask ourselves and projecting it, in the form of a story, on an unreal world, on a time before time began, the time of the gods when man did not yet exist. This history of the gods is our own, transposed into another setting. In that way it becomes the model that man must copy.

For example, people ask about the meaning of the attraction between the sexes or how to obtain fertility. They imagine a world outside time, in which gods and goddesses fall in love, have intercourse, and produce children. If they are fertile, our soil and our flocks will also be fertile, since these deities are simply the unreal transposition of our existence. It is therefore necessary to compel them to be fertile: the aim of religious rites is to force the gods to come together in intercourse. Union with sacred prostitutes, in Babylon or the high places of Canaan, was not an orgy, but a religious rite aimed at securing the fertility of the soil.

So all these mythical stories are extremely serious: they are the first reflections of humanity. We can understand why the Bible took up this language to express its own reflections. However, it transformed the language profoundly. To put it briefly, one might say that it made the photo-romance into a psychological novel.

If we read a good psychological novel, a romance, we will find a couple, with their joys and their problems. . . At first sight it may look just like a photo-romance, but in fact it is the opposite. It does not offer us escape into a dream; on the contrary, it recalls us to our everyday life because it is made up of a thousand and one observations by the author, taken from the lives of different couples. So he compels us to reflect on our existence and take it in hand.

Inspired by these great myths, notably in the creation stories, the Bible rethinks them as a function of its faith in a sole God who intervenes in our history and wills for man to be free.

The diagram above is meant to help you to place the great moments in the history of Israel.

The drawings reproduce paintings or sculptures from different periods. You will find them again, with a brief description, at the head of each chapter, and on pages 4, 20 and, above all, 122.

The diagram is a summary. It is important, because it indicates the route we are going to follow.

The kingdom of David and Solomon

About the year 1000, David captured Jerusalem and made it the capital of a kingdom bringing together the tribes of the south and the north. His son Solomon provided an organization for it.

In this way there was a land, a king and a Temple where God made himself present to his people.

This was also the beginning of literature. People began by writing down their memories of the past: the Exodus, or liberation from Egypt, became the fundamental experience in which God was discovered to be the liberator, the saviour; the story of the patriarchs (Abraham, Isaac and Jacob) was written to show how the promise of God to Abraham had been realized with David. The story even went back to the beginning of the world: God did not want only one people to be free, but all humanity.

The two kingdoms: Judah and Israel

On the death of Solomon in 933, the kingdom broke into two: in the south that of Judah, with Jerusalem as its capital; in the north that of Israel, whose capital was Samaria.

Judah remained faithful to the dynasty of David. The king made the nation a unity and represented it before God, this God who lived in the midst of his people in the Temple. The traditions begun under David and Solomon ended up in a Sacred Judaean History (or Sacred History of Judah). The prophets Isaiah and Micah preached.

Israel broke with the dynasty of David: the kings did not therefore have the same religious importance. It was the prophets who gathered the people together and maintained its faith, threatened by contact with Canaanite religion which revered the Baals (here you can see one riding on a bull). The traditions begun under David and

or the great moments of Israel

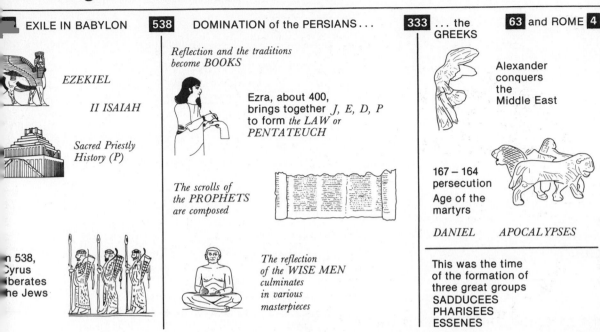

EXILE IN BABYLON

EZEKIEL

II ISAIAH

Sacred Priestly History (P)

In 538, Cyrus liberates the Jews

DOMINATION of the PERSIANS...

Reflection and the traditions become BOOKS

Ezra, about 400, brings together *J, E, D, P* to form *the LAW or PENTATEUCH*

The scrolls of the PROPHETS are composed

The reflection of the WISE MEN culminates in various masterpieces

... the GREEKS

Alexander conquers the Middle East

167 – 164 persecution Age of the martyrs

DANIEL   APOCALYPSES

and ROME

This was the time of the formation of three great groups
SADDUCEES
PHARISEES
ESSENES

Solomon ended up in a Sacred History of the North. The prophets Elijah, Amos and Hosea preached.

Collections of laws were made in the North. When they were taken up later in Judah, they were to become Deuteronomy.

In 721, Israel was destroyed by the Assyrians.

In 587, Judah was deported to Babylon.

Exile in Babylon

The people lived in exile for half a century. They had lost everything, their land and their king; would they also lose their faith in God? Prophets like Ezekiel and a disciple of Isaiah revived their hopes: the priests presented them once again with their traditions, to help them find meaning in their sufferings. This development ended up in the Sacred Priestly History.

Under Persian domination

In 538, the Persian king Cyrus freed the Jews. They settled in Palestine again. The community, purified by the sufferings of the exile, had a wretched existence.

Over the five previous centuries, the people had gone over their history several times, to find meaning and hope in each situation. These three sacred histories, which had already been composed, together with Deuteronomy, were brought together by Ezra, the priest-scribe, to form a unique book: the Law.

In addition, the reflection of the wise men, begun at the time of Solomon and even before, ended up in the production of masterpieces like Job, Proverbs and Tobit.

Under Greek and then Roman domination

In 333, Alexander conquered the Middle East and Greek language and culture spread there.

In 167, a successor of Alexander, king Antiochus, sought to force the Jews to renounce their faith, on pain of death. This was the time of the Israelite martyrs and the people who are known as the Maccabees. These events prompted the reflection of the authors of apocalypses: they awaited the end of time, when God would intervene.

In 63, Rome took over the Middle East. King Herod reigned from 40 BC to 4 BC.

23

1 The Exodus: A People Expresses its Faith

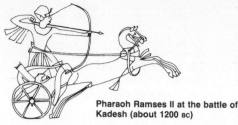

Pharaoh Ramses II at the battle of Kadesh (about 1200 BC)

We are setting out on a journey through the Old Testament: we are going to pass through the key moments in the history of Israel and see how Israel expressed its faith throughout its existence. However, when we leave for a foreign country, before getting into the coach it is a good thing to pause for a moment to review the route that has been suggested to us, to see the reasons for this or that excursion, to gather some information about the customs of the country and the way in which people express themselves. Similarly, before undertaking our journey we are going to stop, in this chapter, at a passage from the book of Exodus. That should get us into practice by discovering a number of things.

First, we are going to familiarize ourselves with reading and studying texts. This may seem a bit complicated, but that is only because we shall try to take an overall view by looking at everything at once. Don't be frightened! Everything will become clear as we go along.

We are going to make the acquaintance of what are called literary genres, or different ways of expressing the same thing. You don't write to your friends in the way that you write to the tax man.

We shall discover that the texts as we now read them in the Bible have a long history: they are made up from even earlier documents. That explains the apparent zig-zag course that we shall follow.

However, this study will not be purely intellectual. We shall discover that for Israel the liberation from Egypt was the foundation event which created Israel as a people. Israel kept going back to it, meditating on it in order to make sense of the present and find hope for the future.

Reading Exodus 12.1 to 13.16

First reading

Begin by reading the text straight through. Do not bother about the titles and notes in your Bible. If there are words and phrases that you don't understand properly, don't worry. We shall come back to them second time through. For the moment, just read the text and ask yourself:

What event is it talking about?

How is it talking about this event? Is it 'narrating it' (in which passages)? Is it deriving laws from it (in which passages)? Is a liturgical celebration being organized to celebrate this event (in which passages)?

Having read the text, try to give a title to the different parts you have discovered. That will compel you to be more precise about the 'literary genre' of these parts.

Second reading

You can now take up certain points with the help of the notes in your Bible, or with other aids.

As you will discover, the texts were produced at different times. Don't spend too much time on this question now; you will understand it better at the end of the chapter.

These are liturgical texts. They show us how to preserve the memory of the event by celebrating it, and what meaning it gives to life today.

Israel took over two already existing festivals, but it changed their meaning and their connection with a historical event. There are, in fact, two kinds of festivals: some celebrate nature and recur every year (we celebrate New Year's Day, the beginning of the year); others celebrate an event which once took place

An Egyptian scribe (fifth dynasty, 2500–2350 BC)

Literary genres

There are different ways of talking about the same thing. For example, we talk about the illness of a close friend in different ways to the sick person's family, the doctor and the social welfare people; we also talk about it after the friend is better in a different way from when he or she was hanging between life and death.

At a deeper level, these different ways of presenting things (or 'literary genres') correspond to different needs in the life of a group. Every group produces a certain number of texts. Take, for example, a small angling club: this will compose documents of a legal kind (the club rules); slogans or short phrases to advertise itself (Relax and go fishing. . .); stories, sometimes embellished stories, real 'epics', in which the catching of a roach is described as though it were the catching of a whale. There are also celebrations: drinks at the bar or the annual dinner.

Thus in order to exist, every society has to create a literature. A nation has its laws, its speeches, its celebrations, its stories about the past, its epics, its poems and its songs.

Consequently, the fact that Israel existed as a people gave rise to a whole literature of different kinds. Here are some of them.

Stories. We have to recall the past to give everyone a common mind. By hearing stories about our ancestors we become aware of belonging to the same family.

Epics. These, too, are accounts of the past, but their chief aim is to arouse enthusiasm and to celebrate heroes, even if it is necessary to exaggerate details in order to do so.

Laws give organization to a people and allow a common life.

The liturgy, celebrations, ritual (sacrifices, for example) express this common life, just as celebration meals bind the family together. Religious actions show the link between men and God.

Poems, canticles and psalms are the expressions of the sentiments and the faith of the people.

The oracles of the prophets – solemn words said to come from God – recall people to true faith.

Teaching by prophets and priests may be given under the form of instruction, but also as stories and tales (parables).

The wisdom writings are reflections on the great human questions: what is life, death, love? Why evil? Why suffering?

Be careful to distinguish literary genres

Each mode of expression, each genre, has its own kind of truth. One does not expect a collection of Asterix cartoons to be as exact as a history book. You don't read the creation story (Gen. 1) as a scientific account. It is a liturgical poem. Similarly, the account of the crossing of the Red Sea is not a newspaper account (Ex. 14): it is an epic.

Thus whenever possible, we should ask what literary genre a particular text is, and what kind of truth it conveys.

---

in history (in France they celebrate July 14, the Storming of the Bastille).

Every spring the nomads celebrated passover: they ate a lamb and used its blood to mark the poles of their tents, to ward off evil spirits. Israel took over this festival (Ex. 12.2–11, 21–22), but made it a remembrance of the liberation from Egypt (12.25–27).

Every spring, peasants celebrated the feast of unleavened bread: they rejoiced over the new crop, doing away with anything which recalled the old one. Israel took over this festival (12.15), but made it a remembrance of the liberation from Egypt (12.17, 39; 13.3–10).

Christians took over these festivals and extended their meanings: they celebrated the definitive freedom brought by Christ.

Israel did the same thing with the old custom of offering the very best to the deity: the firstborn of animals and sometimes of human beings. For them, this custom too became a remembrance of the liberation from Egypt (13.2, 14–15).

📖 Studying a text: Ex. 13.17–14.31

Studying the account of the crossing of the Red Sea will allow us to discover what are called the Pentateuchal traditions.

First reading

Begin by reading this text in your Bible. At first sight it is a story which reads well enough. However, if you look closer, you will notice some strange things. What form does the 'miracle' take? In one instance the wind dries up the sea and the Egyptians get bogged down in the quicksand. In the other, God divides the sea so that the Hebrews can pass through. Sometimes, God himself fights; sometimes he gives orders to Moses, and Moses is the one who acts. The styles differ: sometimes the description is very specific and God is presented as a man who fights, puts spokes in the chariot wheels (in that case we say that the account is anthropomorphic, from a Greek word meaning 'in the form of a man'), and sometimes the story becomes very abstract: God speaks and it is his word which acts.

Observations of this kind made throughout the Pentateuch have led scholars to construct a hypothesis: the Pentateuch was composed from four traditions or documents, at one point collected together to form a single whole.

We are going to try to check this hypothesis by the account given here.

Second reading

Look at the story as it is laid out on pages 28–29. It is set out in three columns: I have taken the text out of a box so that the three traditions can be seen clearly (the fourth is not used here). Of course, there is some guesswork in this division, and sometimes it is by no means clear whether we should put a verse in one column or another. However, even if there are errors in detail, the general impression is important.

When it is laid out in this way, you can read the following text by going from one column to another and keeping to the order of the verses, or you can read each tradition separately by taking only one column. In this story the Elohistic tradition is less important, so to simplify our task, we shall study only the Yahwistic and the Priestly traditions.

Yahwistic tradition

Read this text, which is in the left-hand column. Who are the main characters (you can underline them in different colours)? What do the Egyptians want? Do they know how to get it? Have they the power? What do the Hebrews want? Who will show them how to get it? Who will give them the power?

What is the nature of the event?

Underline the words which keep occurring. Does the word 'see' always have the same meaning (see with one's eyes or with one's faith?)? Has 'fear' the same sense in vv. 1 and 13 as it has in v. 31 (with what other words is it in parallel in this verse)?

The aim of the text seems to be to show how the Hebrews passed from one kind of fear to another. How did this transformation come about? What significance does it have for the faith of the Hebrews and for our own?

Priestly tradition

Read the text, which is in the right-hand column. Here there is only one main character: who is he? What does he want? How does he act? Note all the expressions which keep occurring. Some of them will doubtless cause you problems (God hardened their heart): don't bother about that for the moment; we shall come back to it later (p. 63).

What God seeks is to glorify himself, to make himself known as Saviour. This is not vanity. 'The glory of God is for man to live', said St Irenaeus. God's glory consists in saving his people, and then he appears in the eyes of others as a God who saves, the Lord who protects. But the people have to allow themselves to be saved, to have confidence in God: this is the way in which man can sanctify the name of God, i.e. allow him to show that he is holy, the Lord. We shall see that again when we study the prophet Ezekiel (p. 66).

What is the nature of the event? Note the repetitions: God gives an order, then there is an account of how the order is carried out; this procedure is often used by the Priestly tradition (see the first account of the creation in Gen. 1). Here the important thing is the word of God which creates what it says. Compare the 'miracle' with Gen. 1; a similar theme emerges: God divides the waters and dry land appears (Ex. 14.16, 22, 29; Gen. 1.9, 10).

What meaning does that give to the story of the crossing of the Red Sea? To the creation narrative?

Pentateuchal traditions

Let's begin with a simple example: we have four different texts which tell us about Jesus: the four Gospels.

People have always wanted to bring them together to make a 'life of Jesus', putting into one narrative all the details that we find throughout these four books.

Suppose I ask a literary critic who knows nothing about the existence of the Gospels to study this 'life of Jesus'. He will soon sense that the book does not come from a single hand; for example, he will notice the changes in style (the very detailed descriptions given by Mark and the well-constructed speeches from John), the differences in vocabulary, and so on. And he will put forward the hypothesis that the 'Life' was composed from different documents. He will then try to rediscover these documents by dividing the text back into several columns, corresponding to our four Gospels.

If we now compare the result of his work with our Gospels, we shall doubtless note two things.

'Holes': when Mark and Luke, for example, describe the same episode, the 'life of Jesus' will keep only one version and the other will get lost.

Mistakes: it is not always easy to recognize whether a small fragment of text comes from Matthew or from Luke, and our critic may make mistakes.

Now let's go back to the Pentateuch. These five volumes (which is what the Greek word Pentateuch means) form a single work. However, for a long time scholars have guessed that it was composite, and they have produced the hypothesis that the whole work was a collection of four main traditions written at different times.

Thus the Pentateuch would be written in several stages:

1. Underlying it is the personality of Moses and the events of the Exodus.

2. Subsequently, small units were composed and handed down, orally or perhaps already in writing: stories, laws, speeches, meditations on the event, liturgical celebrations etc.

3. At different periods, scribes (prophets, priests, wise men) collected together these small units to make connected narratives: the four documents.

4. Finally, these four traditions were collected together into a single five-volume work.

We shall have occasion to study these documents in detail. For the moment, it will be enough to put them quickly into context.

1. **The Yahwistic tradition** (denoted by the letter J) is so called because from the beginning it calls God Yahweh (explaining why it is known as J and not Y is rather a complicated business – ultimately this goes back to a less accurate way of reproducing the Hebrew equivalent of Y with a J). It doubtless comes from the time of Solomon, about 950 BC, and originated in royal circles in Jerusalem. The king has an important place there; he is the one who gives the faith unity.

2. **The Elohistic tradition** (denoted by the letter E) calls God Elohim. It came into being, perhaps around 750 BC, in the northern kingdom, after the united kingdom of David and Solomon had split into two. Clearly stamped with the message of prophets like Elijah and Hosea, it attaches great importance to prophets.

These two traditions were brought together in Jerusalem, about 700 BC. This fusion, which is sometimes called Jehovist (JE), was not a simple addition; it was the occasion for completing and developing certain traditions.

3. **The Deuteronomistic tradition** (letter D) is contained above all in Deuteronomy, but it has influenced other books. It was begun in the northern kingdom and completed in Jerusalem.

4. **The Priestly tradition** (letter P) came into being during the Babylonian exile, in the years 587–538 and later. After the deportation, the priests reread their traditions to keep up the people's faith and hope.

These four traditions and their developments were in turn collected together in a single volume: the Pentateuch. This work seems to have been finished about 400 and has often been attributed to Ezra the priest.

In this first chapter we shall simply try to familiarize ourselves with these traditions. In subsequent chapters we shall take each of them up again, one by one. That will take us through the Pentateuch four times, each time keeping to a single tradition.

For further detail about the Pentateuchal traditions, see 'How Israel Became a Nation' by Ernest Nicholson, in *A Basic Introduction to the Old Testament*, edited by Robert C. Walton, SCM Press and John Knox Press 1980, pp. 42–58.

Exodus 13–14

Yahwist	*Elohist*	Priestly

13

[17]When Pharaoh let the people go, God did not lead them by way of the land of the Philistines, although that was near; for God said, 'Lest the people repent when they see war, and return to Egypt.' [18]But God led the people round by the way of the wilderness toward the Red Sea. And the people of Israel went up out of the land of Egypt equipped for battle. [19]And Moses took the bones of Joseph with him; for Joseph had solemnly sworn the people of Israel, saying, 'God will visit you; then you must carry my bones with you from here.'

[20]And they moved on from Succoth, and encamped at Etham, on the edge of the wilderness. [21]And the Lord went before them by day in a pillar of cloud to lead them along the way, and by night in a pillar of fire to give them light, that they might travel by day and by night; [22]the pillar of cloud by day and the pillar of fire by night did not depart from before the people.

14

[1]Then the Lord said to Moses,
[2]'Tell the people of Israel to turn back and encamp

[2b]in front of Pi-hahiroth, between Migdol and the sea, in front of Baal-zephon; you shall encamp over against it, by the sea.

[3]For Pharaoh will say of the people of Israel, "They are entangled in the land; the wilderness has shut them in."
[4]And I will harden Pharaoh's heart, and he will pursue them and I will get glory over Pharaoh and all his host; and the Egyptians shall know that I am the Lord.' And they did so.

[5]When the king of Egypt was told that the people had fled,

[5b]the mind of Pharaoh and his servants was changed toward the people, and they said, 'What is this we have done, that we have let Israel go from serving us?' [6]So he made ready his chariot

[6b]and took his army with him,

[7]and took six hundred picked chariots

[7b]and all the other chariots of Egypt with officers over all of them.

[8]And the Lord hardened the heart of Pharaoh king of Egypt and he pursued the people of Israel as they went forth defiantly.

[9]The Egyptians pursued them,

all Pharaoh's horses and chariots, and his horsemen and his army,

and overtook them encamped at the sea, by Pi-hahiroth, in front of Baal-zephon. [10]When Pharaoh drew near, the people of Israel lifted up their eyes, and behold, the Egyptians were marching after them; and they were in great fear. And the people of Israel cried out to the Lord;

[11]And they said to Moses, 'Is it because there are no graves in Egypt that you have taken us away to die in the wilderness? [12]Is not this what we said to you in Egypt, 'Leave us alone and let us serve the Egyptians? For it would have been better for us to serve the Egyptians than to die in the wilderness.'

13And Moses said to the people, 'Fear not, stand firm, and see the salvation of the Lord, which he will work for you today; for the Egyptians whom you see today, you shall never see again. 14The Lord will fight for you, and you have only to be still.'

15The Lord said to Moses, 'Why do you cry to me? Tell the people of Israel to go forward. 16Lift up your rod, and stretch out your hand over the sea and divide it, that the people of Israel may go on dry ground through the sea. 17And I will harden the heart of the Egyptians, so that they shall go in after them, and I will get glory over Pharaoh and all his host, his chariots, and his horsemen. 18And the Egyptians shall know that I am the Lord, when I have gotten glory over Pharaoh, his chariots and his horsemen.'

19*Then the angel of God who went before the host of Israel moved and went behind them;*

and the pillar of cloud moved from before them and stood behind them, 20coming between the host of Egypt and the host of Israel. And there was the cloud and the darkness; and it lit up the night;

and the night passed without one coming near the other all night.

21Then Moses stretched out his hand over the sea,

21band the Lord drove the sea back by a strong east wind all night, and made the sea dry land,

21cand the waters were divided. 22And the people of Israel went into the midst of the sea on dry ground, the waters being a wall to them on their right hand and on their left. 23The Egyptians pursued and went in after them into the midst of the sea, all Pharaoh's horses, his chariots, and his horsemen.

24And in the morning watch the Lord in the pillar of fire and of cloud looked down upon the host of the Egyptians, and discomfited the host of the Egyptians, 25clogging their chariot wheels so that they drove heavily; and the Egyptians said, 'Let us flee from before Israel, for the Lord fights for them against the Egyptians.'

26Then the Lord said to Moses, 'Stretch out your hand over the sea, that the water may come back upon the Egyptians, upon their chariots and upon their horsemen.' 27So Moses stretched forth his hand over the sea,

27band the sea returned to its wonted flow when the morning appeared; and the Egyptians fled into it, and the Lord routed the Egyptians in the midst of the sea.

28The waters returned and covered the chariots and the horsemen and all the host of Pharaoh that had followed them into the sea; not so much as one of them remained. 29But the people of Israel walked on dry ground through the sea, the waters being a wall to them on their right hand and on their left.

30Thus the Lord saved Israel that day from the hand of the Egyptians; and Israel saw the Egyptians dead upon the seashore. 31And Israel saw the great work which the Lord did against the Egyptians, and the people feared the Lord; and they believed in the Lord and in his servant Moses.

❥ *The Victory Song of the Saved.   Ex. 15.1–21*

In this text, the Exodus has become a poem, a song for celebrating all liberations, of yesterday or today.

Begin by reading this song (aloud – it's better!). You will soon see that there are as it were two choruses responding to each other:

one sings of the power of God in general: vv. 2–3, 6–7, 11, 18;

the other celebrates the specific acts of God: vv. 1, 4–5, 8–10, 12–17.

What impression is made on you by the images they use, particularly in talking about God? Some of them may astonish you, like that of God the warrior (the Greek Bible, two centuries before Christ, turned this into 'God, breaker of war' in the translation). Here we come up against symbolic language (see p. 109); speaking of God the warrior is a way of saying that, 'God is not distant; he is not absent from human struggles for justice and liberty.'

What specific actions of God are celebrated:

in vv. 4–5, 8–10?

in vv. 12–17? The names of the peoples mentioned (Edom, Moab, Canaan, the Philistines) make up an itinerary. What is it? 'The holy abode', 'on thine own mountain', 'the place which thou hast made for thy abode', clearly refers to a building. Which? To what period should we date this stanza?

At this period it was thought that God had a precise purpose in liberating his people (v. 17): what was it?

What does v. 18 teach us about the faith of Israel and its political system?

The Exodus is today

This text leads us to make certain important observations about our faith.

The God celebrated here is not an abstract God, an idea, however lofty. This God is known because his action can be recognized in specific events.

These events are those of today, but the presence of God in them can be discovered only by meditating on the events of former times. Go back to vv. 12–17: we are in the time of the monarchy, the people is settled in Canaan, the Temple has been built, and God is ruling in the midst of his people. Compare this stanza on the passage through the peoples (vv. 12–16) with that on the drowning of the Egyptians (vv. 8–10): it is in the light of what he has just experienced that the author describes the events of the Exodus, and they allow him to decipher that experience.

So this poem is open to the prayer of future centuries: each believing community over the ages is invited to add its own stanza! That is precisely what John does in Revelation, as he shows us the elect, in heaven, singing the song of Moses (Rev. 15.3). Catholic Christianity sings this song during the paschal vigil; it is an invitation to us to extend it by adding other verses celebrating the interventions of God and Jesus in our present-day history, the history of the world and our personal history.

Hebrew poetry

We should look in passing at some features of Hebrew poetry.

Imagery. Hebrew is a very concrete language. In it, objects and things become symbols, suggesting a rich but invisible reality. Rather than develop abstract ideas, the poet prefers to accumulate concrete images, enriched by all his experience. Instead of saying that God is powerful, he shows him wielding a thunderbolt; he is a warrior; his right hand, which wields the sword, is a strong one; he is a guide, gardener, architect etc.

Parallelism. The two parts of a verse.often take up the same idea, but with expressions which are complementary or in opposition. For example,
   This is my God, I will praise him;
   the God of my father, I will exalt him.
Look for other examples in this poem.

The foundation event

'Each one, from generation to generation, must feel as if he himself has come out of Egypt, for it is written: On that day (the day on which the departure from Egypt is celebrated) say to your son, 'That is why the Lord intervened for me, when I came out of Egypt. . .' This extract from the Jewish passover ritual indicates how important this event was for Israel. Throughout its history, the Jewish people – and Christians in turn – have not ceased to meditate on it and discover its significance.

Here we can only evoke some aspects of this richness, but the whole book will allow you to go on discovering it.

The foundation event

'Israel has always considered the departure from Egypt as a special moment in its history, an event which puts it on a different footing from everyone else.' Of course the people existed with Abraham, but only in promise. The Exodus is really the moment when it was created as a people.

When people wanted to understand the meaning of other events (the crossing of the Jordan, the union of the twelve tribes), institutions or rites, and when they wanted to explain the very existence of the people, it was to the Exodus that they turned.

The encounter with God

In this event, Israel began to discover who was its God, and what his name was. It discovered that God is liberator and saviour before recognizing him as creator. That is so important that we shall come back to it. God is 'the one who has brought us out of the house of slavery'. That is his principal title, almost his proper name, used time and again throughout the Bible.

At the time of the vision of the burning bush, God gave his name to Moses, Yahweh, and he explains it by a phrase which can be translated, 'I am who I will be', that is to say, you will discover who I am in what I shall be and do with you, and with your people, in history (Ex. 3.14).

Thus God and his people are united by a blood-tie (cf. the rite in Ex. 24.3–8), by a covenant.

'From servitude to service. . .' This title, given to a commentary on Exodus, is a splendid summary of the essential movement. The people is aware that God has freed them from slavery in Egypt; from now on they may freely put themselves at his service, a service which consists primarily in a daily life led in covenant with God, which is given expression in worship.

A past that is always present

The Jewish passover expresses very well that the Exodus is not just a past event; it is an event which accompanies Israel throughout its existence. When people celebrate it in worship, it becomes present and they participate in it. Reference to this past allows them to understand the present: the whole of life is seen as an exodus, a march towards the kingdom of God. It makes it possible to keep faith in the terrible times of catastrophe or deportation; if God has freed us before, he can do so again. This maintains our hope by turning our attention to the future.

The first Christians continued this meditation. They interpreted the life of Christ as an exodus, and texts like the First Letter of Peter, the Epistle to the Hebrews or Revelation show that all Christian existence is an exodus, following Christ to the definitive kingdom.

As we think of all that, we have gone beyond the texts of the book of Exodus, but as we shall see, everything that meditation on this event has prompted in the course of time also makes up the event and allows us to understand it.

However, can we go back through all this richness of meaning to the event itself? Can we answer the question, 'What actually happened?' That is what we shall now try to see.

What is a historical event?

Before trying to see 'what happened at the Exodus', we must see more clearly what a historical event is.

The answer to this question might seem obvious: a historical event is made up of facts which you can see, or could have seen. However, that definition needs to be qualified.

There are no such things as 'brute' facts, facts which one can account for in an objective way: there are only interpreted facts. Two people describe the same event: they do it in two different ways. That is to say, they do not report the fact in itself, but 'the fact as they saw it', and the same gesture might seem mockery to one and encouragement to the other.

Facts are historical because they are interpreted and given a meaning. There are past facts which have been forgotten immediately because they have no meaning: they are 'in history' but not historical. I open the door, I pick up a pencil . . . these facts exist, but they do not have any special meaning. A historical event is one which leaves a trace in the memory of a person or a group, a fact which lasts in history because it is found to have meaning.

In this sense, however, the meaning is not perceived until afterwards, sometimes long afterwards. As we see the new era which has begun for the Catholic church, we can see the importance of the decision of John XXIII to hold a council; again, the manifold declarations about the 'rights of man' which the French Revolution provoked around the world help us to understand it. So it is by going through history and seeing all that a fact has led to down the ages that we begin to grasp its significance.

Sometimes, too, we have to go back through history: certain events, perhaps minimal ones, have this power of becoming a symbol for a whole development. Suppose we take a well-known example: the fact that insurgents entered the Bastille to free two or three prisoners guarded by a few easy-going soldiers is a modest enough fact in comparison with other dramatic or glorious events. When did this fact become 'historical'? On 14 July 1789? Or after the revolution had succeeded, when it became the symbol of it? Both together! This is because there was a fact on that day which could be made into a symbol; however, only by taking on value as a symbol did it become historical.

With this last example we have come very close to the epic. In an epic narrative, the facts get mixed up; different events are combined, embellished and interpreted to form the account. We cannot tell whether all the events narrated are exact, and yet, beginning from real facts and concentrated on the personality of a number of people, they express something very true: what the people has discovered in depth about its origins, its values, about what it is. The Song of Roland could not have been produced without the personality of Charlemagne, of Roland, and the expedition across the Pyrenees; but its truth is also its expression of the soul of the people at the time it was produced and its vague feeling of being what it is thanks to these heroes.

The Exodus. What happened?

Moses

Underlying these stories is the personality of Moses. Born in the reign of Horemheb (1334–1306) or Seti I (1309–1290), he was educated in a school of scribal interpreters, needed by Egypt in its relations with the Asiatics.

He bore the marks of his time in the desert, in Midian: there he was in contact with a group – of which his father-in-law Jethro was priest – which seems to have been deeply religious and to have worshipped a god Yahu.

Two exoduses?

Some texts present the departure from Egypt as an expulsion, others as an escape. There were probably two exoduses which were then combined in popular memory.

The expulsion will have taken place about 1550. Semites, the Hyksos, had taken power in Egypt round about 1720. They were expelled in 1552. At that time, sons of Jacob, who were also Semites and had profited from the presence of the Hyksos, were also expelled. They took a northern route, and then went down towards the oasis of Kadesh. One day, they entered Canaan from the south.

The escape took place about 1250. Another group of Semites had stayed in Egypt. Galvanized by

Moses, they took advantage of a spring festival to escape (and perhaps some catastrophes had fallen on Egypt, bringing about the death of the children). They took the northern route. Near Lake Sirbonis, an Egyptian detachment caught up with them, but the chariots got bogged down in the quicksand. Safe, the Semites left this dangerous route and went down towards Kadesh.

The 'crossing' of the sea

In the Yahwistic tradition, it is not a matter of crossing 'through' the sea: the wind dries up the waters and the Egyptian chariots get bogged down under the amazed eyes of the Hebrews. We know from ancient historians that the shores of Lake Sirbonis, formed of a narrow band of sand which divides the lake from the Mediterranean, were very dangerous.

It is only in the Priestly account that God divides the waters and makes dry land appear, as at the beginning of the world he divides the primordial waters to produce dry land! The Exodus is presented as an act of creation, and the creation narrative is presented (Gen. 1) as an act of liberation.

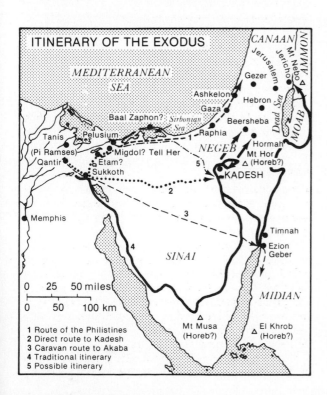

ITINERARY OF THE EXODUS

1 Route of the Philistines
2 Direct route to Kadesh
3 Caravan route to Akaba
4 Traditional itinerary
5 Possible itinerary

Sinai

Depending on the tradition, this mountain is called Sinai or Horeb. Where was it?

Was it Mount Musa, in the south of the Sinai peninsula? This southern itinerary has been traditional only since the fourth century AD; the settlement of monks at the foot of Mount Musa may have influenced this choice.

Near Kadesh, at Mount Hor?

In Midian, east of the Gulf of Akaba?

A theology in epic style

You may be disappointed that everything is so uncertain. That is the result of the nature of these accounts: they are epic, and their importance is primarily theological.

An epic. Different clans claiming the same origin – those who stayed in Canaan, those which were expelled from Egypt, those who escaped with Moses – formed a federation at the time of the assembly at Shechem (Josh. 24). In allying with the rest, each clan contributed its traditions, which were fused to form the common heritage of the new group. The various remembrances were played off, one against the other. So, for example, the remembrance of the 'crossing' of the Jordan contributes towards making the skirmish by the lake into a 'crossing of the sea' (compare Josh. 3.13c with Ex. 14.15a). A number of events marked the settlement in Canaan: the crossing of the Jordan, the capture of fortified cities, the victory at Taanach celebrated by Deborah (Judg. 5). From among these, one event emerged to become the symbol of all the others, the symbol of liberation: the Exodus.

A theology. These remembrances were worked on, not to give us a course in history or geography, but to tell us about God. These stories show us the face of a liberating God, who wants people to be free, to serve him freely and to live their lives in covenant with him. That is the essential element, the motive power throughout the life of Israel and then of Christianity.

This fundamental experience will allow people one day to discover that God does not just want to liberate a people, but mankind: they will then be able to write creation stories which extend this gift of life and liberty to all mankind.

2 The Kingdom of Jerusalem

A reconstruction of the Temple of Solomon

Round about the year 1000 BC, David became king and captured Jerusalem, which he made his capital. This was a new starting point for Israel. How was it reached?

From the Exodus to David

About 1200, the group which had left Egypt under the leadership of Moses and then of Joshua settled in Canaan. The country had already been occupied by various clans, grouped around small fortified towns on the hilltops. These clans made their living from agriculture and trade, and fought among themselves.

By force or by stratagem, sometimes by treaty, the Hebrew group became established in the centre of the country. Later, the book of Joshua came to describe this settlement as a marvellous epic, above all to teach a lesson: the Hebrews had conquered the country, but God had allowed them to do so; the conquest was a gift.

At a great assembly held at Shechem, a religious bond was established between various tribes, which made a covenant with God (Josh. 24).

During what is known as the time of the Judges (between 1200 and 1000), the tribes centred on Yahweh – of which there were now twelve – were divided into three groups: in Galilee, in Samaria and south of Jerusalem. The link between them was very loose, and was principally religious. Sometimes, however, when danger threatened one tribe or another, a saviour (or judge) arose and called the people to arms: then everyone returned home after the victory (Book of Judges).

However, pressure from the Ammonites in the centre and above all from the Philistines, good warriors and mighty beer-drinkers, who had settled in the south near the Mediterranean, made the various tribes aware that they needed a strong central power. The central tribes

A Canaanite king. Ivory (Megiddo, between 1350 and 1150)

had an unfortunate venture into monarchy with Abimelech; the southern tribes did not fare very well with Saul.

In the religious sphere, the inhabitants of Canaan worshipped a God El, but above all they practised a nature religion: they worshipped Baals, who were divinized forces of nature (storms, the earth, etc.), and their consorts, the Astartes, goddesses of love and fertility. The Hebrews who worshipped Yahweh as their God were often tempted by the sensuous cults of the Canaanites in the high places.

David

Profiting from the fact that the three great powers of the Near East were helpless at that time (these were the Hittites, who had virtually disappeared, the Egyptians and the Assyrians), and relying on his personal valour, David succeeded in having himself chosen king successively by the tribes of the south and then the tribes of the north. He conquered the city of the Jebusites situated between the two groups of tribes and made it his capital: Jerusalem. That created a completely new situation for Israel.

So in the political sphere Israel had a king like other nations. That raised a question for some believers: was not Yahweh the only king?

The prophet Nathan then came to play a key role. To consecrate the king in Babylon or Egypt, the priest would proclaim an oracle from the national god over him, in these terms: 'You are my son; I am your father'. Through Nathan, God declares that he will take responsibility for a formula of this kind: on the day of his consecration, the son of David – that is, each of his legitimate successors – becomes the son of God.

We can see how the king, as God's representative, has an essential role: he appears as the one responsible for the well-being of the nation before God; political and religious unity are realized around him.

In the religious sphere, David performed an action with political significance: he decided to install the ark of the covenant in his capital. From the time of the Exodus this ark had been the place of the divine presence for his people. By establishing it in Jerusalem, David bound the presence of God to that of the monarchy. It is not surprising that the faithful challenged this action, because here were two ways of representing God. There was either a static God, installed in a particular place, under man's control, at the disposal of the king and the people; or God remained free, a God who had guided his people, who went where he willed, whose presence and whose action were always unforeseeable (this is shown, in symbolic language, by the itinerary of the ark narrated in I Sam. 5–6). And God, again through Nathan, rejected David's offer to build him a house (II Sam. 7).

These are two ways of conceiving of God that we shall find right through the Bible (cf. Acts 7.48), and which still remain possible even today.

In the administrative sphere, David began to organize his kingdom. Different functions appear: army leaders, priests, secretaries, a ministry of information (II Sam. 8.16–18). And David even held a census (II Sam. 24).

David's foreign policy also had religious consequences. Through his victorious campaigns, David brought a number of tribes into his kingdom; other kingdoms submitted to him. By becoming vassals of the king, these people could also benefit from the covenant with God. The scribes who came to write the history of the people tried to show that this universalism had already been proclaimed in the person of Abraham.

Solomon

Solomon inherited his father's kingdom. Endowed with God-given wisdom (I Kings 3), that is to say, with the art of governing well, he took advantage of peace to organize the kingdom. A more developed government came into being (I Kings 4–5): the country was divided into twelve districts, each charged with providing for one month the provisions and the manpower for his great projects. Imposing stables were built at Megiddo and elsewhere. A fleet sailed over the seas. Riches deriving from trade with Egypt and Syria flowed into Jerusalem, where Solomon built a magnificent Temple for his God and an even larger palace for himself. He was a great king!

And yet there was a darker side to his kingdom. Solomon played the great lord too much, acting like any other king of the time and not as God's representative. The Bible credits him with 700 wives and 300 concubines. Perhaps that's too much! But Solomon had several wives (one of them a daughter of Pharaoh) from foreign nations: they brought their gods with them and the risk of idolatry was great. Solomon exploited his people, and although he succeeded in containing a potential revolt, it broke out after his death. His son, politically incompetent, was the cause of the division of the kingdom into two: the northern tribes went their own way. The united kingdom had lasted only seventy years.

The two kingdoms

From 933 there are two kingdoms:

The southern kingdom, or Judah, with Jerusalem as its capital. All its kings were descendants of David and thus benefited from the promise handed on by Nathan: saints or sinners, they are sons of God.

The northern kingdom, or Israel, with Samaria as its capital. Its kings were not descended from David (of the nineteen, eight were assassinated!). In this kingdom the king was not the one who was held responsible for the salvation of the people before God.

The beginnings of a literature

Because there was peace, because Solomon had organized his court along the lines of that of Pharaoh, a start was made on editing the sacred traditions. The Bible refers to two books which have been lost, 'The Book of the Upright' and 'The Book of the Wars of Yahweh'. Doubtless at that time a history of the ark (I Sam. 2–5) and a history of the Davidic succession (II Sam. 9–20) were composed. Poems were collected together: the song of the bow and the elegy on Abner, doubtless composed by David (II Sam. 1; 3), perhaps some psalms, and sayings later collected in the book of Proverbs.

Above all, a start was made on the Sacred Judaean History which we call the Yahwistic tradition. That is what we are going to read next.

The Sacred Judaean History

Solomon organized his court along the lines of that of Pharaoh: scribes had an important place in it. Trained in the craft of writing, they were also wise men, people endowed with discernment who had learned the art of living: their wisdom was considered to be a divine gift.

The Sacred Judaean History (the sacred history of the kingdom of Judah) is doubtless their work. It is called the Yahwistic tradition (or document) because from the beginning God is called Yahweh. To make things simpler, the author of this tradition is called 'the Yahwist': the word can denote a scribe or group of scribes. It is denoted by the letter J (see p. 27 above).

This tradition was begun in the time of Solomon and continued under his first successors in the kingdom of Judah. The king, son of David and son of God, is the divine representative and brings about the political and religious unity of the nation. The Yahwistic tradition is at the service of the monarchy and shows that this realizes the divine promise to the patriarchs: thus it is also a political writing which supports the monarchy. At the same time, however, the Yahwist criticizes it and calls it to order: the king is not an absolute monarch, but is in the service of God and his people, and even of other nations.

I shall suggest that we read some texts from this tradition, following the theme of the blessing as a guideline. Then we shall study the creation story in more detail.

Some characteristics of the Yahwist

He is a marvellous storyteller. His stories are very vivid, always concrete and full of imagery. God is often represented as a man (anthropomorphism): in the creation story he is in turn a gardener, a potter, a surgeon, a tailor. That is the Yahwist's way of telling us about God and man; he proves to be a profound theologian.

He is a very human God. He walks with Abraham as with a friend (Gen. 2); he invites himself to a meal with Abraham and bargains with him (Gen. 18). Man lives on familiar terms with him and meets him in everyday life.

His is a God who is utterly different. However, this God is the master: he commands or forbids (Gen. 3.16); he calls. 'Go, leave,' he says to Abraham and Moses. He has a plan for history. His blessing will bring happiness to his people and through them will extend to all people. (It is remarkable to find such universalism at this period.) Man must respond to this divine call and obey God.

Man's sin is to want to take God's place. This sin draws down the curse on him: Cain, the flood, the tower of Babel.

His is a God who is always ready to forgive, particularly when men like Abraham (Gen. 18) or Moses (Ex. 32.11–14) intercede with him, and always ready to renew his blessing.

📖 *A key text: Gen. 12.1–3*

[1]*Now the Lord said to Abram,*
'Go from your country and your kindred and your father's house to the land that I will show you.
[2]*And I will make of you a great nation,*
and I will bless you, and make your name great,
so that you will be a blessing.
[3]*I will bless those who bless you,*
and him who curses you I will curse;
and by you all the families of the earth will bless themselves.'

Who are the main characters here?
What words seem to you to be important and keep occurring (how many times)?
Note the tenses of the verb: imperative and futures.
    The word nation denotes a people organized and settled in a territory.
What does this text tell you?
Read Gen. 12.6–9. What new promise is made to Abraham (v. 7)?

Reading some texts

The cycle of creation stories

The table on the right shows you the probable division of the verses of Gen. 1–11 between the Yahwist and the Priestly writer. Here we shall be reading only the J texts. We shall be studying the creation story in more detail later on (page 39).

These chapters are not history but theology expressed in images: they are the reflection of wise men. The author tries to reply to the great questions which people ask about life, death, love, our origins. His starting point is his faith in God, and he reuses ancient myths (see page 21).

The story begins in an optimistic way, but soon the history of mankind appears as that of the proliferation of evil. The curse falls five times in succession (3.14, 17; 4.11; 5.29; 9.25). Each time, God forgives or promises salvation, except on the last occasion. The story of the tower of Babel expresses the feeling that we live in a broken world, in which men no longer understand one another. So is our history accursed?

How does the story of Abraham appear as a response?

Note the reversal of 11.4–12.2 and the five blessings.

The Abraham cycle

The genre here is not yet historical. We have legendary traditions based on a historical foundation and given a religious interpretation in order to provide teaching.

Abraham appears as the guardian of the divine blessing for all peoples. What does he do with it

in Gen. 12.10–20?

in Gen. 18.16–33? Note vv. 17–18.

in Gen. 22.15–18?

If you wish, you can see how the New Testament continues the line of Abraham: Gal. 3.8; Heb. 11.8f.

The Jacob cycle

Here we have the same literary genre as that of Abraham. Traditions about two different clans, those of Jacob and Israel, have been fused together and the two names have been given to the same person, who becomes the grandson of Abraham.

Read Gen. 28.13–16. Why does God make promises to Jacob? What are they?

Gen. 32.23–33. For this episode of the struggle between Jacob and God, see the notes in your Bible or a commentary.

Chapter	J	P
	The creation	
1		1–31
2		1–4a
	4b–25	
3	1–24	
4	1–26	
5		1–28
	29	30–32
	The flood	
6	1–8	9–22
7	1–5	6
	7	8–9
	10	11
	12	13–16a
	16b	17a
	17b	18–21
	22–23	24
8		1–2a
	2b–3a	3b–5
	6–12	13a
	13b	14–19
	20–22	
9		1–17
	From Noah to Abraham	
	18–27	28–29
10		1a
	1b	2–7
	8–19	20
	21	22–23
	24–30	31–32
11	1–9	10–27a
	27b–30	31–32

Benediction

Benediction – the word comes from the Latin – or blessing means saying good things. When God says good things to someone, good things happen to him, because the word of God is all-powerful and does what it says.

By contrast, cursing – malediction – is to say bad things and thus bring them about.

The good things that God says or does can be in the order of having (riches, fertility), but they are above all in the order of being: the very life of God.

The Moses cycle

Moses remains the key figure in the Old Testament. However, his person appears differently in each of the traditions.

For the Yahwist, he is present everywhere, from the departure from Egypt to the arrival in Canaan. But God is the true leader of the people, the only liberator. Moses does not perform miracles, is not a leader in war, does not found a religion; rather, he is the shepherd whom God inspires to make his will known to men.

 ### *Exodus 3.1–8   God calls Moses*

Look at the reaction of Pharaoh in Ex. 8.4; 10.17; 12.31–32. Compare Moses' role as intercessor with that of Abraham in Gen. 18. The people of God must forgive and bless even their worst enemy!

The Balaam cycle

Israel found themselves confronted with the people of Moab. The king of the country brought the seer Balaam from the east to curse Israel. What does Balaam do (Num. 24.1)? It would be a good thing to read the whole of Num. 24.1–19, but you should at least look at vv. 7 and 17.

Here is the way in which Num. 24.17 was understood at the time of Christ, according to the explanatory translation (or targum) which was made then:

Hebrew text	Targum
A *star* shall come forth out of Jacob, and a *sceptre* shall rise out of Israel.	A *king* shall arise from the house of Jacob and a *saviour* (or *messiah*) from the house of Israel.

Does this explanation help you to understand Matt. 2.1f.? What is this star, for Matthew?

The patriarchs

When we want to construct a family tree, we begin with ourselves and go back to our ancestors. We are guided simply by ties of blood. Of course that is important, but sometimes there are ties of friendship or companionship which are stronger than blood ties. A friend becomes a 'brother'. So we can understand how, even now, in certain tribes, when an alliance is made everything is shared: traditions and ancestors. Since now there is only one group, the fact is expressed by setting up ties of kinship between ancestors.

This is what Israel seems to have done in the case of the patriarchs. Round about the eighteenth or seventeenth century BC, various nomadic clans settled in Canaan: those of Jacob, Isaac, Israel, Abraham. . . They adopted the same local god, El. They made an alliance. Once they became brothers, their respective ancestors also became kin: in this way Abraham became the father of Isaac and the grandfather of Jacob was identified with Israel.

There is nothing disturbing about this hypothesis which scholars have put forward. It simply makes us rather more careful when we claim to be reconstructing the history of the patriarchs. However, that is not the essential thing.

The essential element is the religious significance which Israel saw in this history. In this celebration of the deeds of its ancestors, in each generation it found food for meditation and a new strength for its faith. Here the Yahwist discovers a promise of blessing which is given to the king, the son of David: he must pass it on to everyone. The Elohist shows his contemporaries, who are tempted to abandon God for Canaanite idols, that their fathers Abraham and, above all, Jacob were models of faithfulness towards God. The Priestly writer lived in exile: everything seemed to have fallen apart; there was no more possible hope. To strengthen his faith and his hope, he relied on the promise of God to Abraham: God once pledged his faithfulness; he will save us despite our sins.

Paul sees Abraham as the very embodiment of faith: it is not that he wants to be righteous before God through what he does, his works; he puts his whole trust in him. The Letter to the Hebrews invites us to set out in the steps of Abraham, without wanting to know the way in advance.

What are we going to discover in Abraham to enable us to live in faithfulness to God today?

❧ *The Creation Story. Gen. 2.4 – 3.24*

First read this well-known text carefully. Note your reactions and your questions.

Then go through it again asking certain questions (you can underline the text in different colours):

Who are the main characters? What are they doing?

Try to distinguish different parts: what is each one of them about?

Select the themes or expressions which keep occurring. In particular, where is there mention of the tree of life? Of the tree of the knowledge of good and evil? Which expressions explain what one gets from eating its fruit?

Wisdom reflection

What is the literary genre of this text? Clearly it is not an eye-witness account, nor is it instruction in history or geography. Rather, it is the reflection of wise men who are raising the great human questions. Where do we come from? Where are we going? What is the reason for life, suffering, death? Why the mysterious attraction between the sexes? What is the relationship between man and God, man and nature (work), man and his fellows?

To try to reply to these questions, the author relies on his own reflections, but also on those of the wise men of other civilizations. Above all, the starting point for his reflection is his faith: believers before him had already meditated on the Exodus and the entry into Canaan; in these events they discovered something of the aspect of their God. And it is above all in terms of what he already knows about his God in this way that the author tries to respond.

We shall take up some of the questions, and put them back in the context of the thought of the time.

Adam and Eve. First, let's get one difficulty out of the way. You sometimes hear people say, 'Adam and Eve never existed.' That shows that they haven't understood the literary genre of this text. Humanity certainly started one day. With whom? Where? How? Science has to answer these questions, not the Bible. But the Bible calls the first couple, or the first couples, that science may present to us as the first human beings, 'Adam and Eve'. In Hebrew these names mean Mr Man and Mrs Life; thus they are symbolic names representing both the first human beings and every human being: everyman.

The formation of the earth. What scientific idea (of the time) underlies this story? (We shall see that the science of Gen. 1 is different.) Doubtless here we have the underlying experience of the nomad, for whom an oasis in the desert is a paradise.

The creation of man. Of what elements is man formed? Read the passage below taken from a Babylonian poem: what similarities and differences can you see between the two texts? How are the pessimism of Babylon and the optimism of the Bible expressed?

This text does not contradict in any way the theory of evolution, according to which man's origins lie in animal life. It gives a religious significance to the appearance of man. What significance?

The Atrahasis epic (Babylon, before 1600 BC)

The gods are worn down by the tasks that they have to perform:
When the gods laboured in the fashion of men
and were subjected to toil,
the toil of the gods was great,
burdensome their labour, immense their distress. . .
The gods rebelled. To be rid of their buden, they decided to create man. The god Ea advises:
Cut the throat of a god,
with his blood and his flesh
let Nintu (the mother goddess) mix clay,
so that god and man are mingled
in the clay. . .

Man and nature. What is the role of man towards nature (2.15)? Towards the animals (2.19: to name is to give a new being)? Is it not to proclaim that science is legitimate?

The creation of woman. Why was woman created? In what way is the idea expressed that man and woman are of the same nature and that they differ from animals?

For us, to be 'side by side' signifies equality: perhaps we have the same image here. Perhaps, too, the passage takes up an old play on words: in Sumerian, side and life can be written in the same way.

Deep sleep: the Hebrew here has a rare word which expresses a supernatural experience, a kind of ecstasy, as the Greek Bible translates it.

Perhaps here we have the old myth according to which man becomes man only in loving relations with woman. See the text below.

The Gilgamesh epic

Gilgamesh is the hero of the city of Uruk. To counterbalance his power, the gods create a monster, Enkidu, who lives with the wild animals. On the advice of a huntsman, a sacred prostitute offers herself to him. He goes with her for six days and seven nights, and then sated, he wants to return to the wild animals, but they flee. Enkidu wants to follow them, but this is impossible. He has lost his strength, but he has become a man.

Enkidu has no strength,
his knees remain motionless
when he wants to follow his herd.
Weakened, he can no longer run as before,
but his heart and his spirit are lightened.
He returns to sit at the feet of the courtesan
and begins to gaze at her face,
and now he understands
what the courtesan says. . .

The serpent. This creature played a prominent role in mythology. In Egypt the serpent opposed the sun god during the night, trying to prevent him from rising. In Canaan, it was a sexual symbol in certain cults. According to the Gilgamesh epic, it was the serpent which stole the herb of life (see below). All this could have influenced the choice of the serpent. However, the essential concern of the text is to show that sin does not come from within man, that it is not part of his nature: it comes from outside. Thus man is responsible for his actions (compare this view with the Babylonian text below).

Babylonian theodicy (second millennium)

The king of the gods, creator of mankind,
the god Ea who modelled their clay,
the goddess who fashioned them,
gave man a perverse spirit,
they gave him for ever,
not truth, but the lie.

The Gilgamesh epic

Haunted by the idea of death, Gilgamesh leaves in search of immortality. The hero of the flood reveals to him the existence of a herb of life. Gilgamesh succeeds in plucking it from the abyss and wants to take it to his city. He goes for two days and then stops.

Gilgamesh saw a well whose water was cool.
He went down into it to bathe in the water.
A serpent snuffed the fragrance of the plant.
Silently it came up from the earth
and carried off the plant; immediately
it shed its old skin.
Thereupon Gilgamesh sat down and wept,
his tears running down over his face.

The tree of the knowledge of good and evil. Of course, this tree and its fruit are symbols (it's not a matter of an 'apple'), in the same way as we might say that 'we enjoy the fruits of sleep or of our labours'. What does the tree represent?

We must dispose of a wrong interpretation: this is not the tree of knowledge or of science, as though they were forbidden to man. The text affirms the contrary: God gives man the world for him to cultivate, animals for him to name, and thus science for him to create.

In reading this text you will have noticed that this tree was often connected with expressions like, 'You will be like God, knowing good and evil' (3.5); this tree is 'to be desired to make one wise' (3.6); see also 3.22.

If you have time, you might read Ezekiel 28: the prophet takes up the same imagery (Eden or paradise, being like God, cherubim, and so on); the sin of the king of Tyre is to say 'I am god' because he has acquired wisdom.

What is forbidden man, then, is to refuse to be man, to want to make himself God. Only God is 'wise', knowing the roots of happiness and misfortune. One cannot steal this wisdom; God has given it to those who love him with respect or, as the Bible puts it, to those who 'fear' him (see, for example, Prov. 3.18).

The wisdom which man thought he could steal finally left him naked; he discovers that he is only a man, and he shares the serpent's state: naked and crafty are the same word in Hebrew.

Suffering and death. Did man suffer and die before the advent of sin? That is not a good way of putting the question. The author looks closely at the human condition in his day; he knows that there is suffering and death, and tries to make sense of them. And he comes up against the wisdom of God which men cannot know. To want to steal this wisdom is to find oneself naked again, paralysed by this sorrowful human condition. So he discovers a link between suffering and sin. Before sin, Adam would have suffered and died, but he would have gone through this without anguish, trusting in God. (We shall return to this word 'before'.)

Original sin

What Christians call 'original sin' does not appear in the text of Genesis, but in Paul's Letter to the Romans (Rom. 5).

We understand by Genesis that if Adam is man, everyman, his sin is that of everyman, the sin of the world. In this sense, each of our sins forms part of this sin of Adam, increases it and gives it its particular character.

For Paul, the affirmation of original sin is simply the consequence of a much more important fact: we are all saved in Jesus Christ. We are all saved, he goes on, because we all need to be. He then tries to prove this, first of all in terms of statistics, by showing that both Jews and Gentiles are sinners (Rom. 1–3). He then resumes his demonstration in a symbolic way: since Adam represents all of us, and Adam sinned, we are all sinners in him. However, that is merely a consequence. The essential thing is that we are saved in Jesus Christ. Where sin abounded, grace abounded even more. In other words, he tells us that we are not 'gracious', but given grace: sinners who have been reprieved. And that is miraculous. When we survive an accident that could have been fatal, our scars are a miraculous sign: each time we see them, they remind us that we are still alive. The dogma of original sin ought also to encourage us: it reminds us that God saves us in Jesus Christ, that we are more than conquerors in him who loved us (Rom. 8.37).

The tree of life. This appears for the first time in 2.9. According to 2.16, man can eat of it. It reappears in 3.22f. Here we discover the goodness of God. He is not jealous, as the serpent claims. He and he alone has the power of life, and he is ready to give it to man on condition that man wants it: 'I have set before you life and death . . . therefore choose life' (Deut. 30.19–20).

Paradise: a task to be performed

The author wants to express two things which are hard to put into words without losing touch with them. The first is an inference from his faith: God created man to be happy and free; God did not create sin and evil. He knows the second from experience: all men are sinners; all men want to make themselves God, and always have done.

If we pick up a coin, we cannot see both sides at the same time; to do that, we have to cut the coin in half across its circumference, and then it is no longer a real coin. The Yahwist does something like that here. His two affirmations are the two sides of human reality; he separates them to put them side by side, 'before' and 'after'. That's clear enough, but it stops being man! This 'before' is not a historical tense but a theological image; it is simply meant to express God's concern, a concern which is never in fact realized as such.

Some time after the Yahwist, the prophet Isaiah took up the same images again, but projected them on to the end of time: this is what God will bring about one day (Isa. 11.1–9). Perhaps the Yahwist and Isaiah are telling us the same thing: paradise is not in the past, a beautiful dream that we have lost; it is before us, and is a task to perform.

Which God? Which man?

I began this study by saying that the Yahwist is trying to answer the great questions we ask ourselves. Finally, what help has he given you?

What picture of God do you find here?

What is man?

For an explanation of this fresco see p. 122.

Prophets of the Kingdom of Judah

We are now going to make the acquaintance of the first prophets to preach in the kingdom of Judah.

Nathan

He has left no writings, but he played an important role alongside David.

II Sam. 7.1–17. Read this text and put it in the context of the religious and political situation of David's kingdom (see p. 34).

Note the contrasts: dwell in a house/move about in a tent; house (to live in) / house (dynasty); my name / your name. Can you rediscover the two notions of God which were mentioned on p. 35? Can you make them more precise?

What is the role of the king in Israel? Look at the titles given to David: servant, shepherd, king.

If you have time, read I Chron. 17.1–15. The book of Chronicles was written after the exile, more than five centuries after this text from Samuel. Compare II Sam. 7.14 with I Chron. 7.13 (people no longer believed that this son of David could sin), and II Sam. 7.16 with I Chron. 17.14 (the possessive adjectives have changed). This shows that in five centuries the figure of this son of David has increased in importance. Read Psalm 2: now he is said to be king over the whole world. That allows us to understand the sense in which this title son of David could be given to Jesus.

Nathan's other interventions can be found in II Sam. 12 (David's sin) and I Kings I.

Isaiah

Isaiah preached in Jerusalem between 740 and 700. He was a great poet and an acute politician, but above all he was a prophet. He exerted considerable influence on his time. Two centuries later, some disciples inspired by him laid claims to his name, and their work was added to his. So we have to distinguish between the book of Isaiah (which has 66 chapters) and the prophets: Isa. 1–39 is partly the work of Isaiah; Isa. 40–55 comes from a prophet living at the time of the exile, and Isa. 56–66 from a disciple after the exile.

The political situation at the time of Isaiah was a complicated one. The two kingdoms of Jerusalem and Samaria were prosperous (at least as far as the rich were concerned – they were grinding the faces of the poor!), but Assyria was threatening. About 734, the kings of Damascus and Samaria tried to force Jerusalem to join a coalition against Assyria: this Syro-Ephraimite war was to be the occasion for the main oracles of Isaiah. Notes to your Bible or commentaries will give you more details about this social, economic and political context.

To make yourself familiar with Isaiah you might begin by reading the first twelve chapters, or even just Isa. 6–12; 28.16–17; 29.17–24.

The call of Isaiah (Isa. 6) explains his message. Coming to the temple, he experienced the presence of God. He became aware that he was only a man and that he was a sinner: he felt lost. But God made him persevere and purified him. Isaiah saw that the great sin is pride (people think that they can cope by themselves, make themselves God), and salvation lies in faith (putting oneself wholly and humbly, with trust, in God's hands).

Isaiah tries to give his people the same experience. God is like an enormous rock on the way: the people have to choose. Pride is to bump into it (8.14) and

---

'No one can see God and live'

This phrase recurs often in the Bible, and it reflects the experience of Isaiah. It is not that God is wicked, but that he is utterly different from us! Electric current is a good thing, but if we touch a high-voltage transmission cable we are burnt to a frazzle, because we cannot take such power. Similarly, we cannot take God who *is* life, when we only *have* life. That is why God veils his glory when he shows himself: for example, it is a vision of his back which is shown to Moses (Ex. 33.12f.).

Furthermore, of course, we are sinners and cannot stand before the holy God, the God who is both utterly different and perfect. God has to purify us and hold us. But in the end it is only through his Son Jesus that we may 'dare' to call him Father.

find death (5); faith is to rest upon it (10.20–21), or upon this rock which is the Messiah (28.16). Sadly, this preaching will succeed only in hardening the hearts of the majority, but it will also lead to the formation of a small remnant of faithful (6.9–11).

Isaiah was a Judaean. For him the king was son of David/son of God, the guarantor of the faith of the people and their representative before God. He is also tormented by king Ahaz's lack of faith. Panic-stricken at the coalition between Damascus and Syria, Ahaz sacrificed his son to the false gods (II Kings 16.3), thus endangering God's promise to David. Isaiah came to him to announce that despite everything God would keep his promise, that another child was already on the way and that the young woman (Ahaz's wife) was pregnant. And Isaiah put all his hopes on this child, the little Hezekiah, Emmanu-el, God with us (Isa. 7). Isaiah celebrates the era of peace which he foresees when Hezekiah becomes king, becomes son of God (Isa. 9), and he even celebrates in advance the coming of the true son of David who will appear one day to establish universal peace (Isa. 11). These various oracles are important, but they are sometimes difficult to understand. Look at the notes in your Bible or in a commentary.

Micah

Isaiah was an aristocrat. Micah is a peasant: he suffered personally under the policy of the great which led to war and the injustice practised by the rich. One day he went to Jerusalem to proclaim God's indignation.

If we were to keep only one verse from him, it should be Micah 6.8, in which he succeeds in making a magnificent combination of the message of the three prophets of this period: in the northern kingdom Amos, who preaches justice, and Hosea, who preaches God's tenderness; in Jerusalem Isaiah, who preaches a humble faith:

He has showed you, O man, what is good;
and what does the Lord require of you
but to do justice, and to love kindness,
and to walk humbly with your God?

But you might also read his cries against social injustice (2.1–5; 3.1–12; 7.1–7), the announcement of a Messiah who will not be the son of David, king of Jerusalem, but the son of David, the little shepherd of Bethlehem (5.1–5, quoted by Matt. 2.6), or his message of hope (7.1–10, quoted by Luke 1.73).

Prophets

A prophet is not someone who announces the future, but rather someone who speaks in the name of God, someone who has been made privy to God's plans (Amos 3.7) and now sees everything through God's eyes.

Are we to think in terms of extraordinary revelations? That is by no means impossible, but it seems in fact that the prophets discover this word of God in two moments or places: at their calling and in their life. Their calling is the determinative factor: this is the moment when they have the experience of God, as with Isaiah on a visit to the temple, as with Jeremiah in continued prayer, and as with Hosea in an unhappy marriage. This is the light which enables them to discover this word, to read the signs of the times, in life, in great political events and in day-to-day living.

From the time of their calling, everything speaks to them of God: the branch of an almond tree in flower or a boiling pot (Jer. 1.11f.), married life (Hos. 1–3; Ezek. 24.15f.) or enemy invasion. And in this way they teach us to read in our own lives this same word which continues to address us.

The prophets express themselves through words: oracles (declarations made in the name of God), exhortations, stories, prayers, but also through actions. Prophetic actions communicate the Word, and even make history.

If you are working as a group, you clearly cannot study everything suggested here in a month. So why not share out the work? Everyone could read the whole of the chapter, and then individuals could study just one part, looking for particular features. So when the group meets, each person will be able to make his or her own contribution, and you will discover where certain agreements become obvious.

It is in fact important to have a general idea about this period. People were not just at work composing the creation story or the Sacred Judaean History. Prophets were preaching, and wise men expressing their reflections (particularly in Gen. 2–3); people were praying (even if we cannot be sure which psalms go right back to this period). In this enormous period of gestation, the Bible is slowly coming to birth.

43

3 The Northern Kingdom 935–721

King Jehu pays homage to the Assyrian king Shalmaneser III

Only fifty kilometres separate the two rival capitals, Jerusalem and Samaria. Yet in many respects, the kingdom of Israel is very different from its brother and enemy, the kingdom of Judah.

Geographical situation. A look at the diagrammatic map on the right will tell you more than a long explanation.

Jerusalem is in the middle of the hills, near to the desert of Judah. The stony ground produced some cereal crops and allowed the cultivation of vines and olives, as well as the rearing of sheep. The kingdom had no access to the sea – the rich plain of the Shephelah was occupied by the Philistines – and focussed more on the Jordan valley and the Dead Sea.

By contrast, the northern kingdom occupied the hill country of Samaria with its verdant valleys, together with the plains of Sharon and Jezreel. The transfer of its capital gives an indication of its development: Jeroboam, its first king, installed himself at Tirzah, facing the Jordan. One of his successors, Omri, bought the hill of Samaria and built his capital there: the northern kingdom was now focussed on the sea, and had easy links and commerce with the Canaanite princes of the north (present-day Lebanon and Syria). That partly explains its economic and religious situation.

Economic situation. You need to read the description of the inhabitants of Samaria, with their ivory- and ebony-panelled walls, given in the book of Amos (3.12; 5.11; 6.4) to see the prosperity of the country. But you will also see the social injustice which it generated: excavations at Tirzah, the first capital, show a group of well-built houses, separated by a wall from a mass of shanties.

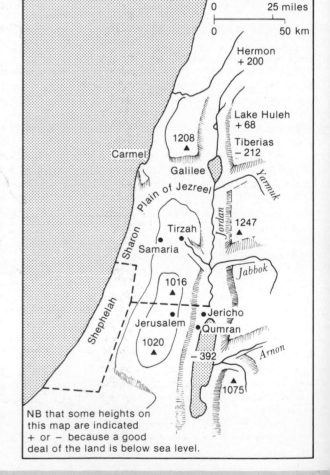

NB that some heights on this map are indicated + or − because a good deal of the land is below sea level.

An official in the king's presence. Hittite bas-relief (eighth century BC)

Religious situation. Israel had more contact with the Canaanites living in its territory than did Judah, and also with the princes of Tyre, Sidon and Damascus. We shall be looking more closely at some of the features of Canaanite religion, which was attractive to an agricultural people because it was centred on a cult of divinized forces of nature, Baals and Astartes, who were thought to give fertility to the soil, to the flocks and to human beings. Israel was tempted to insure itself by backing two religions at once, limping on both feet, as Elijah put it: worshipping Yahweh while serving the Baals.

To prevent his people from going to the Temple at Jerusalem, Jeroboam had set up two bulls (two calves, as the prophets mockingly put it), one at Dan and one at Bethel (I Kings 12.26f.). These bulls were probably meant to serve as pedestals for the true God Yahweh, offering him a place where he could make himself present, as did the ark of the covenant in Jerusalem. However, because the bull was the symbol of Baal, the danger of idolatry was great.

Political situation. The system of monarchy, inaugurated by David and Solomon, continued in Israel. Here, however, the kings were no longer the legitimate descendants of David: eight out of nineteen were assassinated, and one dynasty gave way to another. The king was not son of David and he could not be son of God. 'They made kings, but not through me,' complains God (Hos. 8.4). So the king was not the guarantor of the unity of the people and their representative before God, as he was in Judah. In Israel, the prophet came to play this role, and often opposed the king.

The kings themselves were neither better nor worse than those of Judah, and some of them were great men.

International politics. Israel was deeply involved in the politics of its time.

Egypt was in decline, while Assyria, a powerful nation, made several incursions into Canaan.

To the north of Israel, the small Aramaean kingdom of Damascus prospered. Because of its Semitic origin and its power, it was a near neighbour to Israel and Judah and was ally or enemy in turn. For example, an Assyrian document shows us that in 853, Assyria was confronted with a coalition of Aramaean kingdoms including Ahab of Israel, with two thousand chariots and ten thousand soldiers.

The two kingdoms of Israel and Judah reached the zenith of their power round about 750. Assyria wanted to extend its empire towards the Mediterranean. The first obstacle in its way was Damascus. That was marvellous for Israel and Judah; Damascus was preoccupied with this second front and no longer attacked them. Indeed, as long as it resisted, it served as a buffer against Assyria. It is not necessary to have much knowledge of politics to realize that this situation could not last long. However, for the moment, governed by intelligent kings each of whom reigned for about forty years, the two kingdoms profited and enjoyed their prosperity. This was the time when the prophets Amos and Hosea were preaching in Israel.

However, in 732 the Assyrians captured Damascus, and in 721, Samaria. Some of the inhabitants were deported to Assyria, where they became assimilated: we lose track of them. That was the end of the northern kingdom.

The Samaritans after 721. All the inhabitants were not deported; some of them remained in Samaria. The Assyrians brought colonists to Samaria, deported from other provinces of their empire, who arrived with their traditions and their gods.

This gave rise to a new population, of mixed blood, who served both the God of Israel and other gods. (See the spicy and biased account in II Kings 17.24–41.)

We shall have occasion to look at the disputes between the Samaritans and the Jews who returned from exile in Babylon (pages 74, 79).

We can understand why, in the time of Christ, Jews and Samaritans mistrusted each other.

Literary activity

The Elijah traditions (I Kings 17–19; 21; II Kings 1–2) were certainly brought together after the ninth century, and, about 750, the tales about Elisha (II Kings 3–9), along with fine historical accounts like the story of Jehu's revolution (II Kings 9–10).

The oracles of Amos and Hosea were set down in writing.

The Sacred History of the North, which we call the Elohistic tradition, was doubtless also written down about 750.

Finally, this period also saw the formation of codes of law, to adapt the old legislation to the new social situation. Influenced greatly by the message of the prophets, particularly Hosea, these codes eventually formed the kernel of Deuteronomy.

Prophets of the Northern Kingdom

In the northern kingdom, the prophet, not the king, was the guarantor of faith. So we shall begin by listening to three great prophets.

Elijah

Like Nathan in Jerusalem, Elijah has left us no writings. However, he and Moses are the two great figures of Jewish faith. The New Testament, and above all Luke, presents Jesus as the new Elijah.

His name is a message in itself: Elijah is a version of Eli-yahu, my God is Yahweh. He appears in the ninth century, in the reign of Ahab. Ahab married Jezebel, daughter of the king of Tyre. This alliance contributed to the prosperity of Israel, but Jezebel brought with her her religion, her Baals and her prophets. And the people worshipped God while serving Baal . . . Elijah made his choice.

Read the pages in which he appears: I Kings 17–19; 21; II Kings 1–2. Try to sort out the main features. Here are some of them.

Man before God. The expression 'my God whom I serve' or 'to whom I bow' appears often. Elijah made an unequivocal choice and wants the people to do so as well.

Transported by the spirit. Look at the comic response of Obadiah in I Kings 18.12. This is the source of Elijah's strength of purpose and inner freedom.

His undivided faith. At the time of the sacrifice on Carmel (I Kings 18) he wants to force the people to choose between the living, personal God who intervenes in history, and the divinized powers of nature, the Baals (see the box on the next page). Like us, Elijah believes without seeing; because God asks it of him, he announces the coming of rain . . . but without seeing any on the way (I Kings 18.41f.)!

His intimacy with God. Along with that of Moses (Ex. 33.18f.), his vision of God (I Kings 19) has remained the model for the mystical life: this is the maximum that mankind is allowed to see. However, Elijah remains a man like ourselves, discouraged and afraid (19.1f.). Verse 12 of ch. 19 should be translated, 'there was the sound of a silence': God is not in the divinized forces of nature, he is the mysterious God whose presence one senses in silence and emptiness, a hidden God. Like Moses, in his prayer Elijah does not give himself over to mystical effusions: he tells God of his mission.

Defender of the poor. Confronted with the king and men of power, he defends the poor (I Kings 21).

His universalism. Because he believes in God unequivocally and allows himself to be guided by the spirit, he is completely free to move among the pagans (I Kings 17). However, he asks the pagan woman for unconditional faith (17.13).

A tale of Elijah (II Kings 1). Unfortunately, this popular tale, like all those told of Elisha, has helped to make Elijah into a judge who calls down fire from heaven upon sinners.

The ascension of Elijah (II Kings 2). Probably because people did not know of a tomb of Elijah, they came to think that he had been taken up to God. Luke was inspired by this text to write the account of the ascension of Jesus (Acts 1.6–11); because Elisha sees Elijah ascending, we know that Elisha is to receive his spirit to continue his mission, just as the disciples receive the spirit of Jesus since they see his ascension.

In Luke, Jesus is the new Elijah

Read the texts where Luke refers explicitly to the Elijah story: 4.26 (the sermon in the synagogue at Capernaum); 7.12, 15 (the resurrection of a young man at Nain); 9.42 (the healing of a child); 9.51, 54, 57, 62 (Jesus goes up to Jerusalem); 22.43, 45 (the agony in the garden, Jesus is comforted by an angel). Note, too, that Luke has left out the saying of Jesus which identifies John the Baptist with Elijah (Matt. 11.14; 17.11–13).

In the light of this, you can see how the features that we noted in the case of Elijah help us to discover the character of Luke's portrait of Jesus: his relationship to the Father, frequently expressed in prayer; his inner freedom granted through the spirit; his universalism and his tenderness towards the poor, the sinners, the outcast, the women; his demand that the disciples should place unconditional trust in him. Again like Elijah, Jesus is a man with a single aim: he is going towards his being 'received up' (9.51), which is at the same time his being lifted up on the cross and his ascension into the glory of the Father.

Amos   Act justly

Amos was originally a shepherd from Tekoa, near Bethlehem. He was sent by God to the north at the time when Samaria prospered under king Jeroboam II. A popular preacher with a vigorous turn of phrase, he was struck by the luxury of the houses of the rich, but above all by their injustice. For example, see 3.13–4.3 (luxury); 2.6–16; 8.4–8 (social injustice).

Amos was a prophet; on two occasions he speaks of his call. In 7.10–17 he describes it, and in 3.3–8 he tries to make sense of it. A prophet is someone who is taken into the counsel of God, and thereafter sees everything in the light of it, trying to decipher God's plan in his life and the events of his time.

His social teaching, too, is based on the covenant. The covenant is not an assurance which allows people to live in any way they like. It is a responsibility. 'You only have I known of all the families of the earth,' God declares, 'therefore I will punish you for all your iniquities' (3.1–2).

If God punishes people, it is to bring about their conversion. Amos foresees that there will be a small 'remnant'; some will be saved from the disaster (3.12), and that is a reason for continuing to hope (8.11–12; 9.11–15).

The God of Amos is no longer just a national God: he also watches over the morality of other nations (1.3–2.3, fine examples of oracles). He can do this because he is Creator: Amos quotes a poem (perhaps inspired by a Canaanite hymn): 4.13 + 5.8–9 + 9.5–6.

Hosea   Love tenderly

Hosea came from the north and preached at the same time as Amos. He discovered the tenderness of God through personal experience. Hosea loved his wife, although she behaved badly towards him; through his love he succeeded in restoring to her the feelings she had had when she was young. This is how God loves us: not because we are good, but so that we can become good (Hos. 1–3). God loves us as a husband loves his wife: this theme occurs often in the Bible and gives a new meaning to faith. The law given at Sinai seems more like a marriage contract, an agreement between spouses, and sin is more like adultery, prostitution, a failing in love.

Hosea has an inexorable view of the sinfulness of his people: there is no trust, no tenderness towards one another, no knowledge and love of God. We shall be studying a text from him in more detail, but as we read the whole book, we should stop at those passages which present the love of God (1–3, like that of a husband; 11, like that of a father) or which call for a loving response from the people (4.1–3; 6.4–6, a phrase which Matthew quotes twice: 10.12; 12.3–7). And we can see how sin is the opposite to this (4.4–10; 5.1–7; 7.1–2).

If we are interested in what makes up the life of the people, we might note everything that is said about the institutions of the law, the cult, the land and the prophets. Their importance exceeds that of king and judges. The ideal time was when Israel lived in the desert after the Exodus, under the leadership of the prophet Moses.

God of history or gods of nature?

Israel believed in a God who had intervened in her history: the God of Abraham, Isaac and Jacob, the God-who-brought-us-out-of-slavery. This God guided the people when they were wandering in the desert and he brought them into the land of Canaan.

Now, however, Israel has settled down: the people have fields and towns. What concerns them is how to make sure that the soil and their flocks are fertile. To whom should they pray to have rain in due season? They found an established religion which was well equipped to answer these needs: the Baals, divinized forms of the storm and the rain, and the Astartes, divinized forms of sexuality and fertility (look again at what was said about Canaanite thought on page 19 above).

A God who intervened in history – that was all very well. But one had to make a living, and it was safer to rely on the Baals.

We should not imagine too quickly that this problem is an obsolete one: the Baals have simply changed their name. The Christian may easily experience the same conflict: he believes in a God who has intervened in history and in his son Jesus, but what does this faith have to do with economic necessities? Is it not safer to rely on the 'powers' of nature (one's bank balance, one's own skills and power)?

◆ *Studying a text: Hosea 2.2–23*

Begin by reading this text, paying no attention to the annotations in the margin. Who is it talking about? With what imagery? What does the text say to you?

Note what you like about it, what surprises you, what makes you ask questions, etc.

2 *Plead with your mother, plead –*
    for she is not my wife, and I am not her husband –
  that she put away her harlotry from her face,
  and her adultery from between her breasts;
3 *lest I strip her naked*
  and make her as in the day she was born,
  and make her like a wilderness,
  and set her like a parched land,
  and slay her with thirst.

God *husband*
accused
judge
Baals *lovers*
accused
People *wife*
mother
land

4 *Upon her children also I will have no pity,*
   because they are children of harlotry.
5 *For their mother has* **played the harlot**,
  she that conceived them has acted shamefully, for she said,
  'I will go after my lovers,
  who give me my bread and my water,
  my wool and my flax, my oil and my drink.'

First accusation

6 **Therefore** *I will hedge up her way with thorns;*
  and I will build a wall against her, so that she cannot find her paths.
7 *She shall pursue her lovers but not overtake them;*
  and she shall seek them, but shall not find them. Then she shall say,
  'I will go and return to my first husband,
  for it was better with me then than now.'

punishment

8 *And* **she did not know** *that it was I who gave her*
  the grain, the wine and the oil,
  and who lavished upon her silver and gold which they used for Baal.

Second accusation

9 **Therefore** *I will take back*
  my grain in its time, and my wine in its season;
  and I will take away my wool and my flax which were to cover her nakedness.

punishment

10 *Now I will uncover her lewdness in the sight of her lovers,*
  and no one shall rescue her out of my hand.
11 *And I will put an end to all her mirth, her feasts, her new moons, her sabbaths,*
  and all her appointed feasts.
12 *And I will lay waste her vines and her fig trees, of which she said,*
  'These are my hire, which my lovers have given me.'
  I will make them a forest, and the beasts of the field shall devour them.
13 *And I will punish her for the feast days of the Baals*
  when she burned incense to them
  and decked herself with her rings and jewellery
  and went after her lovers and **forgot me**, *says the Lord.*

Third accusation
'punishment'

14 **Therefore**, *behold, I will allure her,*
  and bring her into the wilderness and speak tenderly to her.
15 *And there I shall give her vineyards, and make the Valley of Achor a door of hope.*
  And there she shall answer as in the days of her youth,
  as at the time when she came out of the land of Egypt.

Exodus

16 **And in that day**, *says the Lord,*
you will call me 'My husband'
and no longer will you call me 'My Baal'.
17 *For I will remove the names of the Baals from her mouth,*
and they shall be mentioned by name no more.
18 *And I will make for you a covenant* **in that day** *with the beasts of the field,*
the birds of the air and the creeping things of the ground;
and I will abolish the bow, the sword, and war from the land;
and I will make you lie down in safety.
19 *And I will betroth you to me for ever;*
I will betroth you to me in righteousness and in justice,
in steadfast love, and in mercy.
20 *I will betroth you to me in faithfulness, and you shall know the Lord.*
21 **And in that day**, *says the Lord,*
I will answer the heavens and they shall answer the earth;
22 *and the earth shall answer the grain, the wine, and the oil*
and they shall answer Jezreel;
23 *And I will sow him for myself in the land.*
And I will have pity on Not pitied,
and I will say to Not my people, 'You are my people';
and he shall say, 'Thou art my God'.

Gen. 2.23

Peace of paradise
Gen. 2.18–23;
Isa. 11.6–8

See Hos. 1.8
This is the negation of
Ex. 3.14

Who are the main characters here? What are the images which represent them?

What are they doing? What are they looking for?

Note the expressions which keep occurring, the words which seem important to you, the play on possessive adjectives (e.g. the grain, my grain. . .).

In these divorce proceedings, which are presented as an ultimatum, note the three accusations made by God (what are they?) and the punishments which he has in mind (what is the third?).

Pay attention to the contrasts: loved / not loved; give / receive; wilderness v. 3 / wilderness v. 14 (is the meaning the same? why?); does being married mean being supported, at the beginning, and also at the end?

Set this text in the context of the thinking of the time (see the box on p. 47); the crucial issue is to know who gives fertility, the divinized powers (the Baals) or the God of history. How does Hosea refer to history (see the references given in the margin)?

What face does God present here? Is he part of nature? He is the one who gives meaning to everything, but nature has its laws which are discovered by science.

What does he expect of man? Note the words which indicate man's response.

The language of love

Tenderness (Hebrew *ḥesed*) is a key word in Hosea, signifying the bond of love between two partners.

Love (*raḥamim* in Hebrew) is a word reserved for God's love towards us. It is the plural (which means, in Hebrew, the superlative) of the word for mother's breast. This is a mother's love, which goes to the roots of one's being.

Faithfulness, fidelity. Words which all come from the same root in Hebrew (*'emet, 'emuna, 'amen*) denote solidity, permanence in an accord between two beings: they can put complete trust in each other.

Knowledge. People know with all their being, with heart and body as well as with understanding (the word can also express the sexual union between man and wife).

Be gracious (*hanan*): a mother's action in leaning over her baby. (In Hebrew the name John is Johanan, God is gracious.)

These are the names which God writes on his 'visiting card': 'The Lord, a God loving and gracious, abounding in steadfast love and tenderness' (Ex. 34.6).

The Sacred History of the North: The Elohistic Tradition

The northern tribes separated from Jerusalem and its king, the successor to David. However, they had the same past and the same traditions. Very soon, in the kingdom of Judah, these traditions were collected together to produce the Sacred Judaean History (or the Yahwistic tradition). Two centuries later, perhaps about 750, in the kingdom of Israel, the same traditions were brought together in the writing of a Sacred History of the North. The tradition is called Elohistic, because in it God is first called Elohim. It is denoted by the letter E.

We have here the same history as that produced in the south, but because the context is different, the history is different also. As we have seen in our study of the prophets, in Israel there was a great temptation to abandon the true God and serve the Baals, or at least to make certain by backing both sides. It was no longer possible to count on the king for the maintenance of the true faith, because he was no longer a descendant of David.

The prophets vigorously reminded the people that there was only one possible covenant: that which God had made with his people. The writers who produced this history had been brought up on the thinking of the prophets and the wise men. For them, to remind the people of their traditions was one way of involving them in the covenant.

This is probably the reason why this history does not begin, like that of the south, with the creation stories, but with the covenant with Abraham.

The religious feeling needed to keep the people faithful to this covenant was the fear of God – not fear as we know it, but respect combined with trust.

We are going to start with a careful reading of two texts in which the Elohist gives good expression to his main convictions: the making of the covenant on Sinai (you will find the text on the opposite page) and the story of Abraham's sacrifice of Isaac, which you can read in your Bible.

We shall then go quickly through this Sacred History of the North, taking as a guideline two elements which are very closely connected: the covenant and the fear of God.

Some characteristics of the Elohist

These characteristics will be clearer if you compare the Elohist with the Yahwist (see p. 36).

He tends to be less vivid, less concrete.

God is utterly different from man. The Elohist usually avoids anthropomorphisms, or ways of talking about God as though he were a man. This inaccessible God reveals himself through dreams. When he speaks in person, he does so through theophanies, or spectacular manifestations. One cannot make any image of the deity.

The Elohist is very interested in moral questions, and he has a developing sense of sin. For example, he explains that Abraham never lied (compare Gen. 12.10f. (J) with Gen. 20 (E)). The law given by Moses is less concerned with how to celebrate the cult than with morality, duty towards God and one's neighbour.

Real worship consists in obeying God and observing the covenant, rejecting all covenants with false gods.

The true men of God are no longer the king and the priests but the prophets: Abraham, Moses (the greatest), then Elijah, Elisha, etc.

The reflections of the Elohist are rooted in the prophetic tradition and the reflections of the wise men.

One possible way of using this guide

We are following a series of great moments in the history of the people and trying to put in context all the texts produced during each period. This necessary backcloth should make it possible for you to follow several courses.

You can follow the approach I have already indicated.

You can also follow a number of great figures: Abraham, Moses and so on. I have tried to indicate the main texts in each chapter. You will find a list of references on p. 120.

The covenant on Sinai. Ex. 19–20

Here are the verses attributed to the Elohist.

19.2 And there Israel encamped before the mountain.³ And Moses went up to God.

⁹And the Lord said to Moses, 'Lo, I am coming to you in a thick cloud.¹² And you shall set bounds for the people round about, saying, ''Take heed that you do not go up into the mountain or touch the border of it; whoever touches the mountain shall be put to death; ¹³no hand shall touch him, but he shall be stoned or shot; whether beast or man, he shall not live.'' ' ¹⁶All the people who were in the camp trembled. ¹⁷Then Moses brought the people out of the camp to meet God; and they took their stand at the foot of the mountain. ¹⁹Moses spoke, and God answered him in thunder.

20.1–17. The Ten Elohistic Commandments (Decalogue).

¹⁸Now when all the people perceived the thunderings and the lightnings and the sound of the trumpet and the mountain smoking, the people were afraid and trembled; and they stood afar off, ¹⁹and said to Moses, 'You speak to us and we will hear; but let not God speak to us, lest we die.'

²⁰And Moses said to the people, 'Do not fear; for God has come to prove you, and that the fear of him may be before your eyes, that you may not sin.' ²¹And the people stood afar off, while Moses drew near to the thick cloud where God was.

20.22–23.33. The Book of the Covenant. This is also Elohistic.

24.3 Moses came and told the people all the words of the Lord and all the ordinances; and all the people answered with one voice, and said, 'All the words which the Lord has spoken we will do.' ⁴And Moses wrote all the words of the Lord. And he rose early in the morning, and built an altar at the foot of the mountain, and twelve pillars, according to the twelve tribes of Israel. ⁵And he sent young men of the people of Israel, who offered burnt offerings and sacrificed peace offerings of oxen to the Lord. ⁶And Moses took half of the blood and put it in basins, and half of the blood he threw against the altar. ⁷Then he took the book of the covenant, and read it in the hearing of the people; and they said, 'All that the Lord has spoken we will do, and we will be obedient.'⁸ And Moses took the blood and threw it upon the people, and said, 'Behold the blood of the covenant which the Lord has made with you in accordance with all these words.'

Read this text carefully.

Note all the characteristics of the Elohist (see the box opposite). What is the role attributed to Moses? Note the various features: prophet, mediator, priest.

Fear: what kind of feeling is this? What is its purpose? For God, the trial is a way of testing the faithfulness of the people.

The covenant: note the ritual; here we have a bilateral contract. God gives his law and the people promise to obey it (in Hebrew, the word understand also means to obey, see Deut. 6.4). Blood is sprinkled on the two parties to the contract; on the altar, which symbolizes God, and on the people. This rite has two aspects: it signifies that if one of the parties infringes the covenant, their blood will be shed, and above all, it shows that the two are 'of the same blood'.

 Abraham's sacrifice of Isaac. Gen. 22.1–13,19

Read this account in your Bible, leaving out vv.14–18, which come from the Yahwist.

Without question, the basis of this is an old story which shows that God does not want the sacrifice of children (a practice sometimes to be found at that time). The Elohist takes up this old story to show us a particularly impressive portrait of Abraham.

Note the features characteristic of the Elohist.

Note the features which we find in both this text and in the account of the making of the covenant.

Put yourself in the place of an Israelite hearing this story: how would Abraham appear to him as the model of what he should be and do?

How is he our model?

Human sacrifice

First fruits are much sought after: what we have first seems to us to be best. And from the beginning of time, the deity has been offered the first fruits of the harvest.

It also happened, at least among the Semites living in Canaan, that the firstborn could be offered in sacrifice, for instance in dramatic cases (invasion, and so on). This was fairly rare, and the Semites coming from the East (Mesopotamia), like Abraham, knew nothing of this rite.

Israel rejected this kind of sacrifice: the firstborn was redeemed; that is, an animal was offered instead.

It is difficult to read this sacred history straight through; when the two parallel traditions, the Sacred History of the South and the Sacred History of the North, were amalgamated after the return from exile in Babylon, in cases of overlap the northern history was usually sacrificed, to such a degree that it now exists only in a fragmentary state. We shall pause for the more certain texts.

Abraham cycle

This history almost certainly began with Abraham and not with the creation narratives, as did the Yahwistic version. The first text is the account of God's covenant with Abraham (Gen. 15). Because it is now extremely entangled in the Yahwistic account, we shall be reading it later (see p. 60).

Abraham and Abimelech (Gen. 20). Here we find the main characteristics of the Elohist: his concern for *morality*. Abraham does not have a very good role, but he did not lie! And only he, as *prophet* (v. 7), can intercede for the king (v. 17). He discovers that the *fear of God* (v. 11) can also be found in a pagan. Furthermore, the pagan did not sin: God, in a *dream*, prevented him (v. 4).

Hagar and Ishmael (Gen. 21.9–21). God intervenes in favour of the oppressed.

Abraham and Isaac (Gen. 22.1–14). We have read this important text. In Jewish tradition the Akedah (or binding) of Isaac to the stake is important. See the box on the right, about the Targum on Gen. 22.10.

Jacob cycle

Jacob's dream (Gen. 28.10f.) is partly to be attributed to the Elohist, with the dream (vv. 11–12), fear before the God who is utterly different (vv. 17–18), and God's protection of the weak (vv. 20–22).

Jacob's journeys (Gen. 29–35). During these chapters we see Jacob visiting the chief sanctuaries of the northern kingdom. Thus the origin of these sanctuaries is given roots in the history of the patriarchs.

The Joseph story

Here again it is difficult to distinguish between the Elohistic and the Yahwistic narratives. Joseph was the father of two northern tribes (Ephraim and Manasseh), and he was buried at Shechem (Josh. 24.32). That explains the interest in this patriarch.

In this story we can discover characteristics of the Elohist. For example, the test (Gen. 42.16), the fear of God (42.18), God's protection of the weak (45.5; 50.20). God pursues his aim of saving men, even through suffering and sin.

Targum on Gen. 22.10

At the beginning of our era Jews read the scriptures in the synagogue in Hebrew, the sacred language; but the people who spoke Aramaic no longer understood it. So a translation had to be made. Instead of translating the text word for word, the Jews made a free translation, which was called a Targum (see p. 81). These Aramaic translations are very interesting, because they show us how scripture was understood at the time of Christ. Sometimes there were small changes, sometimes explanations were added. This was the case with the account of the sacrifice of Isaac. After v.10 the Targum adds:

Isaac answered and said to his father: 'Bind me well so that I may not struggle at the anguish of my soul, and that a blemish may not be found in your offering. . .' The eyes of Abraham looked at the eyes of Isaac, but the eyes of Isaac looked at the angels on high: Isaac saw them but Abraham did not see them. The angels on high answered, 'Come and see these two unique men in the earth; the one slaughters and the other is slaughtered. The one who slaughters does not hesitate, the one to be slaughtered stretches out his neck.'

The binding (Akedah in Aramaic) that Isaac asks for expresses his own inner offering: in struggling, he does not want to risk wounding himself, because in that case he would no longer be a victim that could be offered.

In their moments of anguish, the Jews ask God to remember this Akedah and because of it, to pardon their sins and save them.

Moses

The role of Moses in the formation of the people is more important here than in the Yahwistic history (see p. 38). He has the power to perform miracles; he plays the role of intermediary between God and the people, he acts as a prophet, and his prayer is efficacious; he even appears as a priest.

The midwives and the birth of Moses (Ex. 1.15–2.10). The midwives fear God and prefer to obey him rather than Pharaoh. And God saves the weak, the baby Moses. The author was probably inspired by a story, known in Egypt, about the birth of Sargon of Agade, who lived in Mesopotamia more than 2,300 years before Christ.

The burning bush (Ex. 3–4). God shows himself in an amazing way. He reveals his name to Moses, in a phrase which is difficult to translate. Perhaps the best rendering is 'I am who I will be', that is, 'It is by seeing what I shall prove to be and shall do with you, in your history, that you will discover who I am.' So we can only see who this God is through those who serve him. He is the God of Abraham, of Moses, of Jesus Christ . . . of Mr or Mrs or Miss Smith. The aim of the liberation from slavery in Egypt is for the people to put themselves at God's service (4.23, a phrase which occurs often). Here Israel is called God's firstborn, not the king, as in the Yahwistic history.

The birth of Sargon of Agade

I am Sargon the mighty king, king of Agade.
My mother was poor; I never knew my father. . .
My mother, the poor woman, conceived me, in secret she
  bore me.
She set me in a basket of rushes, with bitumen she sealed
  my lid.
She cast me into the river which rose not over me.
The river bore me up and carried me to Akki, the drawer
  of water.
Akki, the drawer of water, lifted me out as he dipped
  his ewer.
Akki, the drawer of water, took me as his son and
  reared me.
Akki, the drawer of water, made me his gardener.
While I was a gardener, Ishtar granted me her love.
For fifty-five years I exercised kingship.

Moses and Jethro (Ex. 18). Moses' father-in-law helps him to organize the people; he gives him a good position as representative of the people before God (v. 19); one of the criteria for choosing assistants is to be that they fear God.

At Horeb We have already read Ex. 19–20 and later we shall be reading the two law codes (Ex. 20–23: see p.60). In the northern kingdom, the mountain of God is called Horeb and not Sinai.

The golden calf and the vision of God from behind (Ex. 32–34). Here against the Yahwistic and Elohistic traditions are entangled. The sin of the people and of Aaron is obviously idolatry, since they had worshipped an idol; the bull (the calf) is probably the pedestal of the true God (32.5); the people want to force God to make himself present by offering him a throne; in that case he would be a deity under their own control (look again at these two conceptions of God on p. 35). Moses reveals himself as intercessor (33.30f.). He is charged with guiding the people to an encounter with their God: read the impressive account in Ex. 33.7–11. With Elijah, Moses is the one who has advanced furthest towards being intimate with God. However, even he can see only God's 'back' (Ex. 33.18–23).

The gift of the spirit to the elders (Num. 11.16–17, 24–30). We have seen that in the northern kingdom the prophet is the one who maintains the true faith, and Moses is the first and greatest prophet. But the author's ideal is that all the people should be prophets, being guided by the spirit which inspired Moses.

For your work
Remember what I said earlier: when you read a travel guide, you find a general account of what there is to see, but you know that you can't see everything . . . It's the same here. The essential thing is that you should have some idea of the conditions and the ways of thinking in the northern kingdom. Choose the texts that you are going to study. And don't be upset if you can't study them all!

4

The Last Period of the Kingdom of Judah 721–587

A prisoner being led away by an Assyrian warrior (Nineveh, seventh century BC)

When we began our journey, we paid particular attention to the united kingdom of David and Solomon (pp. 34–35). Then we spent some time in the northern kingdom (pp. 44–45). Now we must return to the southern kingdom, Judah: we are in the last period of its existence, which extends from the fall of the northern kingdom (721) to the capture of Jerusalem (587).

Judah from 933 to 721

A tiny kingdom, squeezed between Israel and the Philistines (see the map on p. 41), Judah spread over the hills around Jerusalem and into the Negeb desert. It lived from agriculture and the rearing of livestock, chiefly sheep, and also trade with Arabia and Egypt.

In the political sphere it was, of course, subject to the repercussions of the international situation. For a great deal of this period, the great powers, Egypt and Assyria, were weakened. So political and military activity was concentrated on the territory of Canaan: struggles, alliances, victories and defeats among the little kingdoms of Judah, Israel and Damascus.

The situation changes from 745 with the return of Assyria to the scene. Damascus and Israel formed a coalition to resist Assyria, and wanted to force Judah to join them; this was the Syro-Ephraimite war, the occasion for Isaiah's oracles (see p. 39). The young king of Judah, Ahaz, preferred to appeal to the king of Assyria for help. This came, Damascus was taken in 732 and then Samaria in 722–721.

The repercussions for the kingdom of Judah caused by the fall of Samaria are important both politically and psychologically.

Judah between 721 and 587

All the territory north of Jerusalem (the old northern kingdom) became an Assyrian province. King Ahaz, who was partly responsible for the destruction of the united kingdom because of his appeal to Assyria, remained loyal to Assyria until his death.

Hezekiah, his son, reigned for about thirty years in his own right; his total reign amounted to more than forty years, since for twelve years his father shared the responsibility of government. Despite Isaiah's advice, he adopted a complicated policy of alliances with Egypt, and with a king of Babylon who at one point rebelled against the king of Assyria.

In 701 Sennacherib, the new king of Assyria, embarked on a campaign against Judah. Hezekiah fortified his capital and had 'Hezekiah's canal' dug in the rock. This was a kind of tunnel which brought the waters of the source of the Gihon as far as the pool of Siloah, within the ramparts. However, Sennacherib shut him up in Jerusalem 'like a bird in a cage'. Sennacherib ended by lifting the siege (perhaps because an epidemic ravaged his army), contenting himself with exacting heavy tribute from Hezekiah.

Manasseh, a violent and impious king, reigned for forty-five years, submitting without a fuss to the king of Assyria. The Assyrian king was now Assurbanirpal: this literate and artistic king has left us a library consisting of more than 20,000 tablets of baked clay on which are engraved the annals of the kingdom and the great literary works of the Middle East. However, towards the end of his reign the political map began to change: a new dynasty appeared in Babylon; further east, in present-day Iran, the Medes became powerful, and in the west Egypt began to awaken once more.

It was in this context that Josiah began to rule in Jerusalem. His reign was to last thirty years. After two impious kings, Manasseh and Amon, the accession of this pious king was hailed with fervour, all the more since Josiah succeeded in recovering some of the territory of the northern kingdom. Was Josiah going to be a new David? During his reign, in 622, a scroll was discovered

A Canaanite king. Ivory (Megiddo, between 1350 and 1150)

in the Temple containing laws which had their source in the old northern kingdom: when completed, this collection of laws was to become Deuteronomy. The discovery was to serve as the basis for the great reform which Josiah undertook, with political and religious aims in view (II Kings 22–23).

A new generation of prophets preached in this period: Zephaniah, Nahum, Habakkuk and above all Jeremiah.

There was a dramatic turn of events in 612: Nineveh, the Assyrian capital, was captured. All the peoples of the Middle East applauded the downfall of the enemy. Unfortunately they failed to realize that they had merely changed masters: the victorious Babylonian general was called Nebuchadnezzar, and his first concern would be to set off on a campaign against Egypt.

King Josiah sought to bar the way to Pharaoh Necho, and he was killed at Megiddo. This tragic death of the godly king was a great blow to the faithful: why should someone who trusted in God meet such a lamentable death? It marked the end of the reform launched by Josiah, which did not have time to make a deep impression on the hearts of the people.

In 605, Nebuchadnezzar's victory at Carchemish opened up the way to Palestine for him. He captured Jerusalem in 597 and deported the king and some of the inhabitants. These included a prophet priest, Ezekiel. Nebuchadnezzar had installed a vassal king in Jerusalem, but when his back was turned, this king made an alliance with Egypt. Furious, Nebuchadnezzar returned. On 9 July 587 (or 586) he captured the city, destroyed it, burnt the Temple and the ark of the covenant, and deported the inhabitants to Babylon . . . That was the end of the kingdom of Judah.

The capture of Jerusalem was a considerable psychological shock for believers, as we shall see at our next stage. For the moment, we must go back to the first shock – the capture of Samaria: this partly explains the reflection which began in Judah after 721.

The shock of the fall of Israel in 721

The Germans today know well the trauma brought about by the division of their nation, and they always keep alive the hope of seeing their people reunited.

The faithful in the kingdom of Judah experienced the same trauma, as they saw Assyria destroy Samaria and annex its territory. The trauma was all the greater because it was a blow not only to their patriotic feelings but above all to their religious faith. Granted, the two kingdoms were separate nations, and fought against each other. But they had the same God, the same traditions and the same certainty of being the 'people of God', to whom God had given a country. The annexing of Samaria called in question the two poles of this faith: the people and the land. Was this people to be reduced to Judah alone? Thanks to the prophets and the wise men, there was still a lively hope that one day God would be seen to bring about the reunification of the people: the true people is made up of Israel and Judah.

This political and religious context explains to a large degree the intense literary activity which went on in the kingdom of Jerusalem under kings Hezekiah and Josiah.

Literary activity

The Levites of the north took refuge in Jerusalem, bringing with them the literature that had been produced in their kingdom: the Sacred History of the North (the Elohistic tradition), the collections of laws, the oracles of their prophets etc.

The laws seemed to be too much stamped with the spirit of the north, so for a century they lay dormant in the Temple library until Josiah made them the basis for this reform. Confronted with these laws, scribes undertook a fusion of the two histories, the Judaean history (the Yahwist) and that of the north (the Elohist); this fusion, sometimes called the Jehovist (JE), seemed to be the common property of the tribes of both north and south.

Josiah's reform brought to light the laws which came from the north; when completed, they became Deuteronomy.

In the light of the teaching discovered in Deuteronomy, people began to organize the traditions about Joshua, the Judges, Samuel and the Kings. Rewritten in this way, these books became an illustration, in imagery, of what Deuteronomy was trying to express in theory.

Finally, the oracles of the prophets – Zephaniah, Nahum, Habakkuk and Jeremiah – were put down in writing (see Jer. 36). Many psalms were certainly composed at this time, and the reflection of the wise men continued, above all on the death of the godly king Josiah.

Deuteronomy

The place, Jerusalem. The year, 622. On the orders of king Josiah, work is going on in the Temple. The high priest discovers 'the book of the law' (II Kings 22) and Josiah makes this 'Book of the Covenant' (II Kings 23.2) the basis for the great reform which he undertakes. That was how the central core of what was to become Deuteronomy was discovered.

The book itself has a complex history, and the editing of it stretched over several centuries. So it represents a current of thought we have to note, since this way of reflecting on the history of Israel recurs in a number of books of the Bible.

Deuteronomy as we have it, and its history

The book is presented as a series of speeches by Moses. Before he dies, he gives the people laws, and his last advice on the way in which they should live in the country that they are going to conquer.

The book as we have it now is the culmination of a long history, the main stages of which we can reproduce with some degree of probability.

In the northern kingdom, so before the fall of Samaria in 721, people were becoming aware that the law once given by Moses did not match up very well with reality: this law had been made for a nomadic people, and now Israel had become an organized nation.

New problems had appeared, of a greater or lesser degree of seriousness. For example, the conscription of young married men, the danger of the pagan cults practised in Canaan; the injustice of the rich, who ground the faces of those without rights . . . So it was necessary to read just the law, to make as it were a 'second edition'. This is how, little by little, the laws and customs which one day formed the core of Deuteronomy, the second law, came into being.

The Levites who collected and interpreted these laws and customs were influenced a great deal by the preaching of prophets like Elijah, Amos and above all Hosea. They discovered more clearly that the law given by God to his people was not just any kind of contract, but a covenant, a bond of love like that which unites the betrothed with the one whom he loves (see Hosea 1–3).

After the fall of Samaria in 721, Levites took refuge in Jerusalem, where Hezekiah was king. They

---

Some characteristics of the Deuteronomist

At a formal level:
- the style is very emotional. The author is not content to teach; he wants to convince people that they should obey.
- numerous repetitions, for example: The Lord your God . . . Hear, O Israel, remember . . . Keep the commandments, laws and customs . . .
- a constant mixture of the second person singular and the second person plural. This is doubtless the sign of two stages in the editing. In the book as it is now it becomes the affirmation that the people is a single body, but that each believer among this people keeps his own personality.

Some key ideas:
- The Lord is the sole God of Israel.
- He has chosen a people for himself. In response to this election, the people must love God.
- God has given the people a land, but on condition that they remain faithful to him, remember his covenant with them, today.
- It is above all in the liturgy that the people, an assembly called by God as at Horeb, remembers and understands the word of God.

---

brought these laws with them; they organized them and completed them. They also reflected on the causes of the ruin of their kingdom; what should they have done to remain faithful to God? So their laws are sometimes purely theoretical: they seek more to express a spirit than to make rules which cannot, or can no longer, be applied. Thus, every seven years debts must be remitted and slaves freed (Deut. 15); when a city is captured, all the inhabitants must be killed so that the conquerors are not contaminated by their religion (Deut. 16); people must go up on pilgrimage to Jerusalem for the three great annual festivals (Deut. 16), and so on. This last law is particularly significant: to reconstitute the unity of the people, the Levites want to re-centre the faith upon the sole place where God makes himself present, the Temple in Jerusalem, thus relegating to a secondary level the ancient sanctuaries like those at Shechem and Mount Gerizim.

This first arrangement, made in Jerusalem by the Levites who brought their traditions from the north, forms the old core of Deuteronomy (the passages written in the second person singular between chapters 5 and 26). The reign of the impious king Manasseh made this 'book' sink into oblivion. It was deposited in the Temple, and found there again in 622.

Josiah made it the basis for his great political and religious reform, through which he sought to recreate a people united around Jerusalem. It was perhaps at this period, or later, that the passages written in the second person plural were added, along with the chapters at the beginning and the end.

Finally, after other modifications, this book took its place in the great composite work produced about 400 BC: the law in five volumes, or the Pentateuch.

Because those involved in this work were concerned to be faithful to the thought of Moses; or in other words, because they were certain that the laws they produced were those which Moses would have enacted had he been alive at this time, they put them on his lips as great speeches which he delivered before his death.

'You only had to. . .'

It is all too easy to rewrite history, to say after the event, 'You should have . . . You only had to do that . . .' One wants to retort, 'I would like to have seen you in my position . . .' But if it is God, as it is here, who says it to us . . .?

In their account of the temptations of Jesus, Matthew and Luke show us how, in Jesus, we have seen God in our position! The devil revives in Jesus the temptations of the people and our own temptations. And Jesus retorts with verses from Deuteronomy: he replies as the people should have done. So in him, it is the history of the people and our own history which at last prove successful.

Is it possible to love God? asks Deuteronomy. The New Testament replies: in Jesus, from now on, everything is possible.

A current of thought

However, Deuteronomy is not just a book. People talk about the Deuteronomistic tradition (designated by the letter D): that indicates that we have a current of thought, a way of re-reading history in a precise context, i.e. of the obstacle posed by the fall of the northern kingdom.

In 587 the southern kingdom was destroyed in its turn. Other theologians also meditated on this setback and reread the history that had already been written. As they put the final touches to the books of Joshua and Kings – and also, but in a rather less tidy way, to the books of Judges and Samuel – these writers tried to show how people should have lived in faithfulness to God if they had wanted history to take another course.

Some texts from Deuteronomy

Of course you need to read the whole book to see the love of God for his people, to understand the appeal to respond to him by loving him with all one's being for all one's life, and loving one's brothers and sisters also. However, we can begin with some important texts.

The election (4.32–40). This divine choice is based above all on his love. It is not a privilege but a mission.

'Shema Israel . . .'(6). The beginning of this chapter has become the prayer of every Jew and forms the heart of his faith. 'Hear/obey (the word has two senses), Israel, the Lord is one!' This is the fundamental affirmation, and its consequence is, 'You shall love the Lord with all your heart . . .'

Daily life is like an examination (8.1–5). God tests us to see whether we put our trust solely in him. This text is taken up again in the story of the temptations of Jesus.

The law is not an external code, but a demand to respond to love with love (10.12f.).

The Temple: this is the unique place where God makes himself present to his people (12.2–28); people have to go up on pilgrimage there three times a year (16.1–17).

The true prophet (18.15–22). God announces the coming of the definitive prophet. The first Christians recognized Jesus in this text.

Cursed is anyone who hangs on the tree (21.22). This verse was to play a great role in the thought of Paul about the crucified Jesus (see, for example, Gal.3.13).

Social sense (24.14–22). Here and in many other places we can see the tenderness of Deuteronomy and its love for the insignificant.

The 'eucharist' of the firstfruits (26.1–11). We shall be studying this text on the next page.

The word of God in our heart (30.11–20).

Studying a text: The 'Eucharist' of the Firstfruits. Deuteronomy 26.1–11

Israel had now been living in Canaan for several centuries. The people worshipped a God who had intervened in history; this is recalled by the 'creed' inserted at the heart of the text. Now, however, the Israelite has become a peasant farmer, a trader: what interests him is the fertility of the soil and his livestock. We discover once again the conflict that was there in the time of Hosea (see p. 49): 'The God of history or the gods of nature?' Every year, at harvest time, the Canaanites celebrated a festival in honour of Baal, the god of fertility and vegetation. Israel took over this rite, but what sense did they give to it?

If we don't mind anachronisms, we could say that this text follows a pattern still used in our eucharistic liturgies: offering, narrative (a 'creed', which narrates a history or the account of the last supper), adoration and communion. In what way does the fact of telling a story over our gifts, our life, transform it?

All this, and other things as well, this text invites us to discover.

Begin by reading it carefully, without paying attention to the notes in the margin.

1   When you come into the land which the Lord your God gives you for an inheritance,
    and have taken possession of it and live in it,
2   you shall take some of the first of all the fruit of the ground,
    which you harvest from the land that the Lord your God gives you,
    and you shall put it in a basket,
    and you shall go to the place which the Lord your God will choose,
    to make his name to dwell there,   The Jerusalem Temple
3   And you shall go to the priest who is in office at that time,
    and say to him, 'I declare this day to the Lord your God
    that I have come into the land which the Lord swore to our fathers to give us.'
4   Then the priest shall take the basket from your hand,
    and set it down before the altar of the Lord your God.
5   And you shall make response before the Lord your God:
      'A wandering Aramean was my father,   Creed = a narrative
      and he went down into Egypt and sojourned there,   Object: a land
      few in number;   The Lord is absent
      and there he became a nation,
      great, mighty and populous.   Object: a land of freedom
6   And the Egyptians treated us harshly,
      and afflicted us,   The Lord at the service of his people
      and laid upon us harsh bondage.
7   Then we cried to the Lord the God of our fathers,
        and the Lord heard our voice,
        and saw our affliction, our toil and our oppression;
8   And the Lord brought us out of Egypt with a mighty hand and an outstretched arm
      with great terror, with signs and wonders;
9   and he brought us into this place and gave us this land,
      a land flowing with milk and honey.   Object: happiness in a land one does not possess
10   And behold, now I bring the first of the fruit of the ground,
      which thou, Lord, hast given me.'
    And you shall set it down before the Lord your God,
    and worship before the Lord your God;
    and you shall rejoice in all the good which the Lord your God has given
    to you and to your house,   The Lord recognized as Lord
    you, and the Levite, and the sojourner who is among you.

Begin by reading this text carefully, with the help of the 'tool box' (p. 14).

Who are the main characters? What are they doing? What are they offering? Is the Lord present everywhere? In what places? What are the expressions which recur? Note the play on pronouns: I/you . . . we.

At the beginning of the text, we have only the worshipper as an individual: you. At the end, this 'you' is joined by the Levite and the stranger. What do these three main characters have in common, so that they can be grouped together? How does this grouping change the relationship between the worshipper and his land?

Put this text in the religious context of its time (see p. 44): how does it resolve the conflict between the God of history and the powers of nature?

Some guidelines in case you get stuck (don't read them immediately).
A story begins when someone lacks an object and ends when the object is obtained. Here we can find three stories each inside the other.

v. 5b. The lack of a land has been satisfied since Israel became a great nation. But the way the text continues makes it clear that something has gone wrong. So the object has to be made more precise: a land of freedom. Why have things gone wrong? This is the only passage in the text from which God is absent. Does that imply that a quest without God cannot come to a firm conclusion?

vv. 6–9. Instead of the Egyptians, who bring slavery, God gives the land of liberty (note the appearance of 'we' in a difficult situation).

However, here God seems to be at the service of his people, like the gods of nature.

vv. 10–11, which resume vv. 1–4. Because its history is told, the produce of the soil changes its significance. At the beginning this was 'my fruit which I give you'; it becomes 'the fruit which you give me to grow'. Here God is recognized as Lord.

The relationship to the land is also changed. The Levite and the stranger enjoy a land which does not belong to them. It is the same with 'you'! Our goods do not belong to us; they are to serve our happiness and that of all men.

The former prophets

The Jews gave a different name to the books that we call 'historical': Joshua, Judges, Samuel and Kings. They called them the former prophets, thus putting them on the same level as the latter prophets, Isaiah, Jeremiah and the others.

Here there is more than a change of title. When a modern author chooses to have his book published in a collection of history or philosophy, he indicates something about his concern and shows how he wishes us to read it.

So these books are not history books. They do not seek to give an exact reconstruction of events, and it is not important if, for example, the archaeologists tell us that Jericho was virtually in ruins when Joshua captured it. The author is not a reporter photographing a battle, but a prophet looking for the meaning of the event.

Prophetic books. This indicates that the authors meditated on the traditions which reported events to them, in order to discover what word of God they conveyed. The authors sought less to narrate the events than to discover what these events mean for us. So over the years their work could be taken up again, meditated upon, narrated, in a different way, so as to bring a new word of God in a new historical situation.

In reading Deuteronomy, we have discovered above all a current of thought. The definitive editing of these former prophets was probably carried out by scribes stamped by this current. They had already edited versions of these narratives at their disposal. They took them up and brought them together to derive a lesson from them. After the catastrophe of 587, the account of the failings of Israel and its kings became an appeal for conversion. God remains faithful to his promise to give the land, but this is on condition that the people are faithful to him. God remains present to his people, as he was in his Temple, but on condition that the people return to him. In this meditation on the past, the prophets look above all for light on the present and a hope for the future.

The Jehovist tradition (JE)

This is the name sometimes given to the fusion of the Yahwistic tradition (J), composed under David and Solomon in the southern kingdom, and the Elohistic tradition (E), brought together in the northern kingdom. This fusion was more than a straightforward literary operation; it represents a decision of faith, a reflection in depth on the new situation created by the fall of the northern kingdom.

We are in Jerusalem. King Hezekiah, supported by the prophet Isaiah, is on the throne. He is the successor to David and Solomon, to whom God promised a land, a people, a dynasty. However, for two centuries this united kingdom has been split in two: into the northern kingdom, Israel, and the southern kingdom, Judah. They are aware that both of them, together, are the people with whom God made a covenant on Sinai, and that they inherit the promise made to Abraham.

Now in 721 the northern kingdom was destroyed by Assyria. This event shook the faith of the people seriously, on two fundamental points: the land and the people. The land once given to David had been increasingly invaded by the enemy, who were now encamped almost at the gates of Jerusalem. Was the people from henceforth to be reduced to the tribes of Judah and Benjamin, who made up the southern kingdom?

The faithful among the Israelites from the north who had escaped the massacre took refuge in Jerusalem, bringing their traditions with them. King Hezekiah wanted to stimulate a national and religious renewal, and in his reign an intense theological and literary activity began to develop. The Jehovist tradition was to prove a fine example of it.

This fusion is a response in faith to the agonizing problem raised by the situation of the land and the people. The fundamental hope continued (and has always continued) that the people is made up of both Judah *and* Israel. To show this, the two traditions which had grown up separately were put together in a single work. It was a tricky business, because the two traditions often had the same narratives presented from slightly different perspectives. Those who brought them together tried to respect each of them – which is how modern scholars can rediscover the traces of each – while making sure that the new narrative hung together. They succeeded very well in keeping the hope of the Yahwist, centred on the David dynasty, while incorporating into it the moral and spiritual demands of the Elohist. The result, then, was a work which could be the common property of the tribes of both the north and the south, showing their faith in the God of Israel and their hope in the future. We shall now look quickly at two texts from it.

The covenant with Abraham. Gen.15

This story is probably the beginning of the Elohistic tradition, but it has been amalgamated with a Yahwistic narrative to such a degree that scholars do not even attempt to distinguish the two, being content to pick out the ideas dear to each tradition.

Thus the promise of descendants and a land is added to the blessing of Gen.12.2;13.14, from the Yahwistic tradition. The covenant is a favourite theme of the Elohistic tradition.

As it is now, the text is not without its rough patches, but it is a splendid illustration of the total faith of Abraham. The covenant ritual is important. Normally, the two partners to the covenant would both pass between animals which had been cut in two, signifying that if one or other broke the covenant, they would suffer the same fate as the animals. Here, God alone passes between them, because the promise is his alone. That is essential for Israel, as it is for us; our history as believers starts with this unconditional promise by God, who throws the weight of his faithfulness on to the scales of history. In its sorriest moments, when it was aware of being unfaithful, of being justly punished for its sins, Israel could always turn towards this covenant. God has given an unconditional promise, and he will keep it.

The Book of the Covenant. Ex.20.22–23.19

This is an ancient text, going back to the very beginnings of Israel. It came into being at a period, probably that of the Judges, when there was neither king nor priest. The economy was based on the rearing of livestock, with little agriculture. The text was preserved in the northern kingdom, and Deuteronomy was inspired by it. By paying attention to all the specific sectors of daily life, it teaches that all life must be lived under the eye of God.

At the time of the Jehovist fusion, it was incorporated into the Exodus narrative, and breaks up the framework of that account. However, in this way it contributes by giving the whole narrative the structure of a covenant alliance, in which, this time, both partners commit themselves.

Prophets of Judah in the Seventh Century

Nobody knows quite when the voice of Isaiah fell silent. According to Jewish tradition he was martyred by king Manasseh. But another generation of prophets arose, whose words we are going to hear.

Nahum

You should read his hallucinating vision of chariots fighting at the overthrow of Nineveh. Long before it actually happened – he was probably preaching round about 660 – Nahum 'sees' the ruin of the Assyrian capital in 612. This is an amazing act of faith in the power of God which is evoked in the psalm which begins the book. In fact, at this time Assyria was at the height of its power.

Zephaniah

When Zephaniah was active, the reign of the wicked king Manasseh had just ended: the young king Josiah who was enthroned in 640 had not yet begun his great religious reform.

The first part of the book (1.1–3.8) is a tragic recognition of the situation. The same Hebrew word keeps recurring, though in English it is translated by a longer phrase: draw near . . . in the midst. Zephaniah is dismayed; however hard he looks, in the midst of the people there is no one who is righteous, save God: but he stands alone! Jerusalem does not draw near to her God (3.2). And, the great day of the Lord's wrath is near (Dies irae, dies illa . . . 1.14f.).

Since powerful men, kings, prophets and priests have gone wrong, the prophet turns to those who are poor in heart, those who do not pride themselves in their own strength, but put their trust in God (2.3). In this way Zephaniah is the pioneer of a theme – that of spiritual poverty – which will develop further in the New Testament.

However, the love of the Lord is strongest of all. For the future, God at last sees the time when he will finally be able to be in the bosom of the daughter of Zion, in the midst of his people, and of all the peoples purified by his love. God has only to think of this to begin to dance with joy!

Habakkuk

Habakkuk preached about 600, when the Babylonians were beginning to sweep down on Palestine. For him, they are the instrument of God destined to punish the Assyrians who have oppressed Israel. However, that raises a question for him. How can God use such impure instruments? Why do the wicked always prosper? Habakkuk raises the question of evil at a national level. God replies to him in a phrase which Paul will one day make a summary of his message: the righteous shall live by faith (2.4).

The prayer of Habakkuk (ch. 3) expresses his faith and his joy in God in the midst of the worst trials.

Daughter of Zion

It has been traditional in all civilizations to use a female figure as a symbol for a nation (think, for example, of Britannia!). Hosea compared his people with an unfaithful wife whose heart is transformed into that of a young woman by the love of God.

Micah was the first to use the strange expression 'daughter of Zion'; it probably denotes the northern quarter of Jerusalem, the summit of the hill of Zion where those who escaped the catastrophe of the fall of Samaria regathered after 721. So it indicates a small remnant purified by suffering.

Zephaniah has a vision that in the future this remnant of Israel will be so purified that God can live in their midst, and all the nations who have been purified will join with them (Zeph.3.9). So this image is important for us: it indicates the destiny of each one of us, since here we have the people of the last days.

Jeremiah puts more stress on the sorrowful mystery of the purification that will be needed (4.11; 6.23); so does Lamentations. However, when she is finally purified, this 'woman' will once more search for God, her husband (Jer.31.22).

The disciples of Isaiah who preach at the end of the exile show this virgin of Zion, the Lord's bride, giving birth to many sons (Isa.54.1; 60; 62: 'Rejoice, daughter of Zion . . .'). She will even be giving birth to the new people (Isa.66.6–10).

The first Christians took up this theme once more in order to present the mystery of the church, the woman who was to give birth to Christ through the sorrows of Calvary and throughout history (John 16.21f.; Acts 12). And for Luke, Mary is the image of this church, filled with grace in the last days (Eph.1.6), and welcoming the Saviour into her midst (Luke 1.28–31).

Jeremiah

'Without this extraordinary being, the religious history of humanity would have taken another course, and Christianity would never have happened.' So wrote Ernest Renan, author of a famous Life of Jesus, in the last century.

Jeremiah experienced the terrible drama in which his people were involved, in 597 and then in 587. Furthermore, he had foreseen it, and tried to prepare the people. However, they were thoughtless and simply persecuted him.

Jeremiah began to preach in the time of king Josiah. At that time his preaching was no different from that of the prophets who had preceded him. He wanted to make his people aware that they had gone astray, that the life they were leading would only end in catastrophe. In the first six chapters, which sum up this preaching, two key words recur: the people have *abandoned* God – they must *return* to God, and be converted.

Strangely enough, Jeremiah was silent during the religious reform undertaken by Josiah, though he certainly approved of it.

In 605 the Babylonian king Nebuchadnezzar defeated the Egyptians at Carchemish, in the north of Syria, and in 603 he advanced as far as Jerusalem, which surrendered. Jeremiah understood that the enemy would come from the north, from Babylon. He foresaw the catastrophe and prepared his people for it. When a mishap befalls us (an illness or an accident) and there is no more that we can do about it, there is nothing for it but to try to make sense of what has happened. 'It is afterwards that we understand,' I said at the beginning of this book (p.9). This is what prophets like Ezekiel, and some disciples of Isaiah living in exile in Babylon, tried to do (see the box entitled 'God will punish you . . .'). The great merit of Jeremiah is that he understood beforehand, and made sense of the disaster before it happened. Of course, the people did not listen to him, but rejected him and persecuted him, preferring to follow the false prophets, who reassured them. However, when events proved Jeremiah right, his message was remembered. Thanks to him, the people who endured catastrophe had the possibility of making sense of it as it happened. To a great degree this enabled people to endure the exile in faith and hope, not being overwhelmed by their misfortunes, but rather discovering a new meaning in life.

Of course you won't be able to read all of Jeremiah. But here are at least a few texts that you could read.

True religion. The people are good at practising their religion; they revere the ark of the covenant and go to the Temple; they offer sacrifices, observe the sabbath and circumcise children. They practise their religion, but their heart is not in it. They think that because they respect the ritual, God will have to protect them, along with Jerusalem, the holy city. They have made their practice of religion a matter of security which relieves them of the obligation to love. Jeremiah announces that God will destroy all these false securities: the ark of the covenant (3.16); the Temple (7.1–5; 26); Jerusalem (19), for what God demands is not an outward circumcision, of the flesh, but an inward circumcision, of the heart (4.4; 9.24–25). These attacks seemed so blasphemous that Jeremiah barely escaped death. In this way he prefigures Jesus' attacks on our senseless practices.

The new covenant. Chapter 31 is the climax of his message. He preaches hope beyond misfortune: God will pardon and make things new.

What is this security based on? Read 31.20.

Personal responsibility (vv.29–30): Ezekiel develops this aspect at length (Ezek.18).

What features make the covenant a new one (31.31–34)? Luke (22.20) and Paul (I Cor.11.25) see it realized in the blood of the Last Supper.

Prophetic actions. Like all the prophets, but to an even greater degree, Jeremiah preaches his actions as well as his words. These symbolic gestures are often more than a simple announcement: because the prophet bears the word of God, the effective word, in some sense they make the event announced become present in advance. In this sense the actions of Jesus at the Last Supper are also prophetic actions.

Jeremiah's personal journal. With Paul, Jeremiah is the person in the Bible whom we know best. In fact he gives us his personal reactions; he tells us of his faith and doubts in passages which are extremely personal. They are sometimes called his confessions. Read at least 12.1–5; 20.7–18: how do these 'prayers' help us to understand God? ourselves? our relationship with God?

Jeremiah's call (1.4–19). The way in which a prophet describes his call, his vocation, often sheds a great deal of light on his message. In the case of Jeremiah, there is nothing extraordinary: everything seems to take place in the intimacy of prayer. Using this text as a starting point, try to discover the nature of the mission entrusted to Jeremiah and some features of his character. On what is his certainty based? The two visions (vv.11f.,13f.) show us how a prophet 'sees' God in events. How can that help us to discover the word of God in our life and in world events?

God will punish you . . .

The message of the prophets may well shock us. They often present us with a God who threatens his people with punishment because they have sinned. So are natural catastrophes, wars, human injustice, all punishment from God? We find such a picture of a vengeful God intolerable.

Here is a parable. Imagine a young man, crazy about his motor cycle. One day he has an accident: hospital, long months of convalescence, doctors, nurses . . . and one nurse who soon begins to look after him with more than professional care. One day they get married. This boy might well say to the nurse who became his wife: 'It's lucky that I got smashed up; otherwise I would never have come to know you.' We might accept this remark, but we would find it objectionable if the chaplain went up to him and said, 'You were lucky . . .' Why? In the first case, it is the person involved who himself, out of his own feelings and after the event, makes sense of his accident; it is not imposed on him from the outside. Furthermore, the accident remains a misfortune for him; the good luck is the happy outcome to his troubles.

Now let's change the story and apply it to the prophetic books. Suppose that before his accident this boy had led a dissolute and selfish life. His suffering, the long months of loneliness led him to reflect on the emptiness of his life, and the boy who came out of the hospital was a changed person. He decided to transform his life and to put himself at the service of others. If he even rediscovered faith, one could imagine him saying one day to God, 'It's a good thing you allowed this accident, because as a result I've found meaning in my life.' We can accept this prayer, but we would find objectionable the chaplain who said, 'You see, God's punished you . . .'

The prophets are the boy, and not the chaplain. Ezekiel was deported with the people; Jeremiah was persecuted and bore in advance the sufferings of the people. They reflected on events which for them remained a misfortune. However, from within and after the event (or before it, in the case of Jeremiah), they tried to make sense of these events and to see the good effect that they might have. They led the people to recognize that they had lived badly and had to change their lives. For them, even if the language which they use is sometimes rather abrupt, these events are less divine punishments than occasions for discovering the love of God which invites them to a new life.

An Assyrian warrior cuts off the head of a prisoner (Assyrian painting, eighth century)

5 Exile in Babylon 587–538

Winged bull with a man's head. Assyria (eighth century)

July 587: after a siege lasting one year, the army of Nebuchadnezzar, king of Babylon, captured Jerusalem. That was the end of the kingdom of Judah.

Ten years of madness. 597–587

Nebuchadnezzar had already captured Jerusalem in 597. At that time he was content to accept substantial tribute, to deport some of the inhabitants (including the prophet Ezekiel) and to leave behind a vassal king.

It might have been hoped that that would teach the people a lesson. However, led astray by false prophets who nurtured their illusions and made them feel that they were just having a bad time for the moment, the people experienced ten years of madness. They continued a carefree existence, and made an alliance with Egypt against the Babylonians.

In Jerusalem, the prophet Jeremiah preached the need for submission to the Babylonians. For him, the essential thing was not whether the nation was free or politically subject, but whether it was just and spiritually free, serving its God and acting rightly. The voice of Jeremiah, declared a traitor to his country, was muted by the mud-filled cistern into which he was thrown.

In Babylon, Ezekiel spoke in the same way to the fellow-countrymen who had been deported with him, but to no effect. They were secretly making flags to welcome their brothers who would come to deliver them. In 587, they saw these brothers arrive – at least those who had not been put to the sword – not as liberators, but with ropes round their necks, exhausted by the 1,500 kilometre march, following a king whose eyes had been put out, and retaining in his empty sockets a last sight – that of his sons having their throats cut.

Reconstruction of a ziggurat. The tower of Babel was thought to be like this

The miracle of the exile

The people had lost everything that went to make up their life:

- the land, the concrete sign of God's blessing on his people.

- the king, through whom God handed on this blessing, the guarantor of the unity of the people and their representative before God.

- the Temple, the place of the divine presence.

In the last resort, Israel had even lost its God. At this time, it was thought that each country was protected by its national God, the power behind its armies. So the God of Israel had been defeated by Marduk, the god of Babylon. And one did not go on serving a conquered god.

The great miracle of the exile was that instead of proving the ruin of the faith of Israel, this catastrophe brought about a change in this faith and purified it. The miracle occurred thanks to the prophets, like Ezekiel and a disciple of Isaiah known as Second Isaiah, together with the priests: these led the people to reread their traditions in order to discover there a foundation for their hope. Together, they discovered a new and more spiritual way of living out their faith. Temple and sacrifices were a thing of the past. But it was possible to meet on the sabbath to worship God and to meditate on his word. The king was no more. But was not God the only true king of Israel? The land was lost. But circumcision in the flesh could mark out the bounds of a kingdom with spiritual dimensions. In this way, in exile, what we call Judaism came into being, i.e. a way of living out the Jewish religion which would be that of the time of Jesus and of our own time.

By the waters of Babylon . . .

What was the situation of the Jews who had been deported? That question is not very easy to answer. The people had undergone a terrible psychological and moral shock, and they had also experienced physical suffering. In this period, the capture of a city and deportation meant that women were raped, small children were dashed against the rocks, warriors were impaled or burnt alive, eyes were gouged out and heads cut off. We can read an echo of this suffering in Ps.137. However, we should not imagine that life in Babylon was like that in a concentration camp. The Jews enjoyed relative freedom (though that did not exclude forced labour); Ezekiel was free to visit his compatriots, who could devote themselves to agriculture. At the end of the exile, some of them preferred to stay in Babylonia, where they formed an important and prosperous group. The archives of the bank of Murashu in Nippur (south of Babylon) show us that a century after the exile a certain number of Jews had quite substantial accounts.

The Jews were impressed by the city of Babylon and its traditions. The city had the form of a vast square, covering about thirteen square kilometres, with the river Euphrates running through it. The gate of Ishtar, adorned with multi-coloured enamelled bricks, opened on to the sacred route, flanked by temples, in the midst of which rose the ziggurat (a kind of stepped tower). This was the tower of Babylon, or Babel. Annually, at New Year, they would listen to the recitation of the great poems (Enuma Elish, the Gilgamesh Epic) which told how the god Marduk, god of Babylon, created the world, and how the god Ea saved mankind from the flood. They discovered the thoughts of the wise men about the human condition. In this way the Jews were in contact with a type of thinking which was widespread in the Middle East, and this will clearly have helped them to reflect.

Cyrus the 'messiah'

On 29 October 539, Cyrus seized Babylon without firing a shot, probably thanks to the help of Babylonians who were exasperated with the incompetence of their king Nabonidus.

Cyrus was a petty king of Persia, one of the provinces of the empire of the Medes which extended to the north and east of Babylon. In 550 he seized power in Media, went as far as Asia Minor to seize the fabulous treasure of king Croesus, and returned to Babylon. His amazing rise was followed passionately by the Jewish exiles and Second Isaiah; was not this the man whom God had chosen, had marked out through his anointing (*messiah* in Hebrew) to liberate them?

And in fact in 538 in Ecbatana, his distant summer capital, Cyrus signed an edict allowing the Jews to go home. He even granted them substantial war damages to rebuild their country. Was this because of his natural benevolence, or his political sensitivity? He was actually interested that the Jewish nation, an advance bastion of his empire in the direction of Egypt, should be utterly devoted to him. Whatever his motives, for the Jews this was the end of their nightmare, and at that time a large number of them returned to 'the land'.

Literary activity

The Jews had lost everything. They had nothing left but their traditions. So they began to read these again with great concern.

The prophets Ezekiel and the Second Isaiah preached, one at the beginning of the exile and one at the end.

Priests reassembled the collections of laws which had already been put into writing in Jerusalem towards the end of the monarchy: the Holiness Code (Lev.17–26). Augmented after the return from exile, this law was to become Leviticus.

Above all, in order to sustain faith and hope among the people, the priests once more reminded them of their origins. This rereading of history is known by the name of the Priestly tradition, and is the fourth of the documents which make up the Pentateuch. So all the elements of the Pentateuch were complete: it remained only to bring them together in a single work. This happened around 400.

Disaster, suffering, and also contact with Babylonian and then Persian thought, led the wise men of Israel to deepen their reflection on the human condition. In the centuries after the exile this reflection culminated in works like Job.

We can also easily imagine that the prayer of believers would take on a new tone. Psalms (for example 137 or 44; 80; 89) could be composed at that time as appeals to the God who keeps faith.

In Jerusalem, some Jews spared deportation voiced their lament in the book of Lamentations, wrongly attributed to Jeremiah.

Prophets of the Exile

Ezekiel

Ezekiel was one of the first group to be deported, in 597. For ten years, in Babylon, his message was couched in the same terms as that of Jeremiah, who remained in Jerusalem: he censured the people of God (Ezek.3–24) and the nations (Ezek.25–32) for their wicked conduct.

From 587, when the catastrophe had come about and the people had lost all hope, his preaching became a message of hope: God would restore his people (33–39). Ezekiel was so sure of this that he gave a description, in futuristic terms, of the Jerusalem of the future, transformed by God (40–48).

A disconcerting figure

Ezekiel can never be like anyone else. Like his predecessors, he has visions, but his are flabbergasting: for example, read the account of his call (ch.1). He performs prophetic actions, but sometimes these go beyond the bounds of good taste: see chs.4–5. Some passages in his allegories would make a guardsman blush – so don't read chs. 16 or 23!

However, it is by means of this very excessiveness that Ezekiel achieves the solemn effect he makes, and when he wants to , he can become a very great lyric poet: see his cry against the prince of Tyre (ch.28). Compare it with Gen.2–3: you will see that these two texts exploit, in different ways, the same mythological traditions.

The father of Judaism

Ezekiel's message served as the foundation of what came to be called Judaism, that is to say, the Jewish way of living before God and with others as it took form after the exile.

Ezekiel has a very lively sense of the holiness of God, and he wants this to be expressed with all men's being. Hence the importance he attaches, because he is a priest, to regulations and ritual.

In this way he is inspired by the Holiness Code (Lev.17–26), created by the priests at Jerusalem before the exile (see p.68).

Jeremiah insisted on the inward aspect of religion; his ideals were sustenance for the piety of God's poor. The danger here was that religion might become detached from day-to-day living. Ezekiel also preaches an inward-looking religion, but insists on a complementary aspect: this faith must be expressed through the body, in ritual. The danger here is that people observe the regulations without having their heart in what they do.

▼ Some texts from Ezekiel

The holy presence of God
God made himself present in his temple. However, first Nathan (II Sam.7, see p.42) and then the other prophets had sensed that God does not want to dwell materially in a place, but spiritually, among a faithful people. Ezekiel, living in exile, shows how this can be realized, in his own person.

Read, one after the other, Ezek.9.3; 10.4–5; 11.22–23; then Ezek 1; and finally Ezek.37.26–28; 43.1–12. What is Ezekiel trying to say by means of these extraordinary images? Where is God present? How? (Perhaps Luke was thinking of Ezek.11.23 when he put the Ascension on a mountain facing east, the Mount of Olives.)

I am the good shepherd. Ezek.34; 37.15–18
Who are the shepherds of the people? How have they behaved? Who will be the true shepherd?

Jesus was inspired by these texts (Matt.18.10–14; Luke 15.1–7; John 10). Who is the shepherd? What force and what significance does this give to the words of Jesus?

Behold, I make all things new. Ezek.33.1–11; 37.1–14. The people are in exile, and desperate; they are like old carcases drying out in the sun . . . What does God announce in the vision of ch.37? God recreates his people by his word and gives them life through his spirit. What can this say to Christians today?

Ezek.36.16–38; 47.1–12. What is the spirit doing? Whence does it spring? Jer.31.31–34 makes that plainer: how? How do these texts help us to understand John 7.37–39; 19.34, or Gal.5.22–25?

Second Isaiah. 'The voice which cries.' Isa.40–55

Here is something amazing! To be in exile, scorned, humiliated, having lost everything, toiling without hope, a foreign labourer . . . and then to begin to sing of the God who does miracles, in a voice which is so convincing that it brings hope to a whole people. Where did this disciple of Isaiah, who hides behind his mission and simply calls himself 'the voice which cries', find such strength? In his faith in God. God is always 'the-one-who-brought-us-out-of-the-house-of-slavery' at the Exodus, so he can still free us. He has the power to do so, because he is the creator. And he will do so because he is faithful and loves us more than a mother.

Before we study an important text, let's single out some of the major themes of this moving prophet.

The gospel
Three times, there rings out this good news or gospel, that God will at last establish his kingdom, show himself to be the true king, and make evil, suffering and injustice disappear (40.9; 41.27; 52.7. See also 35.3–6, which comes from the same period). By performing miracles and pronouncing the beatitudes, Jesus proclaims that this is realized in him: the poor will be happy, because from now on their poverty is ended.

God's tenderness. 43.1–7; 49.14–16
This is one of the finest sayings about the love of God, whose feeling for us is the gut-feeling of a mother.

The new exodus
The liberation is seen as a more marvellous exodus than the first. See, for example, 40.3; 41.17–20; 43.16–23; 44.21f.; 48.17–22. The first Christians interpreted the life of Jesus and our own in the light of the Exodus (see the references in the margin of your Bible, if it is an annotated version).

Cyrus the messiah
Here is a fine example of the interpretation of history. Cyrus captures Babylon for personal aggrandisement, He himself interprets this as a call from Marduk, God of Babylon (see the adjacent box). For Isaiah, it is the God of Israel who has called him and anointed him (41.1–5,25–29; 42.5–7; 44.27–28; 45.1–6,11–13; 48.12–18). Faith, and faith alone, allows us to see a meaning in events.

◤ The Servant of God. Isa.52.13–53.12

This text is the climax of the message. There is some controversy over how it should be interpreted.

Begin by looking at those who speak:

God announces the glory which awaits his servant (52.13–15).

The nations who have persecuted this servant are amazed and confess their mistake (53.1–6).

The prophet meditates on the fate of this servant, an innocent victim who has been put to death (53.7–9).

Then he prays:
Lord, ground down as he is by suffering, may he please you; make him a sacrifice of expiation,
so that he may see his descendants and prolong his days,
and fulfil the good pleasure of God.
God hears this prayer. 53.11–12.

This servant is probably the personification of the people of Israel, humiliated, scorned, put to death. Calamity has come upon them and they cannot do anything but try to make sense of it (look again at 'God will punish you . . .', p.63).

How is this situation of the death of the servant transformed? What is the final outcome? Why? (Look at the two aspects, the attitude of the servant and the action of God.)

This servant did a great deal to help the first Christians understand Jesus. How does he help you to discover the meaning
of the mission of Christ (53.12)?
of his death for the many (Mark 10.45; Rom.4.25; the accounts of the Last Supper: Matt.26.28; Mark; Luke)?
The mystery of Easter? Read Phil.2.6–11.

How does this help us to make sense of our lives?

The Cyrus Cylinder

On a clay cylinder discovered in Babylon, Cyrus gives his interpretation of events:

Marduk, the great Lord (of Babylon), the protector of his people, beheld with pleasure the good deeds of Cyrus and ordered him to march against his city, Babylon. He made him set out on the road to Babylon, going at his side like a real friend. Without any battle, he made him enter his town Babylon.

Leviticus

This is a marvellous book, full of sexual tabus and blood! But you need to be brave to venture into it: there are constant repetitions, a boring tone, strange and pettyfogging rules – everything is calculated to put us off. And yet . . .

We need ritual

Because we are physical beings, we express our feelings through specific actions. Watch a family laying the table before a dinner party; everything is set out in accordance with a fixed pattern, with custom, but that is the way in which we show our friends how pleased we are to see them. However, that is also the possible danger of ritual; in a restaurant, the waiter who lays the table may do so with complete indifference.

We also need ritual when we are preparing to meet God. As the fox said to the little prince in Saint-Exupery's story, it's a way of 'dressing up the heart'. For Israelite believers, meeting God was an important matter, the one thing that was worth while. So for them the minute details in ritual were one way of expressing their sense of living in the presence of the holy God.

'Be holy because I am holy'

Many of the regulations in Leviticus belong to a culture which is no longer our own and it would be stupid to want to apply them. But what they tell us is still essential: God is present, and we live before him. God is mentioned constantly (more than 350 times), and 'before him' recurs like a refrain (more than 50 times). Read ch.19: one motivation underlies all the regulations, from love of neighbour (v.18) to justice for the hired labourer (v.13), and taking in all the situations of everyday life: 'I am the Lord your God'. So it is in his love for God that the believer sees the way in which he should live in the world and with others.

This God is the holy God; that is, he is utterly different from us. He is the living God, he is Life. And that explains the mysterious respect there is for blood and sexuality.

'The blood is the life' (Lev.17.11,14)

Blood is sacred because it is life, the very life which comes from God and which flows in our veins. So the blood of men may not be spilt. One may not drink the blood of an animal (much less that of a man); that would be to claim to fortify one's life by human means, whereas God alone is the master of life. So this is not a culinary regulation (don't eat black pudding!), but a matter of respect for life. By contrast, offering blood in sacrifices is a way of recognizing the gift of life which God makes to us. In these sacrifices what is offered is not the victim –

Sacred – sacerdotal – sacrifice

Sacerdotal is an archaic word, meaning 'priestly', but by using it here we can see how the notions of the sacred, priesthood and sacrifice are all connected with the same root. In all religions, the sacred is the sphere of the deity, completely separate from the profane (*pro-fanum*, Latin for 'before the holy place'). Israel largely shared in this mentality. God was the Holy One, that is, the one who is utterly different.

Furthermore, Israel had a keen sense that man exists only in relationship, with others and above all with God. But how was it possible to bridge the gap between the holy God and man?

This was the responsibility of the priest. To fulfil it, he had to enter the sphere of the sacred, and that was achieved through consecration, i.e. separation: separation from the people to be reserved for the cult; separation from the profane and from everyday activities to enter the temple. The culmination of the priest's activities was sacrifice. The word does not mean deprivation, but transformation: to sacrifice is to make sacred: what one offers passes into God's domain. In return, the priest can hand on God's gifts to the people: pardon, instruction, blessings.

With Jesus Christ, this conception was to be completely transformed. In him the sacred became profane. It was no longer possible to make a distinction between the two; through him, everything was sanctified. And he is the only priest, the perfect mediator: his sacrifice is the unique sacrifice (the Letter to the Hebrews develops this aspect at length). However, the temptation of the church is always to express sacrifice and the priestly ministry by going back to the Old Testament pattern: this explains the present difficulties connected with priesthood in the Catholic church today.

---

which is no more than a carcase – but the hot (literally, 'living') blood, i.e. the very life of the victim. We should get into the habit of replacing this word blood by its equivalent, the life which is offered; these texts from Leviticus or the Letter to the Hebrews then become terribly evocative.

The same applies to the sexual prohibitions. Over and above the tabus (which certainly exist), the principal element is the impressive feeling of sharing, through sexuality, in the handing on of the life which comes from God, and which explains the sacred character of sexuality.

The composition of Leviticus

The Holiness Code (Lev.17–26) was composed in Jerusalem before the exile. At the time when Deuteronomy, which came from the north, was being edited, and everything was centred on the covenant and election on the part of God, the Jerusalem priests wanted to codify the customs practised in the Temple, all centred on the cult, to remind people that God is holy, utterly different.

The law of sacrifice (Lev.1–7) and the law of purity (Lev.11–16) were edited after the exile, as was the law of festivals (Num.28–29).

Some texts from Leviticus

Of course you can't read the whole book. But it would be a pity to miss some texts.

Lev.19.1–17: God's holiness is the source of brotherly love and life in society.

Lev.23 reminds you how time is sanctified by the sabbath and the great festivals.

Lev.16 presents the great day of forgiveness, Yom Kippur: this was the only time in the year when the high priest could penetrate behind the veil of the temple, to obtain remission of sins. The author of the Letter to the Hebrews used this liturgy to express Christ's sacrifice. This chapter also takes up an old custom with a touch of magic to it, that of the scapegoat.

Finally, if you want to discover about the various kinds of sacrifices, read Lev.1–7.

Impure or sacred?

For us, purity and impurity are moral notions.

In the Bible, as in all religions, they are notions which come very close to those of tabu or the sacred. A person is impure when he has made contact with a mysterious power which can be good or evil. In that case it is necessary to perform a ritual which purifies, which removes the contagion of this power.

Some illnesses, for example, can make people impure because at that time they are thought to be under demonic influence.

Conversely, contact with God can bring 'impurity'. Thus, only a short while ago, one could read this rubric in Catholic liturgical books: 'After communion, the priest purifies the chalice' (with a linen cloth called a 'purificator'). Had this chalice become impure (in the moral sense) through having contained the blood of Christ? No, it had become sacred because it had entered the divine sphere, and its purification was a rite of desacralization, allowing it again to be put to some profane usage. A woman who has just given birth must also be purified. We might ask whether this, too, is not an act of desacralization: because she had come into contact with God, the source of life, by giving life, she has to undergo a certain ritual in order to return again to everyday life.

This question of purity and impurity is very complicated, and the object of much discussion by scholars. Here I have over-simplified it almost to the point of falsification. However, it's worth at least remembering several points:

- the notions of purity and impurity often have no moral content, but are more closely connected with ideas of tabu and the sacred;

- sometimes, however, these same words take on a moral significance;

- confusion between the two senses of these very words is doubtless partly responsible for the discredit into which sexuality is brought: we have given a moral sense to impurity in places where the Bible gives it a ritual sense.

The Priestly History

In exile, the people had lost all that made them a people. There was a risk that they might become assimilated and disappear, which had been the fate of the northern kingdom 150 years earlier, when they had been deported to Assyria. Who would help them to withstand this test? Prophets like the priest Ezekiel and Second Isaiah, but above all the priests. In Jerusalem these formed a solid group, well organized and with a deep piety. They were the ones who would sustain the faith of the exiles. They succeeded in adapting religion to the difficult situation and giving it a new future.

They invented new forms of practice or gave religious practices a new significance. The sabbath, as a sanctification of time, and circumcision, as a mark of belonging to the people, would become primordial symbols (reread p.64). Sacrifices were replaced by assemblies (or synagogues) where people prayed and meditated on the word of God: this is the origin of what was later to become synagogue worship.

The Priestly History, denoted by the letter P, came into being in this context. The priests reread past history to discover in it a reply to agonizing questions. Why is God silent? How can we believe in God in this Babylonian world which celebrates the god Marduk as creator? What is the place of other nations in God's plans? So this tradition invites us to continue its reflections, and to see how we today, in a new situation, can live out our faith and respond to the world's questions. God's promise is always valid; but we have to work to fulfil it.

A key text: Gen.1.28

And God blessed them, and God said to them,
'Be fruitful and multiply, and fill the earth and subdue
it; and have dominion over the fish of the sea and over
the birds of the air and over every living thing that moves
upon the earth.'

This is an extraordinary blessing, which expresses the faith of the priests in exile. The five verbs are an

---

Some characteristics of the Priestly writer

The style is dry. The Priestly writer is not a story-teller. He loves figures and lists. He often repeats the same thing twice: God says. . .God does. See, for example, his version of the crossing of the Red Sea (p.26 above); the creation (Gen.1); the building of the sanctuary (Ex.25–31;35–40).

The vocabulary is often technical and has to do with the cult.

Genealogies appear often. They are important for an exiled people without roots. They give the people roots in history and connect up this history with that of the creation (Gen.2.4; 5.1; Num.3.1).

Worship has pride of place. Moses organizes it; Aaron and his descendants are made responsible for continuing it through pilgrimages, festivals, and worship in the temple, which is the holy place in which God makes himself present. The priesthood is an essential institution which assures the existence of the people; it replaces the role of the king in the Yahwist and the prophet in the Elohist.

Laws are usually put in a narrative context. So they are attached to historical events which give them significance. See, for example, the law of fertility (Gen.9.1) in the story of the flood, or the law of the Passover (Ex.12.1ff.), attached to the tenth plague.

Because of all these characteristics, the Priestly texts are the easiest ones to identify in the Pentateuch.

---

exact contradiction of their present situation. They express the will of the creator God which will be fulfilled one day, and put an end to evil and to the exile.

You can see how this blessing underlies the book of Genesis, giving a new colouring to the events which are narrated: Gen.8.17; 9.1–7 (the flood); 17.20 (Abraham); 28.1–4; 35.11 (Jacob); 47.27 (Joseph). In Ex.1.7 this is no longer a promise, but a reality which has to be pursued throughout history.

A survey of the Priestly History

Like the Yahwistic tradition, the Priestly History begins with creation and goes as far as the death of Moses (Deut.24.7). On the next two pages we shall be studying the creation story. Here we shall read one or two texts.

The covenant with Noah and the flood. Gen.6–9

The two traditions, the Yahwistic and the Priestly, have been fused in the present account of the flood. Both closely follow the mythical account of the flood told in the Gilgamesh epic. The Priestly tradition stresses the construction of the ark, built with three storeys, like Solomon's Temple: it is in the sanctuary that man finds salvation (6.16).

This narrative ends with the covenant with Noah, with his descendants and with the whole earth (9.8–17). Thus the God of Israel is the universal God and his covenant relates to all men. All nations have a place in God's plan.

But does Israel have a particular place?

The covenant with Abraham. Gen.17

The law of circumcision is attached to a narrative which is made up of four speeches by God. Try to see how the thought progresses from one to the other. What does God ask of Abraham? That he should go in his presence (remember Leviticus) and be whole, without fault or blemish, like the offering for sacrifice (Ex.12.5; Lev.1.3). Circumcision becomes the distinctive sign of the people (compare this text with Gen.15, p.60).

In exile, Israel becomes aware that the people have sinned and broken the bilateral covenant made on Sinai. According to the terms of this covenant, it is natural that God should have let it lapse. As we shall see, the authors pass quickly over Sinai, to return to the covenant with Abraham. Here it is a matter of a promise to which God alone is committed. Whatever its sins, Israel (and we too in our turn) can have recourse to it.

This tradition is interested in Abraham's purchase of land at Hebron to bury Sarah in (Gen.23). This is important for the exiles: their ancestor bought a piece of land and is buried in it (25.9). So they have a right to this land!

The Exodus

These exiles stressed the harsh servitude in Egypt (Ex.1.13–14; 2.23–24) and the promise made by God to Abraham (Ex.6, the calling of Moses). The priests remember the way in which this liberation was celebrated: the cult makes present for each generation the action of the Lord who gives freedom (Ex.12.1–20). The crossing of the sea becomes a powerful act of the creator God (see p.26); he is capable of renewing it for his exiled people. The law of the sabbath is attached to the gift of manna (Ex.16), so the people can cease work on that day without being afraid that God may let them die of hunger.

The covenant on Sinai

This covenant was too important for the exiles to pass it by in silence. However, they transformed its meaning. No actual covenant is made here (as with the Yahwist and the Elohist: Ex.24). God simply announces that he will make Israel a kingdom of priests and a holy nation (Ex.19.5–6). Israel is not governed by kings, like other nations, but by priests.

God does not give a law for his people, but orders to build a sanctuary (Ex.25–27), to establish priests and the cult (Ex.28–29); the only law is that of the sabbath (Ex.31.12–17).

Faced with the failure of the covenant on Sinai, people turned to God's promise to Abraham. And the priesthood was the institution charged with reminding the people of their sin and of God's forgiveness.

The holy presence of God. Ex.25.10–22; 40.34–38

You should read at least the beginning and end of Ex.25–31; 35–40. 'Let them make me a sanctuary, that I may dwell in their midst' (25.8). The text focusses our attention on the mercy seat (the plate of gold which covered the ark), and on this empty space between the mercy seat and the two cherubim. It is there that God makes himself present for his people; and it is on this mercy seat that once a year the high priest sprinkles blood to obtain the divine forgiveness (Lev.16).

To indicate that Christ is the real presence of God and that his blood brings forgiveness, Paul was to write: God put him forward as an expiation by his blood (Rom.3.25).

To study this well-known text, you can use the tool box from p.14.

In these two pages, you will find some help towards answering the questions in the order in which they are given. However, don't read them now. If you try to answer all the questions on p.14 you won't even have to read what follows; you will find it all out by yourself.

So go back to the tool box and your Bible.

When you have finished your study, you can read this next part if you want to.

Here are some of the words or expressions which keep occurring:

God said . . . ten times. These ten words remind us of the ten commandments. God creates the world in the same way as he creates his people on Sinai.

God acts (various verbs). This opposition between creation by the word and creation by action is perhaps an indication of an earlier twofold narrative; or perhaps it is the Priestly Writer's usual style.

And the evening . . . Creation is assigned to six days, culminating in the sabbath. So this is a liturgical arrangement and not a scientific one, to establish the importance of the sabbath.

People tend to forget that this text was produced during the exile. That helps to give it the significance of being an act of faith. At first sight it seems to be poetry, an escape from reality: 'All the world is good.' Now the author is writing in exile, in a broken world. He goes beyond scorn, evil and suffering to affirm his faith in a God who wants a good and just world.

Some expressions or realities had a special sense at that time.

We have seen the importance of the sabbath for the exiles. To show that God himself observed it gives it a sacred character.

The text does not speak of the sun and the moon, but of the two 'lights' (Gen.1.16). This word was part of the cultic vocabulary of the priests; it denotes the lamps shining in the temple (see for example Ex.25.6; 27.20). So the sun and moon are not gods, as they are in Babylon, but signs to indicate a presence (like the light before the sacrament in a Catholic church) and to indicate the times for festivals. The Temple of Jerusalem might be destroyed, but the whole universe was God's temple.

It is interesting to compare this text with the Babylonian myths. There God does not create from nothing; he creates by separation. These accounts took up the old myth which was as well known in Babylon as it was in Egypt; reread the texts on p.19. In Hebrew, the word for abyss is *tehom*, and recalls the Babylonian *Tiamat*. However, there is no trace of struggle here: God is the one God.

We could compare this narrative with many other bibilical texts; however, let's be content with two.

1 The Priestly creation story (Gen.1) **and the Yahwistic creation story** (Gen.2).
The 'science' (as accepted then) underlying the two stories is different. In Gen.2 the land appears like an oasis in the middle of the desert. Here it is an island in the midst of the waters. By successive separations, God makes dry land appear and puts man on it.

In Gen.2, the male is created first to cultivate the earth: then comes the female. Here, humanity (man and woman) is created last. This is another way of showing human dignity; in a liturgical procession, the most important figure comes last. This is mankind, which is created. Only at a second stage is it shown that mankind is made up of males and females.

2 The creation and the crossing of the Red Sea (Ex.14).
We noticed the similarities between these two texts when we studied Ex.14 (p.26): God speaks and acts (directly, or through Moses); he separates the waters so that dry land appears. So the liberation is shown as an omnipotent act of the creator God, and creation as an act of the liberator God who wants not only a people, Israel, but all peoples, all mankind, to be free.

We must now take up some features of these texts in rather more systematic fashion.

A liturgical poem

We should not look for instruction in science or history here. This is a poem expressing the extraordinary faith of priests in their God. The world was created in six days to legitimize the sabbath. This sabbath has a twofold significance. It is the time when God keeps sabbath, that is, ceases to work himself; so the seventh day is the time of human history, the time given to man to work and continue creation; after this will come the eighth day, the last day. However, this sabbath is celebrated by stopping work in order to sanctify time, pay homage to God.

From the liberator God to the creator God

The God whom Israel discovered first was the God who freed them from slavery in Egypt; a God who acts in history. And the exiles in Babylon now turned again to this God in hope of a new liberation. However, as Second Isaiah forcefully puts it, this God is capable of acting in history because he created history.

Man in God's image

How is man the image of God? The story lays stress on two aspects.

Man was created a creator. Man shows God's power through his mastery of the world by science. So he has the responsibility of organizing the universe and making it habitable. That is his concern.

Man is a loving relationship. The image of God who is love cannot be found in a single individual: it is found in a couple, a man and a woman, who love each other and whose love produces life. It was necessary to await the revelation of Jesus to discover all that this image could evoke of the very mystery of God himself. Conversely, however, the human couple are the sacrament of this God who is Trinity.

A God without a name

To give someone a name is to have some power over them; to reveal one's own name is to give something of oneself. So God does not have a proper name (see Gen.32.23–33: God refuses to give his name).

El, Elohim. The first way of naming God was to use the common noun *el*, god. Semites were already addressing their chief god in this way in the third millennium: he was 'the God'. Moslems have kept this usage: Allah comes from *al-Ilah*, the God. People would simply talk about the El of Abraham, of Isaac . . . And that is a first lesson: God remains unknowable. We can only discover things about him through what he is to those who worship him: the God of Abraham, of Jesus, of Mr and Mrs So-and-So. The plural Elohim denotes his majesty, like the royal 'we'.

Yahweh. God seems to give his name to Moses (see p.53). In fact, this is less his name than an indication of a presence. And in any case, we don't know how to pronounce it. As a mark of respect, the Jews never pronounced this divine name. They wrote the four consonants of the word YHWH (you will sometimes hear people talking about the Tetragrammaton, Greek for four letters), but they read it as Adonai, the Lord. The Massoretes (see p.7) put the vowels of Adonai on the consonants of Yahweh producing the barbarism Jehovah, which we find so often in old translations, hymns and prayers.

The Septuagint, the Greek Bible, translated the Tetragrammaton by Kyrios, the Lord. And the first Christians imitated this. Out of respect for the Jews, who are very shocked to hear us pronounce God's ineffable name, we should do the same thing and always read YHWH as 'the Lord'. That happens in RSV, but unfortunately not in the Jerusalem Bible.

6 *Israel under Persian Domination 538–333*

Persian royal guard. Susa (fifth century)

In 538 the edict of Cyrus allowed the Jews to return to their ancestral land and to rebuild their Temple (see this edict in Ezra 1.2–4). This fitted in well with Cyrus' spirit of tolerance and also with his political plans: it was necessary for Jerusalem, the last bastion of his empire in the direction of Egypt, to remain faithful.

For two centuries, the Jews formed part of the Persian empire with its enterprising kings, while Greek power grew. We must find some fixed points in this turbulent history. (For the successions of kings and events, see the chronological table on pp.118–19, and the maps in your Bible.)

The Persian empire

After capturing Babylon, Cyrus pursued his conquests in the east. He died there in 530. His son Cambyses captured Egypt, but came to grief in Ethiopia.

During a long reign, Darius I (522–486) began to organize his immense empire. He divided it into twenty provinces called satrapies, governed by a satrap, a chancellor and a general: they had to pay heavy taxes. He established a remarkable network of roads, including the 'Royal Road', which went from Susa as far as Ephesus on the Mediterranean coast. He conquered Thrace and Macedonia, in the north of Greece, but met his match at Marathon (490).

After Xerxes I, who was also beaten by the Greeks in the sea battle of Salamis (480), Artaxerxes 1 (464–424) first had to pacify Egypt, which had rebelled. The Jew Nehemiah, a royal official at the Persian court, was sent to Jerusalem; having formerly been dependants of Samaria, the Jews became an independent prefecture.

At that time Greece was experiencing its golden age

Assyrian scribe. Assyrian wall painting (eighth century)

– the century of Pericles – in art (the Parthenon), in literature (Sophocles and Euripides), and in philosophy (Socrates and Plato).

Darius II (424–404) had to fight in Egypt. On the island of Elephantine, near to the present-day Asswan dam, there was a Jewish military colony with a temple to the God Yahu. Correspondence with the Jerusalem authorities and the Persian court tells us something about its religion.

When Artaxerxes II became king (404–359), Egypt regained its independence. The province of Jerusalem again became important as a forward bastion of the empire. In 398, the king sent Ezra there. He tried to re-establish peace between Jews and Samaritans, who were to enjoy a special status in the empire: they had to obey the 'Law of the God of heaven' (Ezra 7.21) under the direction of the high priest. This fragile union between Jews and Samaritans only lasted for about twenty years.

The last Persian kings were faced with rebellions in various satrapies before being swept away by a new power, that of Macedon. In 338, Philip of Macedon re-united Greece, to his own advantage. When his son Alexander came to power in 336, a new era in history had begun.

The return from exile

Cyrus put an end to fifty years of exile in Babylon. We can work out that about 50,000 Jews took the opportunity to return home, in two main waves.

In 538, a first convoy led by Sheshbazzar included many priests, a few levites and a great many secondary figures: slaves and Temple servants. Those with less religious motivation, who had made good in Babylon, preferred to stay where they were.

It was difficult to settle in Judah again. The territory had been put under the control of the Samaritans (see p.45), who looked askance at the arrival of the time-honoured owners of the land which they had come to occupy. They wanted to help in rebuilding the Temple, but the Jews rejected the offer because Samaritan religion was not pure. By contrast, the Samaritans were opposed to the reconstruction of the walls of Jerusalem. These difficulties, not to mention the drought and the lack of money, caused an interruption to work on the Temple. It was probably during this period that a disciple of Isaiah whom we call the third Isaiah, Trito-Isaiah, delivered his message.

In 520, in the reign of Darius, a new convoy of exiles led by the prince Zerubbabel and the high priest Joshua arrived from Babylon. Under their direction, and with the support of the prophets Haggai and Zechariah, the Temple was finally rebuilt in 515.

515. The era of the Second Temple

After five years of struggle, the Temple was finally rebuilt. The old men who had known the splendour of the Temple of Solomon could hardly hold back their tears because the new one seemed to be so shabby (Ezra 3.10–13; Hag.2.3). No matter: there was a Temple. Enlarged and decorated by Herod from 19 BC to AD 64, it was destroyed by the Romans in AD 70.

It is important to remember the expression 'Second Temple': it denotes a building, but even more an age, which extends from the return from exile down to AD 70. This is the period of Judaism.

The two missions of Nehemiah (in 445 and 432) made possible the rebuilding of the walls of Jerusalem and mark independence from Samaria. Round about this time the prophet Malachi tried to revive the faith of the people.

In 398, Ezra was charged by king Artaxerxes with reorganizing the area (this is one possible date; the chronology here is very complicated). He re-established purity of faith with an iron fist; he dissolved marriages contracted with non-Jews, and imposed the 'Law of the God of heaven' as the state law. This law was probably the Pentateuch as we now have it, which Ezra edited on the basis of the various traditions.

The solemn ritual described in Neh.8–10 is one of the most important moments in the history of Israel: this is as it were the official birth of Judaism. The gathering does not take place in the Temple, but in the public square. It does not consist of bloody sacrifices, but of reading the law and prayer. Here is the birth of synagogue worship.

Some important aspects

Many details of the history of Israel still remain obscure. However, we can at least note some more general points.

The power of the priests

The priests reorganize the people. They become the real religious and political leaders.

The Jews in the world. The 'Diaspora'

Many Jews remained in Babylon, and formed a lively community there. We know of the existence of a community in Elephantine, in Egypt. The community in Alexandria, also in Egypt, was soon to prove important. So here we see a dispersion (Greek *diaspora*) of Judaism: Jerusalem remains the centre, but other important centres take shape elsewhere.

A common language: Aramaic

Aramaic, which is close to Hebrew, was the international language of the Persian empire for trade and diplomacy (rather as English is today). In Judaea, this language gradually took the place of Hebrew, which simply remained as a liturgical language. At the time of Christ, people spoke Aramaic and no longer understood Hebrew.

This common language and the Diaspora contributed towards opening up the Jews to universalism.

Literary activity

Prophets like Haggai, Zechariah, Malachi, Obadiah and above all Third Isaiah were preaching at this time.

However, this period is characterized above all by the influence of scribes and wise men.

Scribes like Ezra read the scriptures once more, brought them together (the Pentateuch), and completed them (Chronicles, Ezra and Nehemiah).

The wise men brought together earlier reflections and began to produce great works like Ruth, Jonah, Proverbs and Job.

The psalms began to be brought together in collections which soon turned into a book.

Prophets of the Return

Haggai

In 520, Haggai addressed a brief but scathing message to those who had returned from exile: 'What's this? You've been back twenty years. You've rebuilt your own houses, but the house of the Lord is still in ruins.' He wanted to know whether Israel was going to reconstruct its national life with or without God. Always a valuable question!

First Zechariah. Zech.1–8

The fourteen chapters which make up the book as we now have it bring together the preaching of two prophets. We shall read the message of the second of these prophets in the next chapter.

First Zechariah takes up the preaching of Haggai, but he does so in a language of his own which is already that of the apocalypses (see p.89).

Malachi

When Malachi was preaching, the Temple had been rebuilt. Worship had begun again, sacrifices . . . and also the bad pre-exilic habits. The rites were performed, but in any old way, and at the same time people were unjust, unfaithful.

Malachi reacted vigorously, and his message had a great influence, right down to the New Testament.

His book takes the form of a dialogue between God and his people, a prelude to the definitive dialogue of the gospel. 'I was hungry . . . When, Lord, did we see you hungry? . . .' I love you, says God. And you say, In what way do you love us?. . . 'And you say'. This refrain occurs eight times, directed against a nation of arguers. It is repeated eight times to lay bare the sin which is carefully tucked away: the sin of those who offer their left-overs to God (1.6f.), of priests who do not preach the word of God (2.1f.), of those who repudiate their wives (2.10f.: a splendid meditation on marriage), of those who cannot even distinguish between good and evil (2.17f.).

God finally announces that he will send the prophet Elijah to earth before the day of judgment. This text helped to give Elijah a position of considerable importance in Judaism. Jesus declared that John the Baptist filled this role (Matt.17.9f.)

Joel

We do not know when this 'ecological' prophet preached. The pollution everywhere seemed to him to be a sign of the coming of the day of the Lord, the day when God would lay bare men's sins. However, God would put his spirit into those who had been stripped in this way. Peter quotes Joel 3 on the day of Pentecost (Acts 2).

The word of God

Some people lay themselves open to disappointment: they read the Bible in search of the word of God and it seems more and more to be the words of men.

People sometimes have a rather magical view of the word of God, as though it is something which falls from heaven. Whereas God reveals himself in a history, through the events of human life, and these are what we have to decipher.

Doesn't the Christian feel the same bewilderment when faced with Jesus? Christians see him as the Son of God, the Word, whereas his contemporaries saw him as a man like they were. John does not write 'We have seen the word', but 'That which we have seen and heard concerning the word' (I John 1.1); that is, illuminated by faith and the Spirit, we have perceived the word through what we have seen (human actions and words like our own).

God acted in just the same way in the Old Testament. The Jews experienced ordinary events, but believers, primarily the prophets, read in them a word of God, just as we can see words in actions: 'What he did spoke volumes', 'His smile said it all'.

However, we can fool ourselves. Are we sure that the prophets and other believers didn't fool themselves too? It is here that faith in the Holy Spirit which enlightens the believer becomes important. 'The spirit will lead you into all truth,' said Jesus (John 16.13). To look for a word of God which falls from heaven can simply be to reject the spirit and to refuse to live in faith; in such a 'word' we would have God at our disposal, whereas he reveals himself to us, humbly, in human forms.

Third Isaiah. Isa.56–66

Galvanized by the promises of the new Exodus announced by Second Isaiah, the exiles went home. But the happy future to which they looked forward never materialized, and their enthusiasm waned. The resettlement was a sorry affair. But how was it possible to reconstruct a nation when people no longer believed in their destiny? A disciple of Isaiah tried to give them faith in their mission.

The task was difficult, because his audience was divided: people repatriated from Babylon, Jews who had remained at home; strangers who had settled in the meantime, Jews in the Diaspora. Dissension and hatred crept in, together with mistrust of strangers; idolatry threatened, and hopes were shattered. The prophet tries to communicate his enthusiasm to all these groups, despite all the problems.

The book as we have it now takes the form of a fine curve, with matching texts on either side of a peak in chapter 61. Before we study that chapter, we must run through the rest of the work.

56.1–8. Strangers can belong to the people of God because his house of prayer is for all peoples. 66.17–24. God will gather all the nations together again for a new creation.

56.9–57.21. The prophet laments those who think that they are automatically part of the people of God. 66.1–16. By contrast, he shows God giving the daughter of Zion power to bring forth the new people (see p.61 again).

58. True religious practice, true fasting which pleases God, is to share your bread, do away with injustice, free the oppressed . . . 65. Blessings and curses: those who allow themselves to be loved by God and those who refuse.

59.1–15. The prophet's accusation bears fruit: the people confess their sins. 63.7–64.11. A fine psalm of supplication, anticipating the 'Our Father': an appeal to the tenderness of God, asking him to rend the heavens and come down. For Mark, this is realized at the time of the baptism of Jesus (Mark 1.10).

59.15–20; 63.1–6. God is not mocked. Like a vine-presser, he will trample on his enemies. Revelation (19.13) applies this tragic text to Christ: in the last resort, the blood which flows is his own blood, shed for our sins.

Studying a text: Isaiah 60–63

Isaiah 61 is the climax of the book. However, it forms a whole together with chs. 60; 62, which match each other. So we have to study the three together.

Rejoice, daughter of Zion. . .Isa.60; 62
Read these two chapters and try to see how the different protagonists are presented.
God. What aspect does he present? Note the imagery which expresses his feelings. The daughter of Zion. Whom does she denote? Note the imagery which expresses the change in her situation. The sons. . . Who are they? Where do they come from? Who attracts them?

Here we have an extraordinary image of the people of God (and now, of the church): like a cathedral, bathed in floodlights, shining out over the city in the darkness to guide those who are going through the shadows, the people form a luminous sign set up in the world to give a sense of direction. However, the light does not come from the people, but from the God who is in them.

The spirit of the Lord is upon me. Isa.61
This chapter is divided into three parts.

61.1–4. The prophet introduces himself.
How did his vocation come about? What is his mission? To whom is he sent, and what is the news (evangel, *euangelion,* Greek for good news) that he brings? Note the imagery which expresses transformation.

61.5–9. The prophet speaks to his audience.
He speaks, and the Lord speaks through him (v.8) about the future. What promise is given? What will be the people's role?

61.10–11. The prophet or the people express their enthusiasm. Perhaps it is both of them together. Why? What is its source?

Now look back over the whole of Isa.60–62. What is this good news which is capable of bringing new enthusiasm to these discouraged returnees?

Read Luke 4.16–21. In what way could Isa.61, according to Luke, express Jesus' mission? How does it help us to understand the significance of Jesus' miracles and the message of the Beatitudes?

The Law or Pentateuch

When Ezra arrived in Jerusalem in 398 (?), his mission was to reorganize the community and to settle the differences with the Samaritans.

The Law

As a state law, he imposed 'the Law of the God of heaven' (Ezra 7.21) upon everyone. There is agreement that we should see this law as the Pentateuch in its present form, as Ezra had organized it. He had a vast collection of texts at his disposal for doing this:

The Sacred Judaean History (the Yahwist) (see p.36);

The Sacred History of the North (the Elohist) (see p.50).

These two traditions had already been fused into a single account (see p.60: the Jehovist).

Deuteronomy (see p.56).

The Priestly History (see p.70), and Leviticus (see p.68).

Independent traditions, notably laws on sacrifices and festivals, which had been edited by the priests on their return from exile (cf. p.69).

With these texts Ezra succeeded in producing a work which, if it is not always coherent, is at least unified.

The resultant sacred history runs from creation to the death of Moses and brings into relief the two figures of Abraham and Moses.

After the creation narratives (Gen.1–11), the rest of Genesis (12–50) presents the patriarchs, with Abraham in first place. The father of believers, he is the bearer of the divine promise (the covenant: Gen.15; 17); he is the intercessor before God (Gen.18); he has complete trust in God, even when God asks for his son (Gen.22).

With the book of Exodus, Moses comes on stage and occupies it almost to the end. After the reminder of slavery in Egypt and the call of Moses (Ex.1–15), the lion's share is given to the covenant on Sinai, framed by two accounts of life in the wilderness (Ex.16–18; Num.11–12). The Covenant Code has a central position (Ex.20–23, see p.60). Prominence is also given to the various priestly laws: Ex.25–31 and 35–40; Leviticus; Numbers 1–10. Amidst all this, the story of the golden calf (Ex.32–34) is meant to provide a reminder of the ever-present risk of breaking the covenant. The last part presents the march to the promised land (Num.13–36) and the last speeches of Moses on Mount Nebo (Deuteronomy).

Thus Moses is presented as the mediator. He is completely on God's side, his instrument for freeing the people from slavery and leading them to serve God through the law which he gives. Moses is completely on the side of the people, in a solidarity so total that mysteriously it extends even to sin. And along with the people who die in the wilderness, Moses will die before entering the promised land, but, as the rabbis rendered it so magnificently, 'with a divine kiss' (Deut.34.5).

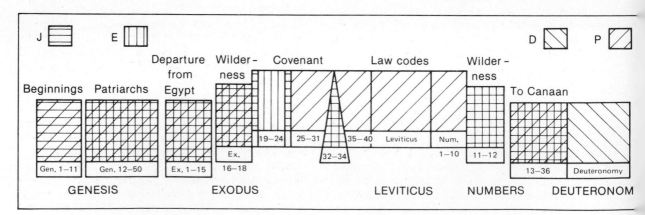

The Law, written and oral

For the Jews, the word of God is essentially the Law (Torah in Hebrew) which God gave his people on Sinai.

It has been set down in written form in the Pentateuch: that is the heart of scripture. However – and the rabbis stressed this very strongly – it has also been handed down, in parallel, by word of mouth. For the Jews, the oral traditions are as important as scripture.

The Prophets are also the word of God, but not quite to the same degree. In the liturgy, their role is above all that of illuminating the Law.

The Writings are revered without having the same importance as the Law and the Prophets.

So we can understand the importance of Ezra, who gave definitive form to the Law. 'If the Law had not been given to Moses,' said one rabbi, 'Ezra would have been worthy to receive it.' Moses and Ezra remain the two great figures of Judaism.

The Samaritans

It looks as though Ezra was successful in imposing the 'Law of the God of heaven' not only on the Jews, but also on the Samaritans, whose origins, as we saw on p.45, were very mixed. In fact, however, this religious union did not last long and soon the Samaritans parted company with the Jews for ever (perhaps in the time of Alexander). They even built their own temple on the summit of Mount Gerizim. However, they kept the Law (or Pentateuch), and their text of it is virtually identical with the Jewish text. That is the only scripture they recognize.

So relations between Samaritans and Jews are very complicated. We know from the Gospels how tense relations between the two communities were at the time of Christ. However, they recognized the same common destiny.

A Samaritan community has survived until today, and every year it is possible to go and see the sacrifice of the paschal lamb on Mount Gerizim.

I & II Chronicles – Ezra – Nehemiah

This work was probably composed at the beginning of the Greek period. The author is unknown. He is usually called the Chronicler. His plan was an ambitious one, to write a history from Adam to Ezra. He was a learned man and quotes his sources: about twenty books, of which some (like Samuel and Kings) are known to us, others not. The two parts of his work have been divided into four books: I and II Chronicles, Ezra and Nehemiah.

It would be fascinating for you to compare some passages in Chronicles with those in Samuel and Kings: you would see how a midrash was written (see p.81 and the brief comparison of passages about Nathan's prophecy on p.42). I shall single out some features of the Chronicler.

First, he offers us a theology of history. In order to show what the life of his contemporaries should be like, he idealizes a period of past history, that of David and Solomon. He moves very quickly from Adam to David (largely by means of genealogies). When it comes to David he spreads himself, chooses his sources, and eliminates episodes which do not favour his hero (David's sin, the luxury and idolatry of Solomon). David is the king after God's heart, the representative of God, who remains the only king of Israel. David had been able to provide his kingdom with a capital, Jerusalem, and to prepare for the building of the Temple and the organization of worship.

The Chronicler passes over the history of the northern kingdom in silence. He is chiefly interested in the history of the Temple and its worship. Priests and levites are very important for him.

He knows how to show that when kings and the people are faithful they are fortunate, and when they are unfaithful they are unfortunate. In a rather simplistic way, then, he tries to show by means of imagery what experience might be like of the kingdom of God on earth.

You might read Nehemiah 8–9

Neh.8. What are the features of this worship? Where does it take place? Who presides over it? What is new about it compared with temple worship?

Neh.9. What points of history are touched on in this confession of sin? What does the speaker rely on: his own merits? God? What qualities are recognized in God? How can this inspire our own prayer?

Wisdom

You and I, indeed all of us, are wise men, but we are not all writers producing wisdom literature.

The wise man is in fact someone who tries to live a good life and discover, in his existence and that of the world, those things which enhance life and those which lead to death. So he reflects on the great human questions: life, death, love, suffering, evil. Does human existence have a meaning? What meaning? Everyone has a philosophy, at his or her own level: the young child and the old man, the professor and the manual worker or the housewife; each of them develops a wisdom, a way of living.

And sometimes poets and philosophers take up all this diffuse reflection, brood on it and produce great works.

That is what also happened in Israel. All the time the people existed, they sought the meaning of their life, reflected on its great problems. We have seen, for example, that the creation stories are 'a wisdom reflection' (pages 39,72). Throughout its existence Israel expressed its reflection in proverbs, kinds of popular sayings; in prayers, in sketches of works.

However, it was only after the exile that writers began to take up all this reflection and, after a long period of gestation, to compose the great works which we are about to read.

So we must be on guard against one possible danger in this study. Over the five previous stages we have listened to the prophets and seen how the Pentateuch gradually developed; we have come to the wisdom books only at this sixth stage. That might suggest that Israel first lived and wrote its history and did not get down to thinking until eight or nine centuries later! Of course, that's not the case. We shall now be reading books, literary works produced at this period. However, we shall see how they take up a long period of earlier reflection, just as the Pentateuch took up elements composed earlier.

Who were the wise men in Israel?

Every Israelite. Wisdom is popular wisdom. For example, many proverbs take up ancient wisdom in a compressed form, with well-constructed maxims.

The king. He was responsible for governing the people and therefore for seeing what was good for them and what was not. He was thought to share in the divine wisdom.

The scribes. Wisdom is popular wisdom, but it is also learned. It was taught at school. The scribes, most often court officials, were the first wise men, and it was thanks to their political acumen that they held power. There were often conflicts between the prophets who defended the weak, and this class of scribes.

The wise men living after the exile are the heirs of all these currents. Having learned to reflect and write, they produced wisdom which was human wisdom, but at the same time they saw this as a gift of God, who alone was wise.

Some features of wisdom

Wisdom is the art of living a good life, seeking what leads to life and not to death. It is a reflection on the great human questions: life, death, love, suffering, evil, men's relationship with God and with one another, social life, etc.

Wisdom is universal and timeless. Suffering and death, life and love, know no frontiers. The sick man who gives vent to his suffering in Babylon or in Israel two thousand years before Christ reacts in just the same way as someone in agony in a modern hospital.

Thus the wise men of Israel drew abundantly on the reflections of other civilizations: Egypt and Babylon, and then Greece. However – and this is where they were original – all this reflection was put into the melting pot of belief in the one God. In the last resort, the true source of wisdom is God, and the only way of getting it is to have a close and respectful relationship with this God, which the Bible calls the fear of God.

Wisdom writings in the Persian period

We shall begin with two books included in our Bibles. One of them is to be found either in the Writings (Jerusalem Bible) or the historical books (RSV); the other in the Prophets. However, both of them belong to wisdom literature.

Ruth

God's sense of humour! To restore the purity of Jewish faith, Ezra had just required Jews who had married foreign wives to repudiate them. Of course God was obliged to approve this, but found that Ezra was going a bit too far, so he inspired this charming story. Boaz, a pious Jew from Bethlehem, marries Ruth, a foreign woman from Moab. They have a son, Obed, father of Jesse and grandfather of . . . David!

This is a lesson in universalism, and a humorous reminder from God to all of us who think that we love him because we observe his regulations: 'You need to love me without fanaticism. Be intelligent, and don't confuse the end with the means . . .' Ruth is mentioned in the genealogy of Jesus (Matt.1.5).

Jonah

Here is a prophet who disagrees with God's methods: Jonah, the hero of this miraculous tale. God sends him to preach to Nineveh, the capital of the Assyrians, that terrible enemy. Nineveh is in the east. Jonah embarks in a boat westwards. He is running away, sleeping in the hold of the ship, out to sea. However, God gets him back by means of a great fish which spews him out in the direction of the east. So off he goes . . .

When he gets to Nineveh he preaches that God is going to destroy the city and is very pleased about that. But the inhabitants repent, and God does not destroy them.

This is a magnificent lesson in universalism. God loves all men. 'He does not want the death of a sinner, but rather that he should repent and live' (Ezek.33.11).

For Jesus, Jonah is a sign of the call to conversion (Luke 11.29; Matt.16;4), and for Matthew, an image of the resurrection (Matt.12.40).

Midrash and Targum

Very soon the Jews were faced with the question how to bring scripture up to date. This word of God had been given in a situation different from that in which they now lived. So scripture had to be reread to see how it might make sense in the present.

Midrash (from the root *darash*, search) is a word used for both the method of interpretation and the works composed by this method.

We can distinguish two kinds of midrash:

Midrash *halakah* (from a root meaning way, road). This is concerned with rules of conduct, laws. In Judaism, *halakoth* (the plural form) is synonymous with laws.

Midrash *haggadah* (from a root meaning to tell). These are chiefly concerned to edify.

The Priestly History, which rereads the traditions in the context of the exile to find meaning and hope in them, and the work of the Chronicler, who looks to history for a way of experiencing the kingdom of God, are the beginning of midrash *halakah*. Ruth and Jonah are more types of midrash *haggadah*.

The Targum is the oral translation of scripture into Aramaic. Hebrew always remained the sacred language. However, a time came when people no longer understood it because they spoke Aramaic. In the liturgy, scripture was read in Hebrew and then a scribe translated it into Aramaic. Instead of making a literal translation, though, he developed the meaning as it was then understood (see the examples on pp.38,52).

At the service presided over by Ezra (Neh.8–9), after the reading of scripture, the Levites explained it to the people. This is perhaps one of the first pieces of evidence about this practice.

The chief targums were fixed in writing towards the beginning of our era. They allow us to see how certain texts were understood at the time of Christ.

The first Christians took over this way of interpreting scripture. They often read it in the light of the targums and they sometimes wrote Christian midrash (the infancy stories in the Gospel of Matthew, for example).

Job

At the time when the great tragedians of Greece were writing plays about history and human life, like *The Persians* and *Antigone,* a Jewish poet began to produce the drama of a believer coming to grips with suffering: Job.

The book of Job as we now know it has a long history. It consists of an old tale in prose (the beginning and end of the book), perhaps already known at the time of Solomon, which from the time of the return from exile served as the framework for dialogues between Job and his friends. Further additions were made at a later date.

The drama of Job is that of every believer who suffers without cause. Job believes in God who is just and omnipotent. He suffers, and when he examines his conscience (in connection with justice and his love for others), he finds that he is innocent.

The task of his friends is to present the traditional arguments: 'If you're suffering, that's because you have sinned . . .' or, 'It's because God loves you: he always chastises those whom he loves . . .' 'That's all eyewash,' cries Job. Confronted with God's silence Job shouts out, rebels, blasphemes.

Finally, God speaks. To explain, or to provide consolation? No! To overwhelm Job by the splendour of his creation and to ask him just one question: 'By what right do you ask me to give an account of myself?' And Job prostrates himself in adoration.

In the end, this does not tell us any more about the reason for evil. However, it is a good thing that in this way a book could express our revolt against evil. We now know that rebellion and blasphemy can be prayers ('Only Job has spoken well with me,' says God, 42.7), that pious explanations are worthless, and that the only possible attitude for the believer is that of trust. 'The terrible moment when God isn't true and yet I still love him,' as one believer wrote. This is the attitude of Christ on the cross.

You might read at least these passages:

Job's despair: 3.6–7; 29–30 (God's absence and silence).

The poem about the wisdom of which God alone has the secret: 28.

Job's examination of his conscience: 31.

God's 'reply': 38.

Proverbs

The book of Proverbs give us a good idea of the wisdom literature and the way in which it developed.

Proverbs appears as a group of nine collections of sayings, differing in length, style and period. The earliest proverbs may very well go back to the time of Solomon (these are in chs.10–22). Two collections (30; 31) are attributed to foreign wise men, which is an indication of the universalism of wisdom. There are affinities between the collection of the wise men in 22.17–24.22 and an Egyptian text, The Wisdom of Amenemope. The beginning (1–9) and the end (31.10–31) were composed after the exile.

You might begin with the earliest collections. It's not a matter of reading these chapters straight through, but of taking them in small doses, rather as you might dip into an anthology of quotations. You might amuse yourself by composing a personal anthology of your own – one easy way of doing this is to mark various themes with different colours. Here are some ideas to help you begin:

The fear of God, the source of wisdom: 10.27; 14.2,26–27.

God is sometimes mentioned. What does he do? 10.22,29; 11.1;12.2,22.

Educational methods: 10.13; 12.1; 19.29.

Some virtues (love, humility, justice . . .): 10.2; 11.2;12.28.

Women (a splendid collection for misogynists!): 11.22; 18.22; 19.13; 21.9,19; 27.15.

Moral vignettes: adultery: 7.6–27; laziness: 19.24; 24.30–34; the businessman: 20.14; the drunkard: 23.29–35.

Sumerian proverbs (from the end of the second millennium)

It is better for the poor man to be dead than alive.
If he has bread, he has no salt;
if he has salt, he has no bread . . .

Anyone who has never had wife or child
has never been led by the nose.

Man's life is like a jug of water in the desert.
His wife is a man's future.
His son is a man's refuge.
His daughter is a man's salvation.
And his daughter-in-law is sheer hell!

Lady Wisdom. Prov. 1–9

Like 31.10–31, the first chapters were composed last, probably in the Persian period. The author takes up the message of Deuteronomy, Jeremiah and Second Isaiah. A master is speaking to his son or disciple; he is teaching him to live in accordance with wisdom, to love his neighbour (3.27f.) and to keep away from debauchery. Human love is celebrated with accents which anticipate the Song of Songs (5.15–23).

In some passages wisdom is personified: Lady Wisdom (contrasted briefly with the foolish woman: 9.13f.). Wisdom is a prophet (1.20–33), a hostess offering a meal (9.1–6), and even daughter of God (8.1–31). We are now going to study a very characteristic text (8.22–31). In the next chapter we shall see how the wise men continued this line of development: wisdom became more and more someone who came from God himself. These texts enabled the first Christians to express the divinity of Christ as God's wisdom (I Cor.1.24).

📖 *Studying a text: Proverbs 8.22–31*

22. *The Lord created me at the beginning of his work,*
    the first of his acts of old.   Before creation
23. *Ages ago I was set up*
    at the first, before the beginning of the earth.   or *consecrated*
                                                                 See Prov. 8.15; Ps.2.6
24. When there were no depths I was brought forth,
    when there were no springs abounding with water.
25. Before the mountains had been shaped,
    before the hills, I was brought forth;
26. Before he had made the earth with its fields,
    or the first of the dust of the world.
27. When he established the heavens, I was there   During creation
    when he drew a circle on the face of the deep,
28. *when he made firm the skies above,*
    when he established the fountains of the deep,
29. *when he assigned to the sea its limit,*
    so that the waters might not transgress his command,
    when he marked out the foundations of the earth,
30. *then I was beside him, like a master workman;*   or *small girl*
    and I was daily his delight,
    rejoicing before him always,
31. rejoicing in his inhabited world,
    and delighting in the sons of men.

Who are the main characters? How are they distributed through the text? Look at words and expressions which correspond.

What does God do? What does Wisdom do? What is the situation for God (see the verbs)? for creation? for men? What is the role of Wisdom?

Some of the expressions are difficult, and you may need a commentary to help you.

At the end of this study you might ask yourself: how does this text help us to understand the role of Christ? See Col.1.15–20.

'amen – 'amon – 'amun

Verse 30 is a good point at which to note the richness – and the complexity – of Hebrew. In Hebrew, as in Arabic, people wrote only the consonants. Vowels were added when the text was read, depending on the meaning. Here we have three consonants making up the root *'mn*, which evokes something solid. In the liturgy, *'amen* means, 'That sure, that's certain'. Here we can read a present participle, *'amon*, the one who founds or who supports, hence architect, master workman; or one can read the passive participle, *'amun*, one who is carried, hence baby, small girl.

7 Israel under the Greeks (333–63) and Romans (from 63 BC)

Winged Victory of Samothrace (about 250–200 BC?)

In 333, by his victory at Issos, north of Antioch, Alexander the Great opened up the way to the Middle East. In 332 he arrived in Egypt and founded Alexandria. In 331 he took Babylon, Susa and Persepolis. In 327 he reached the frontiers of India. And in 323, this young king died in Babylon at the age of thirty-three. In ten years he had won victories during a march of 18,000 kilometres; he had founded more than seventy cities in his immense empire (many of which were called Alexandria); he had spread Greek culture with its art, its baths and its stadiums, and provided a common language as means of unity. This *koine,* or common language, which at that time was spoken in Greece, was to be spoken throughout the Mediterranean basin for eight centuries, down to about AD 500, when it was replaced by Latin. This was the language into which the Old Testament was translated – the version known as the Septuagint – and in which the New Testament was written.

Israel under the Lagids: 333–198

On the death of Alexander, his generals, known as the Diadochi, quarrelled about the future of his empire. In the end they divided it into three, founding dynasties which each bore the name of their first king. So there were the Antigonids in Greece, the Lagids in Egypt and the Seleucids in Syria (their kingdom in fact stretched from the Mediterranean to India).

For more than a century, Palestine was under the thumb of the Egyptian Lagids. These kings, who mostly bore the name of Ptolemy, usually respected the various nationalities and allowed the Jews to live in peace, according to the statute which had been fixed by Ezra. So the Jews enjoyed a considerable degree of autonomy.

During this period the three main centres of Judaism began to go their different ways.

We know little about the community in Babylon, but it continued to survive. Over the next few centuries it produced some important works for Judaism, in particular the Babylonian Talmud.

In Egypt, the Jewish community in Alexandria developed rapidly. At the time of Christ it made up about a fifth of the city. It gave birth to a form of Judaism which was compatible with Greek thinking. It was here that the Bible was translated into Greek (the Septuagint), that books like Wisdom were written, and that in the time of Christ the Jewish philosopher Philo tried to rethink the faith in Greek terms.

In Palestine, the community was divided. Some were tempted by Greek civilization, by its games, its baths and its athletics; some even went so far as to disguise their circumcision by a surgical operation. Others were very disturbed at this tide of Hellenism (or Greek civilization). They were very attached to their Jewish faith and to the way in which it had hitherto been expressed in practices and rituals, and were concerned to show that it allowed people to develop; however, to maintain Jewish faith it was necessary to preserve its particular forms of expression as well. (We know that this is a perennial problem, which can provide an explanation for contemporary clashes within the church.) This is the context in which books like Koheleth, Tobit and Sirach appeared.

The persecution which struck this community at the time of the Seleucids accentuated the division and threw the people into utter confusion.

Israel under the Seleucids: 198—63

In 198, Syrian elephants broke up the Egyptian army, and the age of the martyrs began for Israel. At Paneion, near the source of the Jordan, the Seleucid king Antiochus III wrested control of Palestine from Egypt.

Unlike the Lagids, the Seleucids wanted to impose Greek culture and religion on the Jews by force. In 167, Antiochus IV abolished Jewish privileges, did away with the sabbath and circumcision, desecrated the Temple and installed in it the abomination of desolation, i.e. a statue of Zeus. The crisis was all the greater because the high priests were not in agreement: some of them supported Hellenization.

A priest gave the signal for revolt by killing an emissary of Antiochus who had come to enforce sacrifices to idols. With his five sons he took to the hills. The fifth of these sons was Judas, who was to give his surname to the family; he was known as the Maccabee (Latin, Maccabaeus), the Hammer. By some lucky moves, Judas succeeded in liberating Jerusalem. Temple worship was restored on 15 December 164. Thereafter the event was celebrated by Hanukkah, the feast of dedication. Two of Judas' brothers, and then their descendants, succeeded him, thus founding the dynasty of the Maccabees, also known as the Hasmonean dynasty. They even took the title of king, for a while restoring the monarchy in Israel.

Unfortunately, the history of the Hasmoneans, which began in the blood of martyrs, ended in a morass. The successors of Judas managed to have themselves nominated as high priests by the Seleucids, often resorting to bribery to gain this end; some crucified faithful Jews who were hostile to their actions.

In 63 the Jews, who were divided into rival groups supporting two different kings, were reduced to appealing to Rome for arbitration. Roman authority arrived in the Middle East in the person of the general Pompey. Supporting one side, Pompey captured Jerusalem after a three-month siege. This was the beginning of Roman rule, which was to last until the seventh century AD, the time of the Arab invasions.

The Jewish sects

The religious groups in Judaism are known as sects — not in any derogatory sense. Most of them came into being at this time.

The Pharisees ('the separated ones') belong to the current of Hasidim (derived from the root *hesed,* see p.49), or pious Jews, who from the time of Ezra on wanted to reconstruct the nation on the basis of spiritual values. The Pharisees were profoundly religious, devoted to the Law and the practice of it. As a result of their profound piety and their knowledge of the scriptures they were to become the conscience of Judaism.

The Essenes, who are better known since the discovery of the Qumran manuscripts, were also Hasidim. They probably took refuge in the desert at the time of the Maccabean revolt, forming a community of the new covenant near the Dead Sea. Here they prepared for the coming of the Messiah in prayer and meditation. They were intransigent and broke even with the Pharisees, whom they found too lukewarm.

The Sadducees were made up of high-ranking priests. They supported the Hasmoneans and seemed concerned above all to defend their power by all available means. We should not confuse with this priestly aristocracy the many 'grass-roots' priests who were often very pious and connected more closely with the Pharisaic movement.

Literary activity

A prophet now known as Second Zechariah preached at this time.

Hellenization was to provoke various reactions of defiance or sympathy: Koheleth, Sirach, Tobit, the Song of Songs, Baruch and Wisdom. The scriptures were translated into Greek: the Septuagint.

The persecution of Antiochus and the Maccabean epic inspired several works: Esther, Judith, I and II Maccabees, and the development of a literary genre which began to emerge with the last prophets. This was the apocalyptic trend, represented in the Old Testament by Daniel.

The last psalms were written, and the Psalter came into being.

Prophets of the Greek Period: Second Zechariah

Scholars have divided Isaiah into three; they have also divided Zechariah into two: chapters 9–14, they say, are by a prophet from the time of Alexander.

The arrival of this young king, who overthrew the powerful Persians, raised people's hopes: perhaps God was at last going to intervene. For the prophet, however, radical change could come only from God. So he revived messianic hopes, that is to say, the expectation of a Messiah, one anointed with holy oil (Greek *christos*), by whom one day God would establish his kingdom. The portrait of the Messiah which he draws is unique in the Bible: he combines the features of the royal Messiah, son of David or son of God (see p.42), with those of the suffering servant in Isaiah (p.67). In particular, there are four poems that you can read which were all applied to Jesus by the first Christians. Here they are.

The Messiah king, lowly and peaceful. 9.9–10.

9.1–8 clearly describes Alexander's expedition to Palestine and Egypt in 333. Would he be the Messiah? 'No,' said the prophet.

Read 9.9–10. How is this king introduced? What does he rely on: his strength? on God? What does he bring?

Read Matt.21.5.

The shepherd sold by his people. 11.4–17; 13.4–9

The different images in this story are not easy to decipher. This is probably what they mean. The sheep are the people and the shepherds are the kings or high priests; the merchants or traffickers are the false prophets, wicked priests who hand people over to the enemy. Those who buy are the enemy; the three shepherds who are destroyed are possibly three high priests; the breaking of 'Grace' and 'Union' is probably a recollection of past invasions and the schisms between Judah and Israel in 935 and between Israel and the Samaritans. The author is trying to understand present events in the light of the past.

The shepherd is the prophet, but also God (11.13). To make mockery of him, people pay the price of a slave.

Read Matt.26.31; 27.3–10. Thus Jesus is identified with the good shepherd and with God.

God transfixed. 12.10–13.1

This is the most extraordinary oracle of all: God declares that he himself is afflicted through the person who is pierced.

What is the unexpected result (13.1)? Read Ex.36.25f.; 47.1–12. Who represents this spring? Where does it flow from?

Read John 7.38; 19.34: How does Zechariah help us to understand who Jesus is? Where does the spring come from? John does not claim to give medical information (on which side Jesus was pierced); he is making a theological point. Jesus is the true temple from which the Spirit flows.

Deutero-canonical and Apocryphal books

There is one small difference between Catholic Bibles and those of other Christian churches, in the content of the Old Testament. Catholic Bibles have seven or eight extra books which they call deutero-canonical and others call apocryphal.

The word canon means 'rule': a book is canonical if it is recognized as a rule of faith. The canon of holy books is the total recognized as a rule of faith.

Christians followed the Jews over the Old Testament. However, two different canons had been established. Round about AD 90, the Palestinian rabbis recognized only the books written in Hebrew. The Jews of Alexandria accepted others which were written or known in Greek.

Christians who read the Bible in Greek adopted the canon of the Alexandrian Jews. However, St Jerome, who translated the Bible into Latin early in the fifth century, opted for the Hebrew canon.

At the time of the Reformation in the sixteenth century, the Protestants followed Jerome by printing the disputed books at the back of their Bible (from which they had disappeared by the nineteenth century): they called them apocrypha (kept secret).

At the Council of Trent, the Catholics held that these books had the same level of inspiration as the rest, but they called them deutero-canonical (admitted into the canon at a secondary level). The most important of the books concerned are Judith, Tobit, I and II Maccabbes, Wisdom, Sirach, the Greek passages of Esther, Baruch and the Letter of Jeremiah.

Wisdom Literature

I shall now introduce the wisdom literature composed during the Greek period. Probably you won't be able to study all of it. If you're working as a group, each person could read one work and share his or her discoveries with others.

Koheleth or Ecclesiastes

This is a strange book. The author applies acid to all our security and certainty: action, politics, love, pleasure. All vanity, says Koheleth. One thing matters, and that is to eat well. Is there a God? Yes. But God is in heaven and you are on earth, so stop your stupid chatter.

The author hides behind a pseudonym. Koheleth clearly represents the assembly. He is perhaps the voice of the assembly, listening to a good sermon in which everything is foreseen, God is just and good, and the world goes on in accordance with his plan . . . the voice of the assembly which dares to say: 'That's all rubbish!'

He is an austere counsellor who suggests that we should not take ourselves too seriously, that we should shed our illusions, and act. Since you don't know which of two things will succeed, do them both!

Tobit (deutero-canonical)

This is a very attractive story: a midrash *haggadah*. The author rereads the story of the patriarchs and derives from it an edifying story which he sets at the time of the exile.

Old Tobit, a holy man who has gone blind, is in despair; young Sarah, a virtuous girl, finds that all her fiancés die, and she wants to die herself. Why this absurd evil? Is God absent, or indifferent?

The author shows us how God is present in the life of each one of us, but in a hidden way. We have to know how to discover him.

The story is at the same time a splendid testimony to marriage and human love.

You should read at least the fine prayers (eucharists): the prayer of Tobit in despair (3.1–6), of Sarah on the verge of suicide (3.11–15), of Sarah and Tobit in their marriage chamber (8) and of Tobit when he is cured (13.1–10).

Song of Songs

This is a marvellous poem which celebrates human love in all its physical dimensions, with a realism which modern poets would not dismiss.

The text as it is now has a long history. It probably takes up old love songs sung on the wedding night of a couple; perhaps it is inspired by pagan rites, but without ever mentioning God, it is also a meditation on Gen.2.23–24, Mal.2.14 and those prophetic texts which celebrate God's love for his people in the imagery of betrothal.

The text was to go on to have a long history, also; it became the symbol of the love between God and the people (or the believer) and inspired not only Jews but Christians like St John of the Cross.

At a time when women were men's slaves, these songs in which a couple love each other equally, in the freshness of a tenderness which does not ignore difficulties, are quite extraordinary compositions.

Sirach or Ecclesiasticus (deutero-canonical)

A model grandson translated into Greek a book written by his grandfather round about 190. The temptations of Hellenism were great, and many young men will have been tempted to abandon their ancestral traditions. This book, which has an old-fashioned attraction because of its middle-class piety, seeks to show that faithfulness to the Law and its practices allows a man to gain true wisdom.

As with Proverbs, you might like to make a small anthology of texts (there are some very appealing ones); however, there are some passages on which you should spend time:

The hymn to the fear of God (which is as fine as the hymn to love in I Cor.13): 1.11–20. Wisdom was imparted to us at our mothers' breasts: everyone is born with a grain of it.

The joy of those who seek wisdom: 4.11–19.

Lady Wisdom introduces her role in creation and in history:24. She is identified with the Law. This famous passage inspired John (John 1).

You can find marvellous passages in the praise of creation (42.15–43.33) and above all in the praise of famous men (beginning at ch.44). At least read the portrait of the high priest Simon (50), which inspired Luke 24.50–52.

Literary Offshoots of the Epic of the Maccabees

The epic story of the Maccabees is a brief one (it spans a period of only three years, from 167 to 164), but it left a profound mark on Judaism. Confronted with the firm purpose of Antiochus IV to impose Greek religion by force, believers were led to make a decisive choice between apostasy and martyrdom. The action, and above all the religious concern, of Judas the Maccabee, and his success which led to the purification of the Temple, brought about a revival of faith. However, as we have seen, his successors soon became bogged down in political intrigues and intoxicated with the taste of power.

For a century, this epic provoked three kinds of reaction which we can find in literature. Roughly speaking, they might be classified like this.

1. Sword in hand. The epic story is told in I Maccabees, which supports the combatants. Judith and Esther, written as romances, express feelings at the time.

2. Joined hands. Other believers, especially after seeing the development of the Maccabean dynasty, are very reticent. Only God can bring about liberation. The true religious attitude is not to take up the sword, but to join hands in prayer, asking God to intervene. II Maccabees represents the Pharisaic view: faith leads to martyrdom, and martyrdom will make God act.

The apocalyptic trend, along with Daniel, takes this direction and looks for the intervention of God at the end of history.

3. The outstretched hand. When the storm had passed, and also, because he lived in Alexandria, far removed from the dramas of Palestine, a wise man wrote the Wisdom of Solomon, in which he tried to express his Jewish faith in such a way that it would be meaningful to cultured Greeks.

We shall go through this literature, and pause over two texts: Daniel 7 and Wisdom 7.

Judith (deutero-canonical) – Esther

These two edifying stories (in the form of midrash) express the enthusiasm engendered by the Maccabean epic. They stress one essential point: it is God who acts and who saves. To do this he chooses the weakest instruments: the hands of women.

II Maccabees (deutero-canonical)

This book is not the sequel to I Maccabees. It was even written earlier, about 124. It is a summary of another work in five volumes composed by Jason, who lived a short time after Judas the Maccabee.

Underlying these pious stories we find the spirituality of the Pharisees and their total commitment to God. Let me bring out several points.

A holy war. In relating the exploits of Judas, the author stresses that it is God who gives the victory; hence the prayers before every battle, the miraculous interventions (chs.8ff.).

The martyr. Total commitment to his faith may lead a man to witness to God in the most decisive way possible, that of martyrdom. The martyrdoms of old Eleazar (6.18–31), and above all that of the seven brothers (7), are famous.

The resurrection (7.9,23,29). Here the author takes up, even more exactly, the doctrine already presented by Daniel (Dan.12.2), which was shared by the Pharisees. We shall come back to it when we study Daniel.

Prayer for the dead (12.38–45). This text has played a key role in the Catholic theology of 'purgatory': if we pray for the dead, we should pray that they have not fallen into nothingness and that they can be pardoned after their death. Protestants, who do not recognize this book, simply commit the fate of the dead to God's hands, without seeking to penetrate the mystery.

Creation from nothing (7.28). Hitherto, it had not been demonstrated that God created from nothing (*ex nihilo*); he was thought to have ordered primordial chaos by separating the elements (Gen.1; see p.72).

I Maccabees (deutero-canonical)

The author, who is probably writing about 100 BC, is well-disposed towards the Maccabean dynasty. He tells the history of the first three Maccabees: Judas (3–9); Jonathan (9–12) and Simon (13–16). He wants to write a sacred history along the lines of the former prophets (see p.59), and shows us God at work liberating his people by saving them from the disaster in which sin has involved them.

The Apocalypses

All through our lives, we come up against happy and sad events. We try to get the better of them, to make the best of them, to make sense of them. And we ourselves change when we realize that we are going in the wrong direction.

This is what the prophets did: they interpreted events and discovered a word of God in them: they called on people to change, to be converted.

Sometimes, however, it happens that evil is so great, that a situation is so hopeless, that there is no way out. One cannot hope for better days. And if anyone could then tell us how things would turn out, we would see the light at the end of the tunnel and be given courage to hold on.

The apocalypses are more this kind of material. They generally came into being at a time of crisis. The authors of them had a pessimistic view of the world, believing that it was entirely under the sway of the 'prince of this world' (or a devil). To offer hope, they proclaimed that in the end God would come and create all things new. Until then, people would simply 'cross their arms' and pray. We can see the ambiguity in this trend, which was both pessimistic and optimistic, evoking faith and running the risk of not being involved.

In modern language, apocalypse has become a synonym for catastrophe. It's a pity that only this aspect has been retained, since apocalypse also signifies light and hope.

The Greek verb *apokalyptein* can be translated into Latin as *re-velare*, remove the veil, hence our 'reveal'. History is thought to unfold in a straight line, the end of which is hidden in God's secret. To uphold his people's hope in dramatic times, God lifts the veil which hides the end, revealing the happy outcome to history as a result of God's victory.

The long-jumper

But how does the author of an apocalypse have such a revelation? His technique is rather like that of a long-jumper. The long-jumper wants to jump forward as far as he can; to do that, he first goes back: then he runs as fast as he can for thirty or forty yards and when he arrives at the take-off, he jumps forward, carried by his impetus.

Some characteristics of apocalypses

The author uses a pseudonym. He attributes his book to a holy man of the past. This gives him two advantages. This holy man is near to God, so he can reveal God's secrets. And he is a man from the past, so he can proclaim the future!

Composed in times of crisis, apocalypses are pessimistic about a world doomed to perdition because it is wholly in the hands of the devil, 'the prince of this world'. In the end they are optimistic: God will create a new world.

Their vision of God is somewhat deterministic: everything has been foreseen in advance, and has been written in the heavenly books.

They call forth a total faith in God, but they risk encouraging a lack of involvement: nothing can be done except to wait for God to act.

They are concerned above all to maintain hope.

Restricted to the initiated, they use a special code, expressed in both words and images (see p.90).

The author of an apocalypse is like us. He does not know the future. But he is sure of one thing. God is faithful. To discover how he will bring history to an end, it is enough to see how he has guided it in the past. So the author goes back: he pretends to be writing three or four centuries before the time in which he is living, runs rapidly through history and then, when he comes to his own time, he leaps forward, projecting what he has discovered in his reading of history on to the end of time.

A very widespread trend

There are only two apocalypses in the Bible: Daniel and Revelation. However, many texts in the latest of the prophets already belong within this trend (Isa.24–27; 34–35; Zech. 1–8).

Between 150 BC and AD 70, this trend produced numerous books. It made a deep mark on the minds of believers, making them live in hope and expectation of the end.

The Book of Daniel

This book is very closely bound up with the Maccabean epic. The author is writing about 164. The book itself is classed either with the Writings, as in the Jewish Bible, or with the Prophets, as in the Greek Bible and most modern versions. It makes use of two different literary genres: pious histories and apocalypse.

Pious histories – or black humour! Dan.1–6

In time of war, the morale of the troops is important, and good stories are effective in keeping it up. By introducing fictitious figures, they make it possible to laugh at the expense of the enemy without his taking account of it. Thus it would have been rather dangerous to say that God would make Antiochus IV 'one with the beasts who eat the grass of the earth'; so this description is applied instead to Nebuchadnezzar, who lived four centuries earlier (Dan.4).

However, these stories go beyond humour. They are edifying tales (like midrash *haggadah*, see p.81), aimed above all at strengthening faith. Here are some examples.

Jewish rules about food are very strict. They appeared ridiculous to pagans and even to certain Jews who were tempted by Hellenism, and Antiochus forbade his subjects to observe them. The story of the young people exiled in Babylon is a reply to this: fed on raw carrots and fresh water, they are in better shape than those who eat meat (Dan.1)!

Israel was trampled underfoot by Antiochus, as it had been formerly by others: Babylonians, Medes, Persians, Greeks with their offshoots in the persons of the Lagids and the Seleucids. They felt powerless before this colossus. 'Don't panic,' says Daniel, 'this colossus has feet of clay.' A mysterious stone becomes detached from the mountain and grinds the colossus to dust (2.34). Thus it is God, and not the sword of the Maccabees, who will put an end to history and establish his kingdom.

To those Jews who 'set at nought the king's command, and yielded up their bodies rather than serve and worship any god except their own God' (Dan.3.28), the author tells the story of the three young men thrown into the furnace: 'Do not fear. God will send his angel into the fire with you, to keep you from evil!' (Dan.3). To this story has been added, in Greek, the magnificent 'Song of the Three Children in the Furnace'.

'And even if they kill you, God is capable of bringing you out alive from the tomb.' That is the teaching of ch.6. Daniel is thrown into the lions' den; a stone seals it like a tomb, and the king puts on mourning. Daniel is dead! But he comes out alive. He is the image of the whole Jewish people, put to death by their persecutors but brought to life by their God.

Features peculiar to apocalyptic already appear in some of these texts: the stone symbolizing the intervention of God, visions and dreams. However, it is above all in chs.7–12 that the author deliberately uses the literary genre of apocalypse.

A theology in images

The apocalypses use a system of images which have to be deciphered. Here are the main ones.

Colours
White means victory, purity.
Red means killing, violence, the blood of the martyrs.
Black means death and impiety.

Figures
Seven is the perfect figure, and signifies fullness.
Six (seven minus one) is imperfection.
Three and a half (half seven) is imperfection, suffering, the time of trial and persecution. Be careful! Three and a half can appear in various forms, but its symbolic value remains the same: thus three and a half, or a time, times and a half a time (perhaps 1 + 2 + ½), or three years and half a year all have the same significance as three and half days or forty-two months or 1,260 days!
Twelve means Israel (because of the twelve tribes).
Four signifies the world (the four points of the compass).
A thousand is an incalculable quantity.

Other images
A horn signifies power.
White hair signifies eternity (and not old age: the 'ancient of days' in Dan. 7 is not old, but eternally young!).
A long robe often signifies priestly dignity.
A golden girdle signifies royal power.
The goats are the wicked.
The sheep are the people.

An apocalypse. Dan.7–12

It was the apocalyptic part of Daniel (7–12) which was above all to stamp Israelite thought. The author, as we have seen, is writing in 164. He pretends to be writing at another time of persecution, that of the exile, four centuries earlier, and he takes the name of Daniel, a Canaanite pagan hero mentioned by Ezekiel. So he has no difficulty in 'foretelling' the future between the exile and the time of the Maccabees! However, he does this to discover the broad outlines of the way in which God acts and thus to discover how he will bring history to an end. We shall now study the most important text.

◗ *Studying a text. Dan.7*

First read this text straight through. You will be completely out of your depth! However, this will help you to see how apocalyptic literature works.

Now identify the different parts. Usually there is a vision, which is then interpreted by an angel.

The vision is narrated in 7.1–14, but an important detail is highlighted in 19–22. So read 7.1–8, then 19–22, then 9–14.

The interpretation is given in vv.15–18 and then 23–28.

We shall now go through this in more detail.

There is a contrast between the beasts and a man (in Hebrew, 'son of' is a generic term, so son of man means man); the beasts come out of the abyss, the resort of evil powers, and man appears from heaven. So before we know what these figures represent, we know that the former are evil and the latter is good, on God's side.

What do the four beasts represent? Look at the interpretation given in 7.17. Why is there special interest in the fourth? The most terrible beast represents Antiochus IV, who is persecuting the Jews. See v.25. Who does the man represent? See vv.18,27.

How do the beasts change? How does man change?

How is this vision a message for the Jews under persecution, who accept death rather than deny their faith?

Resurrection of the dead. Dan.12.1–4

This text is the first text in the Bible to give us a clear presentation of belief in the resurrection of the dead. The vision in Ezek.37 was still only an image of the resurrection of the people. Here we have personal resurrection. This text expresses in a different way what is affirmed in Dan.7. Let us look at the situation again.

Antiochus IV persecuted the Jews. Some of them preferred to die rather than to renounce their faith. That raised a serious question: hitherto, people of Israel did not have any conception of a life after death. The only life you had was earthly life. Now these martyrs were prepared to lose all that they had for the sake of God. And God responded. 'You are persecuted and accept death,' writes Daniel. 'That is the visible side of things. Now I shall show you the invisible side of things. Those of you who accept death in this way, people of the saints of the Most High, will be led into glory for a completely new life, in a marvellous kingdom which will last for ever.'

So here we find two ways of speaking, two very important means of expressing the resurrection.

Daniel 12 puts it in terms of before and after. 'Before death, you were alive. Death made you fall asleep, into a deep hole. After death, you will come out of this hole and wake up.' Those who awoke would be the same people as before. However, the new life would not be just the same as what had gone before; the author uses cosmic imagery to describe it: the splendour of the firmament.

Daniel 7 stresses this further dimension. It puts it in terms of below and above. On earth (below) you are put to death. However, above you are brought near to God for a completely new form of life.

We need to remember this imagery when we study the resurrection of Christ: the first Christians used it as a means of expression.

One important detail: man here is an image, a collective figure representing all those who trust in God, even to death. We should remember it when Jesus is presented as Son of man.

**Three lions.
Persepolis (sixth
to fifth century BC)**

91

Wisdom in the Diaspora

We are going to end with two books which were written in the Diaspora, one in Babylon (Baruch) and the other in Egypt (Wisdom).

Baruch (deutero-canonical)

This book is attributed to Baruch, secretary to the prophet Jeremiah; in fact it is made up of four sections coming from different periods and different authors. As it is now, it is a fine expression of penitence. It begins with an affirmation: our sins have broken our relationship with God (1.1–14). Then comes a reflection on sin as being exile far from God; the only recourse we have is to the tenderness and the faithfulness of God (1.15–3.18). So one can meditate on the wisdom of God which is none other than the Law; by practising the latter one acquires the former (3.9–4.4). The last part, the tone of which suggests Second Isaiah, gives consolation to Jerusalem and tells her that God grants her his light and his mercy. Reconciliation is achieved (4.5–5.9).

It is worth reading the fine prayer of the exiles (2.11–3.8), and above all the meditation on God's wisdom: 'It has appeared on earth and lived with men' (3.32–4.1). John says precisely this when he speaks of Jesus.

Jesus the Wisdom of God

To simplify things: the prophets helped Christians to discover the mission of Jesus, what he had to do; the wisdom literature helped them to perceive his being, who he is.

In the Old Testament, the Wisdom of God is sometimes personified, but the language remains figurative, as when I say, 'my heart's in the Highlands'; I personify my spirit as though it were capable of going somewhere without me, but I am well aware that it is my own self, so that I can attribute all my good points and my failings to it. Similarly, the Wisdom of God is God's own self; it is God as he is wise. So one can attribute to Wisdom all the powers of God, like the power to create, and so on (Wisdom 7).

When Christians came to say that Jesus is the Wisdom of God, that made it possible for them to attribute to him the qualities of this wisdom, i.e. the very qualities of God.

Wisdom (deutero-canonical)

This book was written in Greek, in Alexandria in Egypt, about 50–30 BC, and is the last work in the Old Testament to be composed.

The author is a Greek who knows his classics well; he is also a Jew. Living far from upheavals experienced by the community in Palestine under the Hasmonean dynasty, he practises the policy of the outstretched hand. Like the Jewish philosopher Philo of Alexandria at a later date (Philo was a contemporary of Jesus), he tried to think out his Jewish faith in terms of Greek culture.

His book can be divided into three parts.

1. Human destiny in God's plan. 1–5

What is the meaning of life? With a good deal of psychological skill, the author portrays two different attitudes. We were born by chance, say some; life is short and there is nothing after it. And he shows the practical consequences to which this can lead: enjoy life and trample on others to get what you want. In reality, these are friends of death and they forget that God has created man incorruptible by making him an image of his own nature. On the other side there are those who trust in God, who remain firm in his love. They often suffer and are sometimes persecuted, but when they have accomplished their task they will live with God.

The first Christians used these texts, combining them with passages from the prophets to express the death and the crucifixion of the Righteous One.

2. The praise of wisdom. 6.1–11.3

We shall return to one passage from this section, but you should read all these chapters, where the author urges us, like him, to seek the Wisdom of God which is the friend of men, to make it a companion in our lives and to become lovers of his beauty. Then, in an amazing midrash, he takes up the important moments of sacred history to show that Wisdom was in control. Wisdom formed Adam, piloted Noah's ark, allowed Abraham to be braver than a father concerned for his child; it led Moses, and so on.

3. A meditation on the Exodus. 11.4–19.22

Here Wisdom almost disappears. The plagues of Egypt are punishment for some and salvation for others.

Studying a text: Wisdom 7.21–30

It is difficult to single out a precise text, because the argument is a developing one. You should really read all chapters 6–10.

The author pretends to be Solomon, the wise king, and he shows that he owes everything, not to his birth, but to the fact that he prayed and the spirit of Wisdom came upon him. He was instructed by the craftsman of the universe, who organized it (7.22).

Read this text. How does Wisdom appear? She is seen to be endowed with all the qualities, like a beloved. (In 7.22–23 there is a list of three times seven attributes, the superlative of perfection!) In the Bible, some of these qualities are confined to God, while others were attributed by the Greek philosophers to the divine principle which animates the universe: you might try to identify them – but without arguing, as they are not always clear, and the matter is not very important.

As you look at these attributes, try above all to see the relationship between Wisdom and God.

Verse 26 is very strong. For a Jew, the Greek word *eikon*, image, designates a kind of identity, a presence.

As you look at these attributes, try to see the role of Wisdom towards creation and towards men.

Now you might read Gen.1.26–27, God creates man in his image, and Wisdom 2.23. In Wisdom 7.26, Wisdom is the image of God. Does that mean that man reproduces the features of this Wisdom?

Read II Cor.4.4; Col.1.15, then I Cor.11.7; II Cor.3.18; Col.3.10. What does this teach us about Christ? About men's vocation?

You might end by reading all these chapters again, replacing the word Wisdom in your mind by Jesus.

The Septuagint (LXX)

Septuagint (Greek for seventy, hence the symbol LXX) is the name given to the first Greek translation of the Old Testament.

The name derives from a legend told in the Letter of Aristeas, a Greek work from the end of the second century BC. Seventy-two Jewish scholars, working separately, ended up producing, after seventy-two days, translations which were alike in every respect. This is a way of stressing that this translation is miraculous and inspired by God.

In fact the translation was made by various authors between 250 and 150 BC.

The Jewish community in Alexandria spoke Greek and no longer understood Hebrew. Just as in Palestine the Hebrew text was translated into Aramaic (the Targum, see p.81), so in Egypt it was translated into Greek. This translation was probably liturgical in origin, and is often less a literal translation than an adaptation. It is a rereading of the scriptures, bringing them up to date. One example is famous: Isaiah proclaimed, 'The young woman is pregnant and will bring forth Immanuel' (Isa.7.14). The Septuagint translated this 'The virgin is pregnant', which allowed Christians to apply the text to Mary (Matt.1.23).

This translation is very important.

First, it made it possible to acclimatize Jewish belief to Greek culture and provided a language in which it could be expressed. In fact it uses the common language (*koine*), but colours it with various phrases borrowed from Hebrew. The New Testament often uses this language.

The Septuagint became the Bible of Christians, who adopted its list of contents (see the deutero-canonical books, p.86), and often took over its method of interpreting the scriptures. Thus it was a vital link in the preparation for expressing Christian belief.

8 The Psalms

An Egyptian musician
celebrating the Sun God
(about 1000 BC)

We shall end this 'holiday trip' through the Old Testament with the book of Psalms.

Why put them all together in the same chapter? Hitherto we have tried to read texts at the time when they were composed. Why treat the psalms differently? There is a simple reason: it is almost impossible to date them. Prayer is the same at all times. Texts are reread and rewritten, so it is wiser to study them together.

That will help us to understand better how Israel prayed, and it will also be a good way of summing up our journey: the essential features of the experience of this people, their discovery of God and their own situation in the world, is all expressed in their prayer.

In fact the psalms are essentially prayer, the response of human beings to the God who addresses them in every situation of their existence.

Human cries

'We are born with his book in our bellies,' wrote a Jewish poet. 'It is not a long book: 150 poems, 150 steps set up between death and life; 150 reflections of our rebellions and our fidelity, our agonies and our resurrections. This is more than a book; it is a living being who speaks, who speaks to *you*, who suffers and cries out and dies, who is raised again and who sings, on the threshhold of eternity.'

We find all our human cries here: hymns of wonderment at nature or human love, anguish in the face of suffering and death, oppression by society, rebellion against the absurdity of the world or the silence of God. All these cries are here, and they are our own, given to us as the word of God. They teach us that even at the darkest moments of our rebellion, God is present and cries with us, through us, and that both blasphemy and praise can be prayers if they are true and express the way we live.

A blind harpist

Two kinds of language

To be brief, we might distinguish language which conveys information, the language of science, from the language of relationships. For example, a child is in bed and calls out to its mother, 'Mother, I'm thirsty.' What kind of language is this phrase? Perhaps it conveys information, that is, the words 'I'm thirsty' give an exact description of the situation; the mother responds in the same key: 'Get up and get yourself a glass of water', and the child goes to sleep. If the phrase expresses some kind of relationship, after having had a drink, the child will say, 'Mother, I'm still thirsty,' or, 'I'm hot'. 'I'm thirsty' here means, 'I need you, I want you to come.'

In scientific language, which seeks to convey information, the words say exactly what they signify. In the language of relationships they seek to convey something else: the lover who addresses 'her pet' or 'his angel' is not expressing a situation but a kind of relationship, like the psalmist who calls his God 'my rock, my fortress'.

This distinction between two kinds of language is important when we are using the psalms in prayer, and even more generally, when we are reading the Bible. In fact, the word of God is always expressed in the language of relationships and not that of conveying information. Granted, the Bible is concerned to teach us certain things, but above all it seeks to enable us to enter into a personal relationship with God. It addresses us. The language of information is directed towards our intelligence, but often it does not bring about any personal change in us. If a child is really thirsty, the mother is not very bothered. By contrast, the language of relationship changes us. The words 'I'm thirsty' disturb the mother and arouse her maternal instincts.

When we are confronted with an object or an action, our scientific sense makes us ask, 'What *is* it?' The poet or the man of the Bible asks, 'What does it *mean*?' If the science teacher hands a flower to a girl pupil, he is obviously asking 'What is it? What kind is it?' But if a boy gives a flower to the same girl, the question is very different.

So when we open the book of Psalms, indeed when we open the Bible, it is important to remember that we are reading a language of relationships. There are certain images or expressions which we are not to understand in a scientific sense, as information, but which we have to interpret as though they were addressed to us. And they speak to us in terms of our personal experience. The same word means one thing to the country farmer who has just broken his ploughshare on an outcrop of rock; it means something different to the walker in the Alps who, having panicked on a crumbling surface, at last gets a footing on solid rock. These two aspects can also be found in the Bible. God is the 'rock' on which men are broken if they fail to respect him; he is also the solid 'rock' in whom we can trust.

The language of an era

Poetic imagery changes with civilization. 'The solemn action of the sower' might move our grandparents; it is meaningless in an age of automated farming.

The Bible speaks in terms of the culture of its time; its language is no longer ours, and that sometimes presents real difficulties. The notes in your Bible, or those in commentaries, will help you to understand the significance of certain symbols.

The forms of biblical poetry are also different. I have already said something about them (p.30). You may like them, or find that they put you off. However, you might say exactly the same thing about some modern poetry.

The numbering of the psalms

The Greek Bible, followed by the Latin version and the Catholic liturgy, does not have quite the same numbering as the Hebrew Bible, which is followed by the majority of modern Bibles. When the numbering differs, the liturgy always has one figure lower.

So you need to be careful when you are given the reference to a psalm.

The numbering of the Hebrew Bible is being adopted more and more, and I have followed it here.

Very often, two figures are given, e.g. Ps.51(50): this is 51 in Hebrew, 50 in the liturgy.

Literary genres

Scholars have tried to define the various literary genres of the psalms. This is important as we try to understand them, and even more important when we use them in prayer: we don't prepare for a celebration with friends in the same way as we do for a day of mourning. To know the literary genre of a psalm is to know how to prepare to meet God.

The classifications suggested by scholars differ in detail, but broadly speaking they agree. In any good introduction to the Psalter you will find a classification of the psalms into these various genres.

This chapter is meant above all to help you to enter into the prayer of the psalms. That is why I have grouped them according to themes rather than according to literary genres (though the two often coincide).

I am not going to pretend that we can make a complete study of the Psalter. However, simply by reading psalms, some for pleasure and others because of their theological importance or their difficulty, we shall try to discover how these old prayers are still our own.

Some themes of prayer

Praise to God the Saviour and Creator.

Praise to the God who is near: he dwells among his people (in Jerusalem, in the Temple), indeed dwells in his people (the Law).

Prayers of hope. God is king and will establish his reign of justice; he will do this through his king-messiah, of whom the earthly king was a figure.

Prayers of petition and thanksgiving. For Israel, these two aspects were inseparable.

Prayers for living. Here we can include several themes which arose out of the reflections of the wise men: how do we live in our difficult human situation?

Before this, the Psalms of Ascent will give us a first introduction to the Psalter.

For each theme, you will find general comments on the left hand page and suggestions for reading psalms on the right.

The Psalms of Ascent: Pss.120–134

It is easy to find a marvellous small collection within the Psalter: fifteen short psalms, fresh, and all bearing the same title. They are called Psalms of Ascent, probably because they were recited during the ascent to Jerusalem for the three pilgrim feasts. The psalms concerned are Pss.120–134. (Ps. 132 is in fact different, and may not have been part of the collection.)

These psalms belong to different families. They will help us to discover the character of psalms, to see the style of Hebrew poetry, and above all to understand the religious feelings of the authors.

Begin by reading the psalms, simply for pleasure.

After that, you can go back to them and study them from different perspectives.

Literary genres

In which family would you classify each of these psalms? Classifications suggested include prayers of trust, individual or corporate appeals for help, a prayer of recognition, a song of Zion, some psalms of instruction and a liturgy.

Try to discover some of the features of each family, while realizing that the borderlines are sometimes blurred: it is possible to pass from supplication to confidence in the same prayer.

Hebrew poetry

Rhythm. In classical English or French poetry, each verse ought to have the same number of syllables. Hebrew works on a different principle. In fact the voice rests or pauses on certain syllables: only these count. They can be the same number in every verse (for example, 3 + 3), or they can vary (3 + 2). Here is an example:

Out of the *depths* I cry to *thee*, O *Lord!* (3)
   Lord, *hear* my *voice!* (2)
Let thine *ears* be *attentive* (3)
   To the *voice* of my suppli*cations*. (2)

In this strophe the voice pauses on the syllables printed in italics: there is an alternation between three stresses and two stresses.

Parallelism. This consists in repeating the same thing twice in a different way. It happens a great deal. Try to find examples in these psalms (e.g. Ps.122.8–9).

Key words. Sometime each phrase begins by taking up a word from a previous phrase, which it uses as a kind of peg. See, for example, Ps.121.

The imagery

You can study this on two levels.

What imagery is used? What social, economic or cultural milieu does it reveal? It may evoke family

---

Praying together with a psalm

It's clear that there are no fixed ways and that everyone must invent their own way, whether individually or in a group. I can only describe what happens in some places.

The group meets (the atmosphere counts, the way people sit, some focal point of attention). Someone reads the psalm out aloud and then everyone reads it silently: once, twice, ten times, and broods on it. After a longer or shorter period of silent prayer, one person and then another repeats a verse which has made an impression, either reading it straight or rephrasing it in his or her own words. Many verses, words, images of the psalm repeated in this way, rewritten, filled with the life provided by each individual, take on a new significance and renew prayer. Don't be afraid of periods of silence: they are not dead times, but moments when the word of the Bible becomes the word of a brother or sister which resonates within us and calls forth our own words.

Sometimes the refrain of a well-known canticle can be said spontaneously.

Sometimes, too, verses from the Gospels can be included, expressing the certainty that the psalms are also Christ's prayers.

Some editions of the Psalter provide prayers after each psalm which take up the psalm's main themes.

life: mother and child, mistress and servant; or the life of village people in close contact with nature: the herdsman, arrows, building a house, gathering in the harvest; or the stunned gaze of the countryman as he discovers the great city with its enormous buildings and those who live in them. The psalms also display a popular spirit which sometimes verges on truculence: 'they would have swallowed us up alive.'

Try above all to see what they are saying.

What aspect of God appears in these psalms? What is his relationship with man? A simple expression like, 'The Lord will keep your going out and your coming in from this time forth and for evermore' (121.8) is a magnificent expression of what we call providence, the presence of God in the space and time of human history.

What is man's response to this love of God, in ordinary life, in the trials of the everyday world, in anxiety? What sense of sin is expressed? Notice how in every moment of his life, with the family or in his daily work, man lives in union with his God: for him, everything is a sign of God's love.

What is the meaning of pilgrimage, the importance of Jerusalem and of the Temple, the place where God makes himself present?

A link with the scriptures

You might also notice how these psalms take up the spirituality of Ezekiel and the Priestly History, a piety centred on the presence of God in his temple; how they accord with the Deuteronomic code in expressing the presence of God in everyday life; how they take up, in a very simple way, the imagery of the faith of Second Isaiah in God the Creator brought near to man through his love, or again the eucharistic freshness of Tobit.

In depth, the Psalms of Ascent work on four levels. They celebrate an actual ascent to Jerusalem; but this pilgrimage is also a way of reliving the first ascent from Egypt at the time of the Exodus and the ascent from Babylon at the end of the exile. And it is already an anticipation of this ascent of the people towards Jerusalem at the end of time (see Isa.60–62).

Christian prayer

How was Jesus able to use these psalms in prayer? How can we use them today?

God's Poor

In the Bible, poverty can have two significances, which should not be confused.

First, poverty is a specific situation of deprivation. It is an evil and even a scandal, because it shows that the kingdom of God has not yet arrived, since there are still unfortunates who suffer injustice. The prophets of the exile, in particular, announce the coming of the kingdom of God: when that happens, no one will be poor (see p.67). This is the tradition taken up by the beatitudes in Luke.

Poverty is sometimes envisaged as a spiritual attitude: the attitude of the person who submits himself totally to God because he has experienced his own impotence and his poverty. This poverty is a poverty of heart. These poor, the *anawim* (plural of *anaw*, poor), are the ones whom the Gospel of Matthew declares happy.

This idea of spiritual poverty appears clearly with Zephaniah (see p.61). It developed after the return from exile, and led to the formation of this stratum of simple people, with a deep faith, far removed from the political and religious quarrels of the high priests, whom we find at the beginning of our era in the persons of Zechariah, Elisabeth, Simeon, Anna and Mary.

The Psalms of Ascent, composed after the exile, express this spirituality well.

The life of these poor people, these insignificant men and women who were poor in spirit, was very simple. Country folk, close to nature, they enjoyed the simple pleasures of family life, friendship between brothers, and peace. Although they are incapable of expressing themselves in learned words, the imagery they use reveals the depth of their religious feelings: everything speaks to them of God, and is a message of his love. This is the way in which Jesus will speak in the parables.

This God is personal and close to man. He protects him in all his activities and watches over him; he pardons his sins! And the poor man responds to him with a complete and utter faith and confidence.

This God lives in the midst of his people, in his Temple at Jerusalem. So the life of the poor is one long pilgrimage. Israel is a people on the march to the place where their God lives. They have been on the march since the Exodus, because God freed them then; they have been on the march since the departure from Babylon. They will continue on the march until the time when all the people reassembles united by the same faith, in joy and communion with the one God.

Praise to God the Creator and Saviour

There are times when you want to sing, because the world is beautiful, because someone loves you, or because a friend forgives you and takes a great load from your mind. There are times when a jubilant people wants to sing, when there is a great national victory at sport, or a royal wedding. Songs, an explosion of collective joy fuelled by refrains or slogans, praise in one form or another, have been part of festivals all down the ages.

In Israel, praise blossoms or explodes in most of the psalms; it appears in pure form in the hymns, but it is also present in songs of supplication. Here we have one of the essential characteristics of biblical man confronted with God: whatever his particular situation, whether it is joy or sorrow, in the depths of suffering or sin the believer sees his existence as being in the presence of a God whose beauty and goodness he cannot help celebrating.

This praise is not the logical culmination of a process of reasoning. It is an expression of wonderment and joy of one who knows himself to be loved because God has told him, 'You are precious in my eyes, and honoured, and I love you' (Isa.43.4).

God the liberator

As we have seen, Israel's first religious experience was of liberation and salvation: their God was the one who brought them out of slavery. Other books than the Psalter have preserved some very ancient songs: the brief refrain of Miriam dancing for joy with the people at the time of the Exodus (Ex.15.21), or the magnificent hymn of the prophetess Deborah celebrating the victory won at the foot of mount Tabor about 1225 BC (Judges 5).

By celebrating the wonders of God during liturgical festivals, the people make them present once again, and share in them. They revive their awareness of being the people whom God has chosen, renew their faith in the covenant, and their hope. In fact they remind God of past liberations and call upon him to complement them with new ones.

God the creator

Israel then discovered that if God can intervene in history, it is because he is Lord of it, because he has created the world. The prophet Amos was able to quote a fine hymn to the Creator God (Amos 4.13; 5.8–9; 9.5–6: see p.47). Second Isaiah will make this the basis of his theology.

The structure of these prayers

The structure of these psalms is very simple. They begin with an invitation, an exhortation to praise. The development, beginning with 'for', 'because', 'who', proclaims the wonders that God has performed in history, or his qualities. The conclusion takes up the invitation in a more developed or personal way, and often ends with a blessing to an acclamation: 'Hallelujah' (Praise God!), 'For ever!'

Our prayer

We shall probably find it easy to pray these psalms. The only problem is likely to be a cultural one: some images seem rather strange to us (however, the creation stories have already made us familiar with them), and certain allusions to historical events escape us. That is not very important. We do not feel cut off from our grandparents simply because there are things that we don't know about their lives. Similarly, details apart, these hymns should strengthen our conviction that the history of the people of God is our history, and that it is there, in these divine wonders, from the Exodus to the new exodus in Jesus Christ, that we have our roots.

The titles of the psalms

At the beginning, most of the psalms have indications of the author and of the type of psalm, which are often difficult to understand.

The Hebrew preposition which precedes the name can signify that it is attributed to this author or that the psalm is part of a collection made under his name. When rereading the psalms, people wanted to put them in the context of the life of a great personality.

There is often also an indication of the instrument which is to accompany the psalm, and this may indicate its genre.

📖 The God of Exodus. Ps.114

Invitation: Hallelujah. Praise God!

Development

vv.1–2. The purpose of the first Exodus: God wants to make the people his sanctuary, he wants to dwell in a faithful people (see Ezekiel, p.66, and Nathan, p.42).

vv.3–4. The wonders of the first Exodus.

vv.5–6. The author speaks and makes us ask ourselves about these wonders.

vv.7–8. The wonders of the second exodus, the liberation from Babylon. This is at least one possible meaning: inspired by Second Isaiah (Isa.41.15; 42.15; 43.20, etc.), the author celebrates the new exodus.

Jesus' prayer

It was easy for Jesus to take up this psalm (which was recited in the passover liturgy) to celebrate 'his exodus which he was to accomplish in Jerusalem' (Luke 9.31).

Christian prayer

How can we use this psalm today? The New Testament talks of our life in terms of an exodus (John, I Peter, Revelation); what meaning does that give to our existence? We can also apply it to Christ, our rock and the source of living water (see I Cor.10.4).

📖 The God of the oppressed. Ps.113

Invitation

vv.1–3. Who is called on to praise God? Where?

Development

vv.4–6. Which of God's qualities are praised?

vv.7–9. Compare these verses with I Sam.2.1–10, the 'gospel' proclaimed by Second Isaiah (see p.67), and the beatitudes. What do these verses proclaim?

Jesus' prayer

This psalm is the first of a group (Pss.113–118) called Hallel (praise) which were sung in the liturgy of the three great festivals: so Jesus will have sung them on the evening of Maundy Thursday (Mark 14.26). How could he make this his prayer?

Christian prayer

How does God want to show his greatness? How would we translate vv.7–9 today (the dignity of the poor and the oppressed)? Can we pray this psalm without trying to realize in our own actions what is asked for?

📖 The glory of God: living man. Ps.8

Invitation. v.2

This is taken up again at the end, in v.10.

Development

vv.3–5. The psalm celebrates the greatness of God. Perhaps the beginning should be translated like this:

I want to hymn your glory above the heavens in a better way than with the mouths of babes and sucklings.

These babes are probably the stars which sang in the morning of the world (Job 38.6; Bar.3.35): man celebrates God's glory in an even better way than they did. God's abode is heaven: as in Gen.1, creation is seen as God's victory over chaos.

vv.6–9. Man was introduced in v.5. Now he is the centre, but God remains the subject of all the verbs. To proclaim the greatness of man is to proclaim the greatness of God.

With this hymn we are half-way between the two creation stories (Gen. 2 and 1).

The psalm is quoted several times in the New Testament (see the references in the margin of your Bible, if you have an annotated one).

📖 Creation, God's glory. Ps.104

The author is inspired by an Egyptian hymn to the sun god composed about 1350. The few extracts from that hymn quoted on p.18 will enable you to make a comparison. So a human prayer can become a prayer to the living God, just as our daily bread can become the body of Christ. However, the psalmist rethinks his prayer in terms of his faith and of the creation story in Gen.1.

Invitation v.1

Development, vv.2–30

First of all read this text just to enjoy it. Then compare it with the Egyptian hymn: what connections can you see? Compare it with the story in Gen.1: can you see how it follows the days of creation?

Conclusion, vv.31–35

Personal praise, with joy, and hope for a world that will finally be freed from evil.

Christian prayer

God created all things by Christ and for him (Col.1.15–18). He gives us life through his breath, the Spirit. And the bread and wine become symbols of a world made new in the Spirit.

Praise to the God who is Near

God is the God who is utterly different, Lord of history, the Creator. However, the wonder which Israel never ceased to extol was that God had come very near. He dwells *among* his people: in Jerusalem and in his Temple, the place of his presence to which people go on pilgrimage. He dwells *in* his people. 'For this commandment is not too hard for you, neither is it far off. But the word is very near you; it is in your mouth and in your heart, so that you can do it' (Deut.30.11ff.). Here I have brought together psalms which scholars classify into various genres: psalms of Zion, of pilgrimage, of instruction.

Immanu-el: God with us

Some psalms celebrate the joy of being invited to God's house, of being his guest, sharing an intimate relationship with him. So we should watch out for expressions like 'be with', 'with you', 'be your guest', 'dwell in your house', 'be sheltered by God', 'God before us', 'under your wings'.

It is worth studying Ps.139.

God present in his Temple

Jerusalem – or Zion, the hill on which the city is built – and the Temple are the places where God makes himself present to his people. As we read Isaiah's call (p.42) or the priestly texts about the presence of God upon the ark (p.71), we could see the extraordinary impression it made upon the people.

People went up to Jerusalem three times a year, on the pilgrimage feasts (Passover, Pentecost and above all the Feast of Tabernacles). In this way they once again had the experience of being a community around God. However, there was a danger: the presence of God might be thought to be a piece of magic, dispensing righteous living. Prophets like Jeremiah disabused the people of this idea (p.62), and the exile and the destruction of the Temple forced them to understand that this presence of God was not an automatic assurance. God does not live primarily in a place, but in a faithful people.

Christian prayer. The presence of God is a real fact in Jesus Christ, our true temple. And the church is his body, animated by his spirit. These prayers remind us that the church is a people on the march to the heavenly Jerusalem, the ultimate city where evil will disappear because God will be wholly in us.

God present through his Law

The law gets a bad press. So does obedience!

For Israel, the law is not a matter of orders and commandments. It is the word, a tender word like the smile of a woman responding to her lover, brusque, like a team leader organizing his group for work; precise, like a guide indicating the only firm hold on crumbling rock. And this word – Shema Israel! Listen and obey, Israel! – simply says: 'I love you. . . Do you love me?'

As the etymology of the word reminds us, obey (*ob-audire*) means to get in a good position to listen to someone who is talking, to prepare with all our being to receive his words so that they may resonate in our heart and produce a response which will stem from our whole being. In this sense, the conversation between two lovers is mutual 'obedience'.

It is essential to remember this when you read these 'prayers of obedience' if you are to understand how these believers could sing of the law with such tenderness, as happens, for example, in Ps.119.

Christian prayer. It is easy for us to pray these psalms now. For us the law has taken human form, Jesus Christ, word of God laid down in our hearts by the spirit. And these old words can help us to tell him once again of the passion which inspires us.

With abounding love hast thou loved us, O Lord our God, and great and overflowing tenderness hast thou shown us. O our Father, our King, for our fathers' sake, who trusted in thee, and whom thou didst teach the statutes of life, be also gracious unto us and teach us. O our Father, merciful Father, ever compassionate, have mercy upon us; O put it into our hearts to understand and to discern, to mark, learn and teach, to heed, to do and to fulfil in love all the words of instruction in thy Torah. Enlighten our eyes in thy Torah, and let our hearts cleave to thy commandments, and unify our hearts to love and reverence thy Name . . . Thou hast chosen us from all peoples and tongues, and hast brought us near unto thy great Name for ever in faithfulness. Blessed art thou, O Lord, who hast chosen thy people Israel in love. . .

A prayer from the Jewish liturgy.

📖 Lord, you have known me. . . Ps.139

At some time we have all dreamed of being known as we really are, with our personal qualities and failings, and being loved for what we are. This is the way in which believers know themselves to be known and loved by their God.

However, this intimacy is not entirely a tranquil matter. As in the case of Jeremiah (p.62), the temptation may be that we find this word too heavy to bear, and may seek to evade it.

Verses 1–18. Note the imagery and expressions which indicate proximity and intimacy. Humility is also a matter of recognizing ourselves as the most marvellous gift which God gives us: 'Thank you, Lord, for making me in such an amazing way.'

Verses 19–22. However, this believer still has a sorry question: why evil? In what we may feel to be rather a simplistic way, he asks God to destroy whatever is opposed to him.

Verses 23–24. His final prayer is even more moving: he is no longer sure that he is going on the right way and asks God to protect him.

Christian prayer
God has freely bestowed grace on us through his beloved (Eph.1.6). In him, we can become sons and know something of his intimacy with the Father through the Spirit, which makes us pray, 'Abba, Father!' And we know that the Son protects those whom the Father has given into his care (John 17).

📖 My whole being cries out with joy. . . Ps.84

This hymn of a pilgrim arriving at the temple expresses his passionate love for God.

Look for the imagery and expressions which speak of the march, the habitation (dwelling, house, nest), the happiness (joy, rampart, shield). It is worth looking for those images which express the same realities for us; if we do that, we shall already be half way towards composing a prayer for today.

Christian prayer
From now on the real temple is the body of the Risen Christ. So we can celebrate it in the same words.

And his church is his body all through history. We can celebrate the joy of living as brothers, but ask at the same time that this church should be purified, should become more like what it ought to be, and also ask that God allow us to work in it.

📖 I am thirsty for God. . . Pss.42–43

Originally, these two psalms were one; a refrain (42.6,12; 43.5) divides it into three strophes of equal length.

A temple servant is in exile in Lebanon and cries out in his suffering. In his exile he feels only one pain: being far from God.

42.2–6. What is his desire? (See Ex.34.23.) What is his suffering? What comforts him?

42.7–12. One can pray to God from exile, from any place of exile. This psalm takes up the classic imagery.

43.1–5. The prayer.
Look for images and expressions which are nostalgic (thirst, faint . . .) – water – light – joy – salvation.

📖 The wonders of your Law. . . Ps.119

176 verses! 176 verses to say one thing: 'Lord, I love your law.' Twenty-two strophes, one for each letter of the Hebrew alphabet; the eight verses of each strophe all begin with the same letter which is successively every letter of the Hebrew alphabet. And one of the eight names of the Law appears in each of these eight verses: law, precepts, commandments, and so on. This psalm – which it is better to use in small sections – is as bewitching as an incantation. Just as the lover keeps telling the beloved of the same love in a thousand ways, so the psalmist constantly tells God that he loves him, this God who has brought himself near through his word: 'Thou art near, O Lord' (v.151).

In this loving conversation between the God who speaks and the believer who listens, we might look for those images and expressions which present God: the Law is God, who makes himself near (it comes from his mouth, it teaches him) . . . but remains mysterious.

We should also look at the images and expressions which present man and his attitude: he is turned towards God (he examines, meditates, cherishes, studies . . . the law), he obeys, goes, seeks . . . He is brought back to God, because, in the past, he has sinned.

Christian prayer
You can use this psalm as a prayer by putting Jesus instead of law, for he is the word of God which has been set in our hearts by the Spirit: Jesus, 'the way, the truth and the life'.

Prayers of Hope. God the King. The Earthly King

Two different genres of psalms have been brought together here: common to both is that they celebrate the kingdom, in one case of God, in the other of the earthly king. They direct our attention towards the future, to that moment when God will finally show himself as he is, a faithful and just king, through the intermediary of the one whom he will establish as Messiah king.

The Lord is king

In Israel, God alone is king: the earthly king is only his representative. That was the faith from the beginning.

During the exile in Babylon and afterwards, there was no longer a king. So belief in the kingdom of God developed. Thus Second Isaiah shows that God is king because he is Creator (Isa.40.12–31) and liberator of Israel (41.21; 42.15; 44.6 . . .). The prophet calls on all the people to recognize God as king by celebrating him (42.10–12). He announces that God will finally come to establish his kingdom (52.7).

Five very similar psalms celebrate this kingdom of God: Pss.93,96,97,98,99.

There is an outburst of rejoicing; you might think that it was a festival. Israel, the most distant peoples (the islands) and all the elements of the universe share in this universal joy.

Taking up the good news, the gospel, of Second Isaiah, these psalms proclaim the time when God will bring an end to all wretchedness and poverty (see p.67).

Ps.47 probably has the same origin. Ps.24.7–10 is perhaps an ancient psalm celebrating the entry of the ark into Jerusalem at the time of David: verses 1–6, added after the exile, take up the whole theme from a universalist perspective.

These songs were formed in the liturgy: in the cult, the eternal kingdom of God begins to become effective on earth.

Christian prayer

By proclaiming the beatitudes and performing miracles for the poor, Jesus shows that in him the kingdom of God has begun. However, it has only begun: the disciples must realize it. So these psalms reinforce our expectation ('Thy kingdom come') and invite us to work for it.

The 'birth' of the king

Seven psalms (2,21,45,72,89,101,110) and perhaps some others celebrate the king of Israel.

Unlike other peoples, Israel never divinized its kings. However, as the prophet Nathan announced to David (p.42), they became son of God in a special sense on the day on which they were enthroned. On this day of their birth as kings, they were begotten as sons of God.

Perhaps some of these psalms are very old. At all events, they were reread after the exile, at a time when there was no longer a king. At that time they became the bearers of a new hope: one day, God will send his Messiah king to establish his kingdom.

Christian prayer

The Christian recognizes Jesus as this Messiah king; so he is invited to celebrate him and to pray that his Lordship over mankind may increasingly be realized.

Psalm 2 in the New Testament

This psalm helped people to understand and express:

The resurrection of Christ: this is the time when he was begotten (his birth) as son of God, messiah king and Lord of the universe (Acts 13.32; Rom.1.3; Heb.1.5; 5.5; Rev. 12.5). This is not his birth at Bethlehem, and the expression 'son of God' does not have the meaning we attach to it today: it does not denote his divinity but his establishment as king and Lord of the universe.

The death of Christ: he is rejected by the leaders of the people; so these are the 'evil men' of the psalm, who rebel against the Lord and against his anointed (Acts 4.23–31 and probably also Matt.26.3–4).

His coming at the end of the world: one day he will be definitively enthroned as Lord of the universe (Acts 19.15; 21.1–5). Here is the ultimate foundation of our hope, and John promises that we shall share in his glory (Rev.21.7; 2.26).

God is king! Ps.96

It is worth noticing how this psalm makes the message of Second Isaiah into a prayer (as do other royal psalms). Here are some connections:

vv.1–3. An invitation to all the earth to sing a new song (Isa. 42.10). In bringing liberation from the exile, God shows his salvation, his justice, his glory before the nations (Isa.45.14–25; 52.10).

vv.4–6. That shows that God is God and the other deities are nothing (Isa.41.21–29; 43.9–13).

vv.7–9. All the people are invited to praise God.

vv.10–13. In proclaiming God as Creator, vv.11–12 say why God can finally reign as a just king (vv.10–13).

Note the images and expressions which evoke glory and creation, peace and social justice, universal praise.

My son – sit at my right hand. . . Pss.2; 110

It would be a good thing for you first to reread Nathan's prophecy to David (II Sam.7, see p.42).

Ps.2, vv.1–3. The 'wicked' ones, kings and peoples, plot against God and his messiah; thus they make common cause (as in I Chron.17.14).

vv.4–6. God mocks them; he has his plan against which revolts are of no avail.

vv.7–9. The Messiah king recalls this plan: on the day he ascended the throne, God made him his son. However, this monarchy goes beyond Israel: it now extends to all the people of the universe. So this is not just an earthly king.

vv.10–12. A warning to the rebels. Be still!

Ps.110 takes up the same themes with different (and sometimes obscure) expressions.

Sit at my right hand: the image begins from a specific situation, since the royal palace was on the right of the temple; it thus evokes a unique, almost divine position accorded to this king.

You are priest . . . In Israel, as with other peoples, the king is also a priest. In fact he is above all the patron of the priests, and the two functions tended to be kept separate.

Christian prayer
See the boxes: Pss. 2 and 110 in the New Testament.

Faith in the faithless God! Ps.89

'The terrible moment when God isn't true and yet I still love him'. This phrase applies not only to personal situations (like that of Job, p.82), but also to collective situations, as here.

In 587 the monarchy disappeared. Now God has promised always to maintain the dynasty of David. Might he then be faithless? Might he have perjured himself?

vv.2–3. This praise of the love and faithfulness of God is an act of total faith, made in the dark: apparently everything tells against it. That is why the author clings desperately to these two words which he keeps repeating: tenderness and faithfulness (*hesed* and *emunah*, translated steadfast love and faithfulness by RSV). They occur in vv. 2,3,9,15,25,29,34,50 (see the box about the language of love on p.49).

vv.4–5. God is reminded of his promise to David.

vv.6–19. God is Creator and he is king. So he is all powerful. He has no excuse for not keeping his promise!

vv.20–38. A detailed recollection of God's promise to David and his descendants.

vv.39–46. With a bold leap of faith, the author shows that God is unfaithful.

vv.47–52. An agonized appeal for God to act.

v.53. The prayer began with a sheer act of faith. It ends with thanksgiving, for a work which God has not yet performed!

Christian prayer
First of all we learn an attitude: to rebel against situations which makes God false, in prayer, in sheer faith, and in confidence.

Now we can experience this attitude in Jesus' prayer in Gethsemane and on the cross.

Psalm 110 in the New Testament

Jesus applies this psalm to himself when he is before the Sanhedrin (he does the same with Dan.7, the passage about the Son of man).

Jesus is seated at the right hand of God: so the creed affirms. Peter proclaims this on the day of Pentecost to express what happened at Easter (Acts 2.34). The theme is often taken up again in the New Testament: Acts 5.31; 7.55; Rom.8.34; Col.3.1; Eph.1.20; I Cor.15.25; I Peter 3.22.

The Letter to the Hebrews makes v.4 the basis of its argument: Jesus is high priest (Heb.5.6).

Prayers of Petition and Thanksgiving

More than a third of the psalter consists of intercessory prayers, supplications, appeals for help. Scholars distinguish between individual supplications and collective supplications. The only difference lies in what is asked for, so we can study the two together.

These prayers are usually made up of four parts (the order of which may vary): invocation of God and cry for help – an account of the situation – reasons for being heard (above all the love, the faithfulness and the glory of God, and also the confidence of the person who prays) – conclusion, which is often a confident prayer, a thanksgiving in the certainty of being heard and a promise to offer a sacrifice out of gratitude.

The situations which call forth prayer can be very different. Here are the main ones:

- Prayers of sick people who already feel on the edge of the grave.
- Cries of the poor who are oppressed by injustice.
- The prayer of exiles.
- Prayer for victory for the armies of Israel.
- Prayers against the enemy. These cursing psalms raise a particular problem, which we shall study separately.
- Confession of sin.

Christian prayer

It is both easy and difficult for us to pray these psalms.

It is easy to take them up, because they express our own situation at one time or another.

The difficulty comes from several sides.

These prayers are expressed in imagery which will often be strange to us. Sometimes the notes in our Bible or a commentary may help. And in poetry, we need not always understand everything!

Fortunately, we are not always in such situations. The psalms, which are as it were universal prayers, compel us to come out of ourselves, to take into our prayer all those who are in such a situation. The first person in the psalms is almost always a collective; here we are the voice of suffering humanity.

Intercessory prayer bothers us. God is not a stopgap for our inadequacies. That's true. But love between two people can also be expressed by asking: we know very well that this does not prevent us from acting: on the contrary, we draw on our love for others to find strength to take action ourselves.

Prayers which express only thanksgiving or trust are quite rare; that is because these themes appear in almost all the psalms of supplication. We may keep finding the same parts, but often there is mention of the lesson which is drawn from the event: 'See the power and love of God, which are capable of drawing us, though we are sinners, out of this hopeless tangle.'

Cursing psalms

Some passages in the psalms, and sometimes whole psalms, scandalize us. How can we ask God to kill our enemies, to disembowel them, to break their teeth? Perhaps there are two ways of using these psalms in prayer.

Sometimes they are the only true prayer that we can utter. When we feel incapable of finding our place in the New Testament ('Father, forgive them'), we can at least take up these prayers, which are a step in that direction. So to pray them, humbly, can be one way of making scriptures warm our hearts, so that one day the word of God may take us to the foot of the cross.

However, with Christ, these prayers have changed their meaning and have become prayers of consecration. Read the terrible poem of the divine vintner (Isa.63.1–6, see p.77). God tramples on all his enemies, their blood spurts on to his garments. When Revelation takes up this poem and shows us Christ in bloodstained garments (Rev.19.13), we understand that Jesus had taken upon himself all the sin of the world (II Cor.5.21), and that the blood which flows is henceforward his own.

Praying these psalms today, Christ continues to take on himself this sin of the world, to suffer death and to destroy it by exorcizing it with his love.

Praying these psalms with him, we say in a sense to God, 'Put me on the cross with your Son and blot out all this sin in me, all this sin of the world in which I share. With your Son, I consecrate myself so that all men may be consecrated in the truth.'

📖 My God, why have you forsaken me? Ps.22

vv.2–3. Invocation of God and cry for help.

vv.4–12. The believer begins by giving the reasons why he should be heard: God is near; he has delivered those of former times; he has protected the believer since his birth.

vv.13–22. An explanation of the situation with the help of expressive imagery.

vv.23–27. Thanksgiving. Whether in reality, or whether in hope, he has been heard. He urges the people to join him in praise and invites the poor to share in the sacrificial meal which he is offering.

The opening individual's prayer probably stops here. When it became a collective prayer, by being taken into the psalter, vv.28–32 were added. The announcement of the conversion of the nations and the kingdom of God is dependent on the message of Second Isaiah and corresponds to the psalms which celebrate God as king. Verse 30, which recalls the worship given to God by the dead, must be dependent on Dan.12 (cf. p.91). Thus the prayer becomes the expectation of eternal life.

Christian prayer

According to Matthew and Mark, on the cross Jesus expressed his anguish with the first verse of this psalm, and the passion narrative takes up some of its imagery.

Having become a prayer of Christ, this psalm can become our own, with him and in him.

📖 Lord, slay them all. . . Ps.109

This psalm is probably the worst of the cursing psalms. People have tried to tone it down by putting the curses of vv.6–19 in the mouths of the enemy, directed against the faithful. It is better to accept it as it is: even a saint like Jeremiah could resort to such 'prayers' (Jer.17.18; 18.21–23; 20.11–12). It is easy to identify the different parts of this psalm.

Christian prayer

First of all, remember that Jesus used this psalm in prayer like all the rest. So it must be possible to turn it into a Christian prayer. You might find inspiration in the box on the left, or in some other way. However, we cannot suppress this psalm and those like it, and exclude them from liturgical usage, because they too are the word of God.

📖 Lord, be merciful (Miserere). Ps.51

vv.3–4. An invocation of God and an appeal for forgiveness.

vv.5–8. I have sinned against you. . .

vv.9–14. A request for purification.

vv.15–19. A promise of thanksgiving: the sacrifice which the believer is going to offer will be himself, with his humbled pride.

vv.20–21. A prayer for Jerusalem. These verses, with their mention of physical sacrifices, do not fit in well with what has gone before and have probably been added.

The believer uses three main types of language to weave together his confession: that of sin (see the box below), that of purification, and that of love (see p.49. Tenderness, love, thanksgiving in v.3). Try to identify them all. What colouring do they give to this prayer?

You might also note how this psalm takes up the message of Ezekiel: the believer has the feeling of belonging to a people of sinners (Ezek.16; 20; 23); he knows that only God can give him a pure heart (Ezek.36.26f.); this will be the work of the Holy Spirit (Ezek.36.26f.; 37.14; 39.29; 47).

What are the themes on which the sinner relies in asking for pardon?

Christian prayer

If Christ could only pray this prayer in solidarity with us, it is easy for us to take it up. Love fully revealed in Jesus Christ, and the Spirit spread abroad in our hearts, allow us to use it in complete trust.

The language of sin

Fault (*hatta*). The root denotes 'to go wrong', 'not to attain one's end'. So to sin is to lack God and therefore to lack happiness (vv.4,5,6,7,9,11,15).

Revolt (*pesa'*). This is the deliberate transgression of another's rights, whether individual, people or God. The prophets often use it to reproach the people for refusing to obey God (vv.3,5,15).

Perverseness (*'awon*). The root signifies to twist, to deviate. The twisted heart of the sinner needs to be converted (vv.4,7,11).

Evil (*ra'*). This is the most common name for sin; it denotes wickedness and immorality (v.6).

Prayers for Living

The reflections of the wide men after the exile led to a deepening of all these themes and the appearance of new subjects like the praise of the righteous, or of the law, or the difficult problem of retribution.

We can also find these subjects in prayer.

Praise of the righteous, or the cult of the saints

It is enough to read the description of the perfect housewife (Prov. 31.10–31) or the ancestral portrait gallery in Ben Sirach (Sir.44ff.) to know how fond the wise men were of this kind of portrait.

Read Ps.111: this is a fine eulogy of God (each verse begins with a different letter of the alphabet, in alphabetical order). Now read Ps.112 (constructed in the same way): is it not amazing that much of the praise given to God is applied to the righteous man? Or take Ps.1 or 26 ('I will wash my hands in innocence. . .'): how can we truthfully say these prayers? There are perhaps two ways in which we can use them.

First, with the simplicity of Mary extolling the work of the Lord within her: 'The Lord has done wonders for me . . .' Sin is not a matter of recognizing one's qualities, but of failing to see them, and refusing to give glory to God for them.

And secondly, with humility. I know very well that I am a long way from having allowed God to realize in me the dream which he cherishes for me. To say these psalms again is to put before one's eyes an ideal, to recognize that one has yet to attain it, and to ask God to show the way to it.

The cult of the Law

We have already read the magnificent Ps.119, with its 176 verses in honour of the Law. You can go on to read Ps.19.

We have seen how, for the Jew, the Law is the word of God, his wisdom (Sir.24; Bar.4.1). Paul could move from 'The Law is my life' to 'Christ is my life'; he was only giving the same reality its true name.

For the Christian – and we shall return to this on p.109 – the Law has not perished. Now that Christ enables us to understand it (Luke 24.25), it remains the way which leads us to him by making our heart burn to recognize him.

The problem of retribution

'If you do good, you will be rewarded; if you do evil, you will be punished': there is nothing to be said against this principle, which is so vigorously recalled by the Deuteronomist, except that the facts often contradict it! Noble souls try to defend it even today by appealing to heaven: the balance will be restored after death. That is open to discussion, but at all events it was an unthinkable view in Israel until people belatedly came to believe in life after death. Meanwhile, they found consolation by hoping to survive in their children, or explaining misfortune as being the result of collective solidarity. It is always easy to say to someone who has suffered unjustly, 'That's because of your grandfather's sin!' Ezekiel (ch.18), and then Job and Koheleth, challenged these easy ways out.

About twenty psalms deal with the problem. We can see in them four main stages in deepening faith.

1. Peace through lack of awareness
People were happy to affirm the traditional doctrine (for example, Ps.138). By transposing what is hoped for into spiritual terms, can we perhaps express a hope for heaven?

2. Astonished suffering
'If God existed, would he let innocent children die?' These psalms (e.g. 10; 94) express the question; sadly, without giving an answer. This may sometimes be our prayer. It is the prayer of many people. These psalms may, fortunately, disturb our security as believers who too often have the answer to everything.

3. Peace in faith
The wicked are seen to prosper; it is said that this prosperity is unreal. Man's dignity lies elsewhere. God will certainly triumph over present trials. Pss.49; 91; 139.

4. Joy in love
Psalm 73, which we are going to read, is a climax. Nothing is explained. The believer has utter confidence, despite the darkness, in God, because he is sure of God's love and also of our own. And it is in this magnificent act of faith, in this self-abandonment to God, certain of his love, that we find joy. Despite everything.

▌❧ Mankind, beasts to the slaughter. . . Ps.49

You should read Koheleth again before praying this psalm. You will find there the same disillusioned tone, the same way of applying acid to our big ideas and our illusions. 'The satisfied man is like a beast for the slaughter' (vv.13,21).

This psalm is a good counterbalance to those which praise the righteous. It invites us to look elsewhere than in human success for the dignity of mankind. It was the greatness of Koheleth to reject false solutions, even though he did not have others to put forward. Man is greater than all the embellishments with which he bedecks himself. This is the austere lesson of a believer. A necessary lesson.

Christian prayer

We should not be too confident that we know better, that the Christian has an answer to everything. By living as a man, Jesus taught us that one could make sense of human life, but he lived it out in all its harshness, without anaesthetics. And he invites us, with him, to live out our human role with courage.

▌❧ I am always with you. . . Ps.73

Here is an honest believer who does not disguise the scandal of belief. He affirms with simplicity, 'I was within a hair's breadth of falling. . .'

What he finds scandalous is that because he believes in God and loves him, he wears himself out trying to live an honourable life. The result is that he is poor and scorned, while those who do not believe in anything are fat and sated. 'What is the use of being honest?' (v.13).

All this is too sad, too difficult to accept. So the believer feels that he is stupid, a great beast, before God (the actual word he uses is *behemoth*, the most amazing animal in the Israelite menagerie).

But now he understands: 'I am always with you. You hold me by the hand. You will direct me according to your plan. And one day you will receive me in glory. What else can I want, seeing that I have you?'

Here we have reached a climax: love has the last word, even if the psalmist does not use the term. The believer cannot explain. But he loves, and knows that he is loved. That enables him to hold fast, with joy, to this great certainty: 'I do not know what is to happen, but I love you too much now not to be able to continue to go on loving you.'

Hippopotamus in enamelled pottery (between 2000 and 1800 BC, Egypt). It is decorated with the lotus flowers on which it feeds. Along with the rhinoceros, it is the biblical Behemoth.

Journey's End

Our year's 'holiday' travelling through the Old Testament has come to an end. A companion volume to this one is available, inviting you to a similar journey through the New Testament.

Before we say good-bye, it might be useful, at the end of our journey, to sum up what we have discovered. Along the way, a number of questions have probably occurred to you; now we shall look at them. Why read the Old Testament now that we have the New? Is the Bible the Word of God or the words of men? Finally, on a more personal level, I shall try to say what I hope you have discovered en route; I shall sum it up under the term 'eucharist'.

1. Finishing the course

You have just entered this world of the Bible; you have come to know something of the history of Israel and the surrounding nations; you have met numerous persons, some already known to you and some not; you have read or glanced through texts and books on some of which you would have liked to spend more time. Now that you've come to the end, you probably have the feeling that you've seen a great many things – and forgotten them all. That's natural, but not quite true.

You may well have forgotten facts and dates; you may no longer know at what period a particular book was written. But that doesn't matter too much; when you need this information, you will easily be able to discover it in this book or elsewhere.

That is because – and this is perhaps the first thing this book will have taught you – you have learned to make use of your Bible, to go back and find texts, and to use the notes or to refer to commentaries and other books.

And you've acquired a degree of background. The various dates, and above all the great moments in the history of Israel which were summed up in the diagram on p.22,

will allow you now to give some body to the story of the life of Israel, and to place a book within that life.

More important, perhaps, you have acquired a certain way of approaching the Bible. Probably you have now lost the capacity to approach it freshly and naively. However, you should also feel that you have gained in truth. You have seen that the Bible is not an eye-witness account of a history, but an interpretation made by believers. You have acquired certain reflexes. When you read a text, you don't first ask, 'What happened?', but rather, 'What do these believers tell us about what happened? What word of God have they perceived?' Now you are no longer at the level of the event, but at the level of its being put into writing.

I could list all kinds of other discoveries: texts which have become familiar, figures who have become friends, a new aspect of God, a way of relating ourselves to the world. I shall leave you to draw your own conclusions. What we must now do is to take up some questions which you may still want to ask.

2. Why still read the Old Testament?

Do we have to spend time on this question? The course has surely persuaded you that the Old Testament is interesting. It should be enough simply to bring together what you've discovered yourself.

Why still read the Old Testament? There are, in fact, three main reasons. We need it to understand the New Testament. It is a reflection of our own life. The promise which it announces has yet to be realized.

1. We need the Old Testament to understand the New Testament

It is always illuminating to begin a book by reading the Contents page. If it has been put together well, we immediately have an overall view of the subjects to be discussed. However, it is obvious that each chapter title will mean much more when we have read the chapter in question.

The New Testament, the Contents page of the Old Testament

It's the same with the Bible. In the New Testament we come across many terms which are not explained because they form part of the culture of the time. If anyone talks to us, twentieth-century Westerners, using terms like Pentagon, Oval or Red Cross, we know that they are not referring to geometrical figures; these words are part of our culture and are all symbolic, with profound historical connotations.

Similarly, many of the words used by Jesus or his disciples are part and parcel of the religious culture of the time, and have far more than a surface meaning. Now above all, scripture (the Old Testament) formed the basis of this culture. Thus titles applied to Jesus (Messiah or Christ, son of David, son of God, suffering servant, prophet), and expressions like vine, marriage, Zion, water, breath, are like chapter headings, with a rich content which has come to maturity over a long period in the history of Israel.

However, to speak of a Contents page is too mundane. What we have, rather, is a universe of symbols.

A universe of symbols

Earlier (p.94), I distinguished between two types of language: that of science, which gives information, and that of relationship, which uses symbols. Let us now put these two kinds of expression in context again, with the help of a simple example.

If I say to a child, 'That's a brave man', I'm using the language of science; the word 'brave' has a quite precise sense, defined by the dictionary, and I am applying it to this man. The word sums up what I know of him, but it does not enrich the knowledge I have of him. If I say, 'This man is a lion', I am using symbolic language; the child will not imagine that this man is an animal, with claws (using language which gives information), but he will transfer to the man all that the image of lion evokes, always supposing that he knows other lions than his cuddly toy! At this point we are touching on both the riches and the limits of symbolic language: it enriches our knowledge of the object to which we apply it, but it makes sense only to people who have had the same experience. If a child does not know what a lion is, he has to be taken to the cinema, or to the zoo: it is only when he has some experience of a lion that I can use the word as a symbol.

The Old Testament, a world of symbols

From what I've just said, we can draw two practical conclusions for reading the Bible.

When we read anything from the Old or New Testament, we have to ask whether it is providing information or acting as a symbol; in the latter case, we must then ask what connotations it had at that time. Otherwise we run the risk of making ridiculous mistakes. To take one example: for a present-day Christian, Son of God has a precise meaning, signifying great strength, whereas Son of Man conjures up weakness. Now we have seen that for Israel, Son of God was the equivalent of Son of David; it was an important title, but not a supernatural one. By contrast, in some instances Son of Man conjured up the heavenly figure of the book of Daniel, to whom God entrusted the judgment at the end of time. This figure therefore had divine, supernatural characteristics; it was much stronger than Son of God!

We may draw a second conclusion: when we read the Old Testament we should resist seeing Jesus in it as long as possible. Let me explain that with an example. Suppose we are studying Daniel 7. If, when we read the phrase 'Son of Man' there, we say 'That's Jesus', we have applied to Christ a meaningless title, or one with an inappropriate meaning (like saying that a man is a lion to a child who knows lions only as cuddly toys). So to begin with we must forget Jesus and look for the meaning of the expression Son of Man in the book of Daniel. When we see that the Son of Man is a collective figure, that he represents all believers brought into the presence of the glory of God because they have put that above their lives, we shall be able to apply it to Jesus: and in this way our knowledge of Christ will be remarkably enriched.

So the Old Testament is indispensable to our understanding of the New. That is important, but we are still talking on an intellectual level. We shall now see that on a more existential level, the Old Testament is the reflection of our own human life.

2. The Old Testament as a reflection of human life

We could say that God made his people live through great hopes and great human experiences. So reading the Old Testament is like reflecting in depth upon our own lives. We discover this, simply by reading it, and Jesus and Paul tell us the same thing.

Reading the Old Testament

This first journey through the Old Testament will have allowed you to discover a certain number of texts. After spending the time needed to get used to the vocabulary, the imagery, the historical situation, you will certainly have noticed, here or there, that the fundamental elements in your own life have in fact been evoked here. Perhaps that is more immediately evident in the wisdom writings: the innocent Job who suffers and wants to know why; Koheleth expressing the absurdity of the human condition; the freshness of the love of the betrothed couple in the

Song of Songs; the cries of suffering or wonderment in many of the psalms. In all this, it is almost our own life which is being presented to us, as though in a mirror, so that we can reflect on it. However, that is also true of the other texts: our thirst for liberation and our desire to be free men is expressed through the epic of the Exodus or the expectation of the new exodus; the cries of the prophets demanding justice and respect for the poor are added to our social concerns; reactions, whether violent or non-violent, to the persecution of Antiochus express our present-day alternatives and their ambiguities. You could certainly continue the list, but we must stop there.

At this first level, anybody can have this experience, whether or not they are believers. The Bible is one of the great works of humanity, and the characteristics of these great works is to express the essential quality of being human. The Bible does this in its own way, like Greek epics or Babylonian myths. Luke and Paul show us that this is still more true for the believer.

How Jesus taught – according to Luke

On Easter Day, two discouraged disciples were going back home to Emmaus. 'We had hoped that he would be the one to deliver Israel. . .' This remark reflects a bitter experience and dashed hopes. Jesus does not reproach them for it, but contents himself with noting that they have kept to the Old Testament hope. He goes through the scriptures with them again, and they find that their hearts are afire, so that they recognize the risen Lord in the breaking of the bread.

Like these disciples, we too sometimes get 'cut off'. The Old Testament is there to re-establish all our human connections and to bring us, if we have patience, towards the one whom it announces.

The history of Israel as a 'mock up'

Paul expresses this in theological terms. He declares that the events in the history of Israel are types of what we are (I Cor.10.6,11). The Greek word *tupos* (type) is usually translated 'model' or 'example'. However, the type is precisely the opposite of the model; it would be better translated 'mock up' or 'pattern' (of a garment).

In the case of a model or example, the important thing is the model and not the copy. With the mock-up or pattern it is the other way round. If an engineer constructs in his laboratory a mock-up of the dam he is to build, or if the couturier cuts out of newspaper the pattern of the garment that she wants to make, it is the dam or the garment which are important. The mock-up or pattern are a kind of anticipation of the reality which a human mind is imagining in advance.

The case of Israel is a special one. The events in its history have a value in themselves. However, for the believer, they are something more: they are an anticipation of his life. In some way God was thinking of us when he was talking with Israel.

It is important to understand this if we are to avoid a moralizing approach. One example should make this clear.

The temptation of Jesus in the wilderness

Our imagination sometimes works like this: Jesus was tempted and resisted; I must imitate him. So we have the pattern: Jesus (model) + us. That's not wrong, but it can lead us to a kind of moralizing (we have to be kind like Jesus), or worse, discourage us: if someone presents me with too good a model I may admire it and say to myself, 'That's not for me.'

Now Matthew and Luke show that Satan repeats for Jesus the fundamental temptations experienced by the people in the wilderness. Thus Jesus again takes up the history of Israel, but he makes it succeed because he responds as the people should have done (see 'You only had to. . .' on p.57).

These temptations experienced by the people in the wilderness, a 'mock up' of our own, are still ours today. So Jesus experienced our own temptations. This gives us the pattern: Israel, a mock-up of ourselves, + Jesus + ourselves.

Jesus is not primarily a model to copy; he is the one in whom our life has succeeded and in whom we now can and should live.

3. The time of the promise goes on

To a large extent, the Old Testament is promise. Remember, for example, the prophetic texts, the royal psalms or the apocalypses, where the good news is announced. One day, God will establish his kingdom; then the poor will be happy, because that will be the end of poverty: evil, injustice, suffering and even death will be overcome.

We only have to look around us (and within ourselves) to know that this has not yet been realized, that evil, suffering and sin still exist. The Jews looked for a Messiah who would establish this kingdom of God by himself, all alone, and in a flash. Christians recognized Jesus as this Messiah, but they discovered that he had only inaugurated the kingdom, leaving it to his disciples, given new life by his spirit, to work for it.

The coming of Christ did not suppress this expectation. On the contrary, it strengthened hopes. The promise contained in the Old Testament remains the programme for Christians to carry out, as it was for Jesus.

3. Word of God and words of men

We have already come up against this question (p.76). We ought to return to it now, because you will certainly be asking it as you come to the end of this study.

People usually approach the Bible with the conviction that it is the Word of God (whether they accept the conviction as believers, or reject it as non-believers); the Bible is the holy book of Jews and Christians, a sacred book.

Now throughout this study you may have had the impression that I was robbing the Bible of its sacred character. We have been studying it with analytical methods as though it were a secular text. We have watched the way it came into being, starting with the reflection of the people, prophets, wise men, priests. In the end, there is a risk that it may seem to us above all to be the word of men. 'God said to Abraham . . . to Moses . . .'; we probably feel that it would have been better to say, 'People said that God said to Abraham. . . They interpreted. . . They divinized their human words by turning them into the word of God. Who can guarantee that they were right?'

Perhaps we should revise our conception of the word of God. The analogy with the incarnation will help us here. That leads us to recognize the importance of the Holy Spirit and its role in the faith.

Jesus, the Word of God made man

Our amazement at the way in which this Bible, the Word of God, is so strangely human is exactly the same as that of the contemporaries of Jesus. After the resurrection, they became aware that they had lived in intimate association with the son of God, the word incarnate. However, they had only seen and heard a man, human words. The word of God does not come down from heaven in a visible way, as though by magic. Humbly, it makes itself one with us, and we have to know how to discern it with the eyes of faith.

'The word is very near you; it is in your mouth and in your heart, so that you can do it' (Deut.30.14). So it is in man's heart, in his actions, in his everyday behaviour, as in the great events of the world, that we have to decipher this word. At an ordinary human level, actions and objects say something: 'That was an eloquent action. . . That smile spoke volumes. . .' In the same way, we have to decipher the word of God through human words, attitudes and events.

The role of the Holy Spirit

There is a risk that we may describe as the 'word of God' what is only the expression of our human choice. What guarantees that the biblical authors did not do the same thing?

The believer who recognizes the Bible as the word of God recognizes it, by the same token, as being an inspired word. He sees here an action of the Holy Spirit. 'When the Spirit of truth comes, he will guide you into all the truth, for he will not speak on his own authority', says Jesus to the disciples (John 16.13). To dream of a word of God in a pure state, fallen down from heaven, is perhaps to want to do the work of the spirit! And of faith!

The role of faith

We want proof. We are like the Jews who asked Jesus for great signs in the heavens. And Jesus said to them, 'No sign shall be given to this generation except the sign of Jonah. For as Jonah became a sign to the men of Nineveh, so will the Son of man be to this generation' (Luke 11.29f.). Jonah preached without performing miracles or giving proofs; he simply preached, and the inhabitants saw in his words the word of God inviting them to be converted. Similarly, in Jesus' human words, in his human form, people were to perceive the mystery of God.

The consequence of this is important. If the Word of God had fallen in a pure state from heaven, we could do nothing but repeat it. If, however, it is the humble deciphering of human events by generations of believers, it continues to present itself to us in events of today. Reading the Bible perhaps invites us less to repeat what was discovered by our ancestors in the faith than to do what they did: to read the Word of God in our lives and in the life of the world.

4. Eucharist

Very often, when we have come to the end of a course of this kind, I have been asked, 'What did you have in mind when you suggested this course to us? What is the "ideology" of this book? Where is it meant to take us?'

Whether asked in a friendly way, or with some more sinister motive, this question is important. It shows that we never read the Bible objectively – any more than any other text. Nor is the course presented here completely innocent in this respect. I'm not going to give you my 'ideology' – ideology exercises a force without our being aware of it. My final concern is more modest. I shall give up the impersonal tone I've been using so far and go over to the first person. I would like to tell you what this study of the Bible has given me, and what I hope that it will give others.

Christian and intelligent?

I believe very strongly that God wants us to use our minds and that he does not ask us to sacrifice our intelligence when we begin to read the Bible. We are men and women of the twentieth century, moulded by science, in the arts as well as in the applied sciences, and it is as people of the twentieth century that we should become believers, without having to give up either our faith or science.

So a first benefit that studying the Bible has brought me is the discovery that one can be both Christian and intelligent. And that's quite something. Let me give you a rather crude example (you can think of others for yourself). Believers have often come under a great deal of fire – and still do – over the creation stories. As a Christian, someone might feel obliged to accept what these texts seem to affirm (direct creation by God, in six days, and so on); at the same time, however, because he or she is also a twentieth-century person, they will hear a little voice muttering inside, 'But I can't believe that!' A matter-of-fact study of the stories, as of many others, will show us that there is no clash between science or history and faith. We can belong completely to our age and still believe, without being pulled two ways the whole time.

Christian and free?

Too often the Christian seems rather alienated, hemmed in by beliefs and prohibitions as by a barbed wire fence. However, one conviction stands out from all the Bible: God wants men and women to be free and responsible.

But it is true that the way in which we approach the Bible is not completely open. A story may make the point as well as anything. I was studying a teaching problem with students from many different countries: in what order should the texts of the Old Testament be presented to people coming to them for the first time? Various possibilities were mentioned: to follow the pattern of 'sacred history' (creation – the fall – Abraham – Moses), or to follow the pattern now adopted in catechetics (Abraham – Moses – the creation stories), or again, to begin with the Exodus as we have done here. A nun from Latin America said to us: 'At home, the Bible is part of the teaching given in schools. So there are recognized textbooks and they follow the pattern of sacred history. We've formed a catechetical centre where we train teachers who want to begin with Abraham and deal with the creation stories later.' She added: 'So far the government hasn't noticed. But when it does notice, there will be trouble. . .' On reflection, that's obvious. The pattern of 'sacred history' is essentially conservative: it gives pride of place to an all-powerful God, absolute master, creator of mankind which has only to obey him. Granted, mankind rebelled through sin, but God remains master because he punishes and forgives. . . And we can understand how an authoritarian government will find such a pattern congenial: it can make an unconscious assimilation between this God and the masters of the country. By contrast, the other pattern – the one which God made his people follow – is subversive: it brings to light that God above all a God who liberates, who wants man, all men, to be free and responsible.

Thus the way in which we begin the Bible can have a great influence on our religious mentality, and also on our human attitude; it can also contribute to the formation of docile citizens or responsible human beings.

The humanity of God

I might put the same thing in a different way by talking, like the book of Wisdom, of the humanity of God and his humility. God is the one who is utterly different, the Lord of history, Creator of the universe, the transcendent God. That is what he is and that is what he remains. However, above all he seeks to be the God who is near, who goes with his people step by step, with an infinite respect for mankind, who does not violate their faith by miracles and never destroys it. He is a God who wants mankind to stand on its own feet, free, and he gives mankind the world to shape and history to make.

And this God is faithful. We have seen how the Bible expresses his involvement with Abraham. Once for all, God has thrown the weight of his faithfulness into the balance of history. Here is the ultimate and definitive security of mankind, which makes people perfectly free: whether we are saints or sinners, we know that we are unfailingly loved by God, who is faithful. We know how important it is, humanly speaking, to be loved if we are to act: we need someone to count on us, to have confidence in us. Here is the enormous and unshakable security of the believer: he knows that God loves him, that God has confidence in him, despite everything.

History, both the history of the world and the history of the church, can have its setbacks and failings. However, that should not lead us to despair: in silence, invisibly, God goes with men and puts his trust in them.

The eucharist

If I had to sum up the fundamental attitude which studying the Bible can instil in us, I would say, without hesitation, it was that of thanksgiving, of the eucharist.

A scholar gave a magnificent summary of this in the title which he gave to his commentary on the Book of Joshua: 'The gift of a conquest'. That says it all. The entry into Canaan was a conquest: if Joshua and the people had not fought, they would not have conquered this land. They were the ones who occupied it. But at the same time they recognized that it was a gift. When we studied a text from Deuteronomy (p.58), we saw how the fact of telling a story – the credo – changed the significance of the produce of the soil; at the beginning, the Israelite could put his hands on the fruit and vegetables which he had grown and say, 'This is my produce.' The story of the action of God for his people led him to recognize, with joy, and with open hands, that his produce, his life, were a gift of God. 'Blessed art thou, O Lord, who givest us this bread and this wine, the fruit of man's labour', declares a prayer from the Catholic liturgy, taking up a Jewish formula.

It seems to me that the Bible leads us to recognize that everything depends on man, that he has to shape himself, the world and history, but that at the same time he is the finest present that God gives. 'I praise you, God, for having made me the amazing wonder that I am' (Ps.139.14). 'The Lord had done marvels for me. . .' (Luke 1.49).

Ebil-il the steward, at worship
(Alabaster, Mari, the middle of the third
millennium.)

If You Want to Know More . . .

Throughout this book I have made few references to other books or commentaries. That was deliberate: you can get a long way with just a good Bible and this guide. However, if you want to explore further, here are some useful works.

Reference books

A wealth of information about the content of the Bible can be found in two dictionaries: James Hastings, *Dictionary of the Bible*, T. & T. Clark, and the five-volume illustrated *Interpreter's Dictionary of the Bible*, Abingdon Press. Two convenient atlases are Lucas Grollenberg, *Shorter Atlas of the Bible*, Penguin Books, and the *Oxford Bible Atlas*, edited by H. G. May, Oxford University Press: each has an illustrated text as well as the maps. There are many commentary series, with a separate volume for each book or a small group of books: the Cambridge Bible Commentaries are simple and factual; in America the Layman's Bible Commentaries published by John Knox Press are very readable; the Old Testament Library, published by SCM Press and Westminster Press, is harder going, but the substantial volumes are very rewarding. Big one-volume commentaries also contain articles on general topics; there are three good ones to choose from: *The Jerome Biblical Commentary*, edited by R. E. Brown, J. A. Fitzmyer and R. E. Murphy, Geoffrey Chapman/Prentice-Hall; *The New Catholic Commentary on Holy Scripture*, edited by R. C. Fuller, Leonard Johnston and Conleth Kearns, Nelson; *Peake's Commentary on the Bible*, edited by M. Black and H. H. Rowley, Nelson. Texts relating to the world of the Old Testament can be found in: *Near Eastern Religious Texts relating to the Old Testament*, edited by Walter Beyerlin, in the Old Testament Library, and *Ancient Near Eastern Texts*, edited by J. B. Pritchard, Princeton University Press (there is a fascinating companion volume of *Ancient Near Eastern Pictures*).

General Works

Some valuable studies of the Old Testament as a whole are:

Bernhard W. Anderson, *The Living World of the Old Testament* (American title *Understanding the Old Testament*), Longmans/Prentice Hall.

G. W. Anderson, *The History and Religion of Israel*, Oxford University Press.

John Bright, *A History of Israel*, SCM Press/Westminster Press.

Alan T. Dale, *Winding Quest*, Oxford University Press.

John H. Hayes, *An Introduction to Old Testament Study*, SCM Press/Abingdon Press.

Henry McKeating, *Studying the Old Testament*, Epworth Press.

Roland de Vaux, *Ancient Israel*, Darton, Longman & Todd.

Robert Walton (ed.), *A Basic Introduction to the Old Testament* (American title *Bible Study Source Book – Old Testament*), SCM Press/John Knox Press.

Books on particular subjects

The following books deal with subjects that we have explored in this guide. They are listed in the order in which we came to them.

George W. Ramsey, *The Quest for the Historical Israel*, SCM Press/John Knox Press.

E. W. Heaton, *Solomon's New Men*, Thames & Hudson/Universe.

E. W. Heaton, *The Hebrew Kingdoms*, Oxford University Press.

Gerhard von Rad, *The Message of the Prophets*, SCM Press/Harper and Row.

Walter Zimmerli, *The Law and the Prophets*, Blackwell.

J. Lindblom, *Prophecy in Ancient Israel*, Blackwell/Fortress Press

P. R. Ackroyd, *Exile and Restoration*, SCM Press/Westminster Press.

P. R. Ackroyd, *Israel under Babylon and Persia*, Oxford University Press.

Martin Hengel, *Jews, Greeks and Barbarians*, SCM Press/Fortress Press

D. S. Russell, *Between the Testaments*, SCM Press/Fortress Press.

D. S. Russell, *The Jews from Alexander to Herod*, Oxford University Press.

One book will lead you on to another and there is no end to reading them; however, don't forget the most important thing – not to lose sight of where you started from!

Jewish Literature outside the Bible

In Bibles which follow the Protestant tradition, like the Revised Standard Version, the last book of the Old Testament to be written, Daniel, comes from the second century BC; in the Catholic tradition, presented by versions like the Jerusalem Bible, the last books of the Old Testament were written about a century before our era (except for the Book of Wisdom, which does not form part of the Jewish Bible). In a Catholic Bible, there is nothing between this book of Wisdom, written about 50 BC, and the first book of the New Testament to be written, I Thessalonians. Was this a century without literature? At all events, it is a particularly interesting century for Christians, since this was the century in which Jesus lived.

In fact, literary activity at that time was intense, and biblical scholars are now hard at work in this area.

The Law, written and oral

God gave his Law to Moses on Sinai. However, for the Jews, only one part of the Law was put into writing: the rest was handed down orally (see p.79).

The written Law is essentially the five books of the Law (the Pentateuch). The Prophets shed light on it; the Writings meditate on it. Together, all these books form the Bible.

Following after the Writings, a large number of books were written round about the Christian era. Some of them have been known for a long time; others have been discovered recently, like the writings from Nag Hammadi in Egypt, found in 1945, and the Qumran writings found in 1947.

The oral traditions are more difficult to follow, precisely because they are oral. They hand on traditions which run parallel to the written Law; they meditate on the scriptures, relate them to the present day, produce new traditions. . . And it is often very difficult to tell at what particular period this or that tradition came into being.

Jewish writings

Writings of an apocalyptic nature

Many of these works have been known for a long time. They include, for example, the books of Enoch, Jubilees, the Psalms of Solomon, the Testaments of the Twelve Patriarchs, the Assumption of Moses, the apocalypses of Elijah and Abraham, IV Esdras (which appears in the Latin Bible, the Vulgate), and so on. Not all these books are apocalypses in the strict sense, but they are all stamped by this trend. The trend is especially important for understanding the New Testament.

The Qumran writings

These manuscripts, discovered from 1947 onwards in caves near the Dead Sea, have made known to us the thinking of the Essenes, pious Jews who withdrew to the 'monastery' of Qumran at the time of the Maccabees and lived there until it was destroyed by the Romans in AD 70 (see p.85). The best guide to these writings is Geza Vermes, *The Dead Sea Scrolls in English,* Penguin Books 1970.

Other writings

We should at least note the work of the Jewish historian Flavius Josephus, who was born about AD 30 and died at the beginning of the second century. He rewrote the Bible in his *Jewish Antiquities.* In his many books, Philo of Alexandria, who lived from about 13 BC to AD 50, tried to express his Jewish faith in the context of Greek culture. He was writing at the time when the Gospels came into being.

Oral literature

People also talk about rabbinic literature. The rabbis are

the Pharisee scribes who at the time of Christ were already beginning to fix the way in which the Law was to be put into practice (see, for example, the rabbi Gamaliel in Acts 5.34). They did this by their knowledge of the Law and the commentaries which they produced on it. After the fall of Jerusalem in AD 70, these Pharisee scribes moved to Jabneh (near modern Tel Aviv), reorganized Judaism and gathered the traditions together. The oral literature is not entirely rabbinic, but it was collected together by these rabbis.

I shall mention the chief collections so that you can give a context to the names which you will have heard mentioned (for example, the Talmud). It will also show how intensely these Jewish believers worked in reflecting on the Law. This is interesting for those wanting to know more about Judaism; it is also interesting as we try to understand how the New Testament came into being. The first Christians were Jews, trained in the same methods of relating scripture to the present. The Gospels underwent a long period of oral formation and transmission before they were put down in writing, and in this way they are parallels to the rabbinic traditions.

I have chosen the title oral literature rather than rabbinic literature to stress this fact: the collections I shall be mentioning have come down to us in written form, but for the Jews they are essentially collections of oral material. To suggest a comparison: a composer writes the score of his symphony, but it is not produced to be read, but to be played and listened to; it is only put into writing as an aid to the memory.

Oral traditions

The rabbis handed on to their pupils what they themselves had received (cf. I Cor.15.1–3). These traditions are of two kinds: the Halakah gives interpretations of the Law aimed at helping people to act on it, practical rules for living (the root *halak* means way, road); the Haggadah is meant, rather, to be edifying (see p.81).

A systematic editing of these traditions began at the end of the first century AD. The first collection produced by this oral editing is called the Mishnah. Rabbis provided comments on this Mishnah in both Palestine and in Babylon; their commentaries came to form the Gemara.

The Talmud (instruction) is a collection of all these traditions: the Mishnah is the basic text, supplemented by the Gemara and other traditions which had not found a place in the oral collections (the Tosephta). The Jerusalem, or Palestinian, Talmud was only formed in the fourth century; the Babylonian Talmud, which is fuller, was finished towards the end of the fifth century.

Midrash

Researches into scripture, or scriptural commentaries made in the schools and synagogues, culminated in collections of midrashim (see p.81).

Targum

The Targum is the translation of the text of the Bible, read in Hebrew in the synagogue, into Aramaic. This translation was made orally, and was an adaptation which related the text to its new setting. So it is very interesting in showing us something of how scripture was interpreted at the time of Christ (see two brief examples on pp.38,52. For more details see R. C. Musaph-Andriesse, *From Torah to Kabbalah,* SCM Press 1981 and OUP, NY 1982).

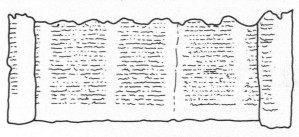

Qumran manuscript. Temple scroll

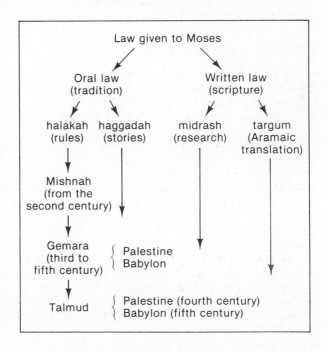

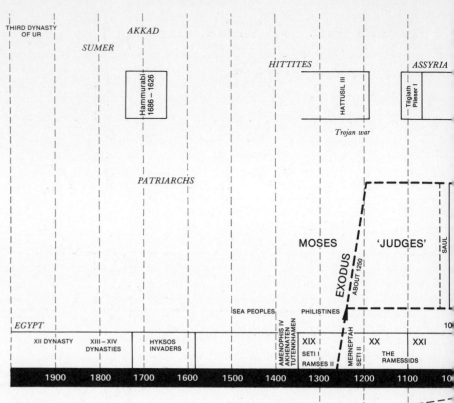

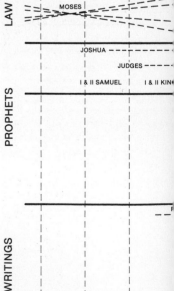

The history and the literary history of Israel

This diagram is a summary, so don't begin here!
The dotted vertical lines divide up history into centuries, from 2000 BC to AD 100.

1. History: the upper part of the diagram

The rectangle running right through the diagram, above the figures indicating the centuries, represents Egypt: its history is divided into the various dynasties.

The rectangles above that appear one after the other in succession: they represent the peoples of Mesopotamia (the Sumerians, Akkadians, Assyrians, Persians, Babylonians), of Asia Minor (the Hittites), or of Europe (Greeks and Romans), who in turn became masters of the Middle East.

The rectangle in blacker lines represents Israel. It was divided into two when the United Kingdom of David and Solomon broke into two parts: the Northern Kingdom (or Israel, Samaria), and the Southern Kingdom (or Judah, Jerusalem).

2. Literary history: lower part of the diagram

This part of the diagram shows the particular period in which a book of the Bible was composed (sometimes this is pure hypothesis). The straight lines ————— indicate the composition of a book. The broken lines – – – – represent an oral tradition on the way to becoming an edited text.

The dots surrounding a straight line . . . ————— . . . indicate a probable period.

The vertical grill between 600 and 500 represents the time of exile in Babylon.

The two horizontal grills between 1000 and 700 represent the northern kingdom. For the Law, the letters JEDP represent the traditions edited at different periods. J = Yahwistic tradition (at Jerusalem in the time of Solomon); E = Elohistic tradition (in the northern kingdom, about 750); JE = the Jehovistic tradition (a fusion of the Yahwist and the Elohist in Jerusalem); D = the Deuteronomic tradition (a core formed in the north was taken up and completed in the south); P = the priestly tradition (during and after the exile in Babylon).

These four traditions, regrouped after the exile, constituted the Law (or the Pentateuch), divided into five books: Genesis, Exodus, Leviticus, Numbers, Deuteronomy.

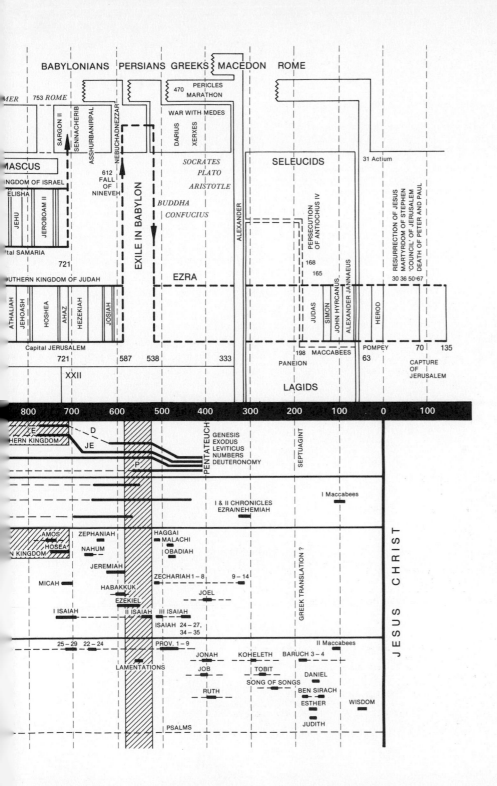

BABYLONIANS PERSIANS GREEKS⌇MACEDON ROME

...MER   753 ROME

...MASCUS

...INGDOM OF ISRAEL

...ELISHA

JEHU	JEROBOAM II

...tal SAMARIA

SARGON II
SENNACHERIB
ASSHURBANIRPAL
NEBUCHADNEZZAR

612
FALL
OF
NINEVEH

EXILE IN BABYLON

470   PERICLES
       MARATHON

WAR WITH MEDES

DARIUS   XERXES

SOCRATES
PLATO
ARISTOTLE

BUDDHA
CONFUCIUS

EZRA

ALEXANDER

SELEUCIDS

31 Actium

PERSECUTION
OF ANTIOCHUS IV

168
165

RESURRECTION OF JESUS
MARTYRDOM OF STEPHEN
'COUNCIL' OF JERUSALEM
DEATH OF PETER AND PAUL

30 36 50·67

721

...OUTHERN KINGDOM OF JUDAH

ATHALIAH	JEHOASH	HOSHEA	AHAZ	HEZEKIAH	JOSIAH

Capital JERUSALEM

721   587 538   333

XXII

| JUDAS | SIMON | JOHN HYRCANUS | ALEXANDER JANNAEUS | HEROD |

198 MACCABEES   POMPEY   70   135
PANEION   63   CAPTURE
                                    OF
LAGIDS   JERUSALEM

800   700   600   500   400   300   200   100   0   100

JE
...HERN KINGDOM

D
JE

P

PENTATEUCH
GENESIS
EXODUS
LEVITICUS
NUMBERS
DEUTERONOMY

SEPTUAGINT

I & II CHRONICLES
EZRA/NEHEMIAH

I Maccabees

AMOS	ZEPHANIAH
HOSEA	NAHUM

...N KINGDOM

HAGGAI
MALACHI
OBADIAH

JEREMIAH

MICAH

ZECHARIAH 1 – 8   9 – 14

HABAKKUK
EZEKIEL

JOEL

I ISAIAH

II ISAIAH   III ISAIAH

ISAIAH 24 – 27,
34 – 35

GREEK TRANSLATION ?

25 – 29 22 – 24   PROV. 1 – 9

LAMENTATIONS

JONAH   KOHELETH   BARUCH 3 – 4

JOB   TOBIT

SONG OF SONGS

RUTH

DANIEL

BEN SIRACH

ESTHER   WISDOM

JUDITH

PSALMS

II Maccabees

JESUS CHRIST

Analytical Index

God. Some ways in which he makes himself known

Jesus. Titles given to him

Figures from the Bible

Groups or peoples

Some themes

Literary questions

Principal texts studied

Cherubim. Ivory panel from the palace of Ahab at Samaria (ninth century BC)

This wall painting, measuring 2.50 metres by 1.75 metres, adorned the great hall of the palace of Mari (destroyed in 1760 BC) on the Euphrates. It is now in the Musée du Louvre, in Paris.

It has been called the Investiture Fresco, or, sometimes, the Paradise Fresco.

In the upper rectangle in the centre, the king, probably Zimri-lim, is receiving the staff and the ring, attributes of power, at the hand of the goddess Ishtar, goddess of war. She has her foot on a lion, which is her emblem. The goddess and the king are surrounded by deities.

Below, two goddesses are carrying jars from which four rivers flow.

On each side there are two trees, one very stylized, the other representing a palm tree. The first kind is guarded by three 'cherubim': a winged sphinx, a winged griffin and a bull with a man's head.

Many of the details depicted here recur in the stories of earthly paradises: the authors certainly drew on the same common source. In particular, we find again the two types of tree, the four rivers and the cherubim. However, we can see one important difference: in the Bible the centre is occupied not by the king, but by man, whom the one God makes master of creation.

Table of Contents

A Canaanite prince, seated upon a throne made up of two cherubim, is drinking from a cup and taking a lotus flower offered to him by the queen. A girl is playing a nine-stringed lyre. She is followed by officers, and two kings in chains. The winged disc of the sun is above them. (An ivory found at Megiddo)

The Books of the Bible

Abbreviations, and the pages in this book on which they are mentioned

Old Testament

(The Deutero-Canonical books are printed in italics)

Amos	Amos 47	Judith	Judith 88
Bar.	*Baruch 92*	I Kings	I Kings 42, 45, 46, 55, 59
I Chron.	I Chronicles 79	II Kings	II Kings 45, 46, 55, 59
II Chron.	II Chronicles 42, 79	Koh.	Koheleth 87
Dan.	Daniel 88, 90	Lam.	Lamentations 65
Deut.	Deuteronomy 45, 55, 56	Lev.	Leviticus 65, 85
Eccles.	Ecclesiastes (also called Koheleth; for references see below)	*I Macc.*	*I Maccabees 88*
		II Macc.	*II Maccabees 88*
Ecclus.	*Ecclesiasticus (also called Sirach; for references see below)*	Mal.	Malachi 76
		Micah	Micah 43
Esther	Esther 88	Nahum	Nahum 60
Ezra	Ezra 79	Neh.	Nehemiah 75, 79
Ex.	Exodus 26, 30, 38, 51, 53, 60	Num.	Numbers 53
Ezek.	Ezekiel 40, 66	Obad.	Obadiah 75
Gen.	Genesis 36, 51, 60, 70, 72	Prov.	Proverbs 82, 83
Hab.	Habakkuk 60	Ps.	Psalms 94
Hag.	Haggai 76	Ruth	Ruth 81
Hos.	Hosea 47, 48	I Sam.	I Samuel 35, 55, 59
Isa.	Isaiah	II Sam.	II Samuel 35, 55, 59
	(I Isaiah, chs. 1–39) 42	*Sir.*	*Sirach 87*
	(II Isaiah, chs. 40–55) 67	S. of S.	Song of Songs 87
	(III Isaiah, 56–66) 75, 76	Tob.	Tobit 87
Jer.	Jeremiah 62	*Wisd.*	*Wisdom 92*
Job	Job 82	Zech.	Zechariah
Joel	Joel 76		(I Zechariah, chs.1–8) 76
Jonah	Jonah 81		(II Zechariah, chs.9–14) 86
Josh.	Joshua 34, 55, 59	Zeph.	Zephaniah 60
Judg.	Judges 34, 55, 59		

New Testament

Acts	The Acts of the Apostles	Luke	The Gospel of Luke
Apoc.	The Apocalypse: also called the Revelation of St John the Divine (see below)	Mark	The Gospel of Mark
		Matt.	The Gospel of Matthew
		I Peter	I Peter
Col.	Colossians	II Peter	II Peter
I Cor.	I Corinthians	Phil.	Philippians
II Cor.	II Corinthians	Phlm	Philemon
Eph.	Ephesians	Rev.	The Revelation of St John the Divine (also called Apocalypse)
Gal.	Galatians		
Heb.	Hebrews	Rom.	Romans
James	James	I Thess.	I Thessalonians
John	The Gospel of John	II Thess.	II Thessalonians
I John	The First Letter of John	I Tim.	I Timothy
II John	II John	II Tim.	II Timothy
III John	III John	Titus	Titus
Jude	Jude		